An Obsession with Anne Frank

AN OBSESSION
with ANNE FRANK

Meyer Levin and the *Diary*

> > > > > >

LAWRENCE GRAVER

University of California Press

Berkeley   Los Angeles   London

University of California Press
Berkeley and Los Angeles, California

University of California Press, Ltd.
London, England

© 1995 by
The Regents of the University of California

Library of Congress Cataloging-in-Publication Data

Graver, Lawrence, 1931–
    An obsession with Anne Frank : Meyer Levin and
The diary / Lawrence Graver.

        p.   cm.
    "A Centennial book."
    Includes bibliographical references and index.
    ISBN 0-520-20124-8 (alk. paper)
    1. Levin, Meyer, 1905–   .   2. Frank, Anne,
1929–1945. Achterhuis.   3. Jews—Public
opinion.   4. Holocaust, Jewish (1939–1945), in
literature.   I. Title.
PS3523.E7994Z7   1995
813'.52—dc20   94-48123
                                                CIP

Printed in the United States of America
9 8 7 6 5 4 3 2

The paper used in this publication meets the minimum
requirements of American National Standard for
Information Sciences—Permanence of Paper for Printed
Library Materials, ANSI Z39.48–1984.

For Suzanne, Ruth, and Elizabeth

> CONTENTS

> ABBREVIATIONS

BU	The Meyer Levin Collection, Special Collections, Boston University Libraries
BE	Personal papers of Barbara Epstein (Barbara Zimmerman)
GH	Goodrich and Hackett Papers, State Historical Society of Wisconsin, Madison
JM	Personal papers of Joseph Marks
KB	Kermit Bloomgarden Papers, State Historical Society of Wisconsin, Madison
PWRW&G	Papers of Paul, Weiss, Rifkind, Wharton, and Garrison, New York
SCSNY	Supreme Court, State of New York
SHSW	State Historical Society of Wisconsin, Madison
TF	Personal papers of Thelma Frye
TT	Personal papers of Tereska Torres Levin

PREFACE

and ACKNOWLEDGMENTS

Since it first appeared in Amsterdam in the early summer of 1947, Anne Frank's *Diary* has become one of the most widely read, powerfully affecting books in the world, but it has also been in startling ways one of the most controversial. Early on, it was rejected in manuscript by dozens of publishers in Holland, Germany, England, and America, mainly because editors doubted that people so soon after the war would want to buy the private jottings of a Dutch girl who hid with her family for twenty-five months and then died in a Nazi concentration camp. Once accepted, the *Diary* soon proved all the skeptics wrong. Acclaimed as an astonishing story of eight fugitives, an indelible portrait of a gifted girl growing up, and a remarkable document of the Holocaust, it has been—as a book, play, film, school text, art work, ballet, and musical—read, seen, and talked about everywhere, turning Anne Frank from a singular girl into a cultural myth and one of the most familiar, best-loved figures of history. As the critic Alvin Rosenfeld has observed, "streets, schools, and youth centers bear her name, just as public statues, stamps, and commemorative coins bear her image. Youth villages, forests, and foundations have been named after her . . . requiems, cantatas, poems and songs composed for her. Public figures of every kind, from politicians to religious leaders, regularly invoke her name and quote lines from her book. In all of these ways, her name, face, and fate are kept constantly before us."

But if the ubiquitous girl and her book are now legendary, they have also been the persistent subject of fierce dispute. From the late 1950s to the present moment, countless individuals and groups have used (and continue to use) the diary of Anne Frank for their own personal and political designs, often forcing her father, Otto, his heirs, and the Anne Frank Foundation into painful, protracted quarrels and lawsuits. Most of these fights have centered on baseless yet continuous claims by Nazis and neo-Nazis about the authenticity of the work itself. The first allegations that the girl's diary was a forgery were published in Swedish and Danish newspapers in 1957, and from then on, essays and books repeating and embroidering the charges have appeared with dismal regularity. Among the most notorious are Richard Harwood's *Did Six Million Really Die?* (1974), David Irving's *Hitler and His Generals* (1975), A. R. Butz's *The Hoax of the Twentieth Century* (1975), Ditlieb Felderer's *Anne Frank's Diary—A Hoax?* (1978), and Robert Faurisson's *The Diary of Anne Frank—Is It Authentic?* (1980) and *The Diary of Anne Frank—A Forgery* (1985). The growing number of such publications in the late 1970s prompted the Netherlands State Institute for War Documentation to prepare the authoritative *De Dagboeken van Anne Frank,* (Amsterdam, 1986), to respond to "the slurs . . . intended to cast doubt both on the personal integrity of the author and on the relationship between the original manuscript, the published version, and its many translations." The massive "Critical Edition" (which reprints nearly all the different versions of the diary) also includes a sixty-three-page summary of an exhaustive handwriting and technical study by the Netherlands State Forensic Science Laboratory of the Ministry of Justice, proving beyond all reasonable doubt that the girl's work was genuine. Yet despite the definitive evidence presented there, pamphlets and books questioning the authenticity of the *Diary* continue to appear. Late in 1993, the Anne Frank Foundation asked the Dutch courts to stop dissemination of *Anne Frank: A Critical Approach*, coauthored by Faurisson and the Belgian historian Siegfried Verbeke, which had been published in 1991 and was circulating in the Netherlands. (For a detailed history of extremist assaults on the *Diary*, see David Barnouw's essay on pages 84–101 of *The Diary of Anne Frank: The Critical Edition* [New York, 1989] and Deborah Lipstadt's *Denying the Holocaust* [New York, 1993], pp. 229–35.)

If the recurring attacks on the legitimacy of Anne Frank's *Diary* now make up a long, ongoing chapter in the history of the malignancy known as Holocaust revisionism, the other notable dispute concerning the book is equally fascinating and instructive. In the early 1950s the novelist Meyer Levin, after helping the *Diary* achieve great popularity in America, became involved in a bitter disagreement about adapting it for the theater, an argument that brought him into conflict with Otto Frank and scores of other people, lasted thirty years, and was widely reported in the press at the time. My own interest in the extraordinary Levin-Frank dispute began in the late 1980s, when I was teaching a course called Imagining American Jews at Williams College. I was struck by how intensely many contemporary writers—John Berryman, Alfred Kazin, Philip Roth, C. K. Williams, Francine Prose, Anne Roiphe, Scott Spencer, as well as Meyer Levin and others—were gripped by the Anne Frank story. At first, I thought of writing a book about the different ways these American writers depicted the girl and her fate, but as I explored the subject I found that Levin's preoccupation was by far the most complex and resonant, for it not only shaped his entire personal and literary life but reached into the realms of publishing, marketing, theater, film, law, religion, politics, the media, and popular culture. The story of Meyer Levin's relationship with Anne Frank also reveals what many people (American, German, Dutch, English, Israeli; Jewish and gentile; famous and obscure) wanted, needed, or hoped to make of the afterlife of the girl and her book, an afterlife that has taken on the shape and implication of myth. I have four main aims in this study: (1) to provide a thorough narrative of a controversy that up to now has been inadequately and misleadingly described, either by the participants or by onlookers who had only a sketchy idea of what was happening and what was at stake; (2) to explore the effect of the prolonged dispute on the life and career of a neglected but important writer; (3) to shed light on evolving American attitudes toward Jews in the 1950s and afterwards; and (4) to reflect on the continually vexed issue of how people bear witness to and represent the Holocaust.

At every stage of my work I have benefited from the generosity, support, and sensitive criticism of many people.

Tereska Torres Levin gave me permission to read and quote from the Meyer Levin papers in Special Collections, Mugar Memorial Library, Boston University. She has also answered countless questions and shared many documents with me. Although she has not read this manuscript and is not responsible for any of the interpretations or errors, I could not have proceeded with the project without her assistance, candor, and encouragement.

Eli, Gabriel, and Mikael Levin, the writer's sons; Dominique Torres, his daughter; Judith Klausner, his cousin; and Leonard Schroeter and Leon Wells, his friends, have also been extraordinarily helpful to me, providing published and unpublished material, responding liberally to inquiries, and offering cheerful hospitality. They, too, have not seen any of this text and should not be held accountable for my arguments or mistakes.

Several other participants in the history described here have also been uncommonly forthcoming with recollections and documents: Joseph Marks made it possible for me to reconstruct the events of June and July 1952 by sharing a file of letters and memoranda from his years at Doubleday; he also read and commented on part of the first chapter. Barbara Epstein, who edited *Anne Frank: The Diary of a Young Girl* when it first appeared in America, permitted me to read and quote from her correspondence with Otto Frank and others. Edward Costikyan of Paul, Weiss, Rifkind, Wharton and Garrison (Otto Frank's attorneys) granted me access to extensive files of the lengthy litigation. Samuel Fredman (Levin's attorney) and Robert Gottlieb (his editor) also shared memories and letters with me. Mordecai Kaplan, who twice directed Meyer Levin's

Anne Frank at the Lyric Stage in Boston, talked with me at length about the productions and gave me copies of sketches, playbills, reviews, and photographs.

Librarians and archivists are indispensable to a scholar's work. I am particularly indebted to Bruce Abrams, archivist, Supreme Court, New York County Court House; Alice Birney, Library of Congress; Donald Crafton, Wisconsin Center for Film and Theater Research; Howard B. Gotlieb, Mugar Memorial Library, Boston University; Harold Miller, State Historical Society of Wisconsin; and Dienke Hondius, Joke Kniesmeyer, Yt Stoker, and Hans Westra at the Anne Frank Stichting in Amsterdam. The reference and interlibrary-loan staffs at Sawyer Library, Williams College, have been unfailingly helpful, notably Lee Dalzell, Helena Warburg, Walter Komorowski, Peter Giordano, and Jean Vankin.

I also received valuable practical help from Adriana Millenaar Brown, who worked with me in Amsterdam in 1990, translating documents, introducing me to staff members at various institutes, and making my stay in the city a pleasure. My cousin, Shep Ellman, tracked down essential material in Jerusalem libraries and inspired me with his excitement about the project. Elfriede Frank and Vincent Frank-Steiner were wonderfully hospitable to me when I visited Basel in 1991, allowing me to read correspondence between Otto Frank and American publishers.

I am also pleased to acknowledge my indebtedness to others who shared recollections and documents with me or assisted me in other important ways: Larry Frisch, Thelma Frye, Herbert Gold, Vahan Hogroian, Judith Jones, Susan Kerner, Dennis Klein, Shimon Lev-Ari, Howard J. Levitz, Ken McCormick, Frederick Morton, David Passow, Carl E. Rollyson, Louis A. Rachow, Abram Rothberg, Charles Simmons, Karen Shawn, Benjamin Weiser Varon, C. K. Williams, David Zinder, and Louise Zutra.

I wish also to thank the following for permission to quote from unpublished material and to reproduce photographs: Paul Berkowsky, Edward Costikyan, Barbara Epstein, Samuel Fredman, Martha Gellhorn, Robert Gottlieb, Robert Gurbo, Garson Kanin, Floria Lasky, Archie Lieberman, Joseph Marks, Simon and Schuster, and the editors of the *New York Times Book Review*.

Williams College provided research support, travel grants, and sabbatical leaves, which allowed me to complete my research and writing more quickly than I had anticipated.

To seven readers of this book in typescript, I owe very particular thanks: Robert Bell and Ellen Schiff read an intermediate draft, responded with characteristic enthusiasm and meticulous attention to arguments and details, and made many valuable suggestions. Morris Dickstein proposed several crucial revisions that significantly improved the shape and impact of the entire study. Michael Grunebaum helped me sharpen a number of my points about the psychological dimensions of the history. My daughters, Ruth and Elizabeth Graver, read the manuscript with a combination of imaginative probing, analytical rigor, and special feeling for the author. They will recognize many of their recommended revisions (and even some of their phrasings) in the text. Their other contributions are incalculable. My wife, Suzanne, as always my most devoted, sympathetic, and discriminating critic, read the book chapter by chapter and improved it everywhere, in conception, structure, and style.

Williamstown, Massachusetts
L.G.
November 1994

> **I**

"Some day
a teller would arise"

THE AMERICAN WRITER Meyer Levin first read *Le Journal de Anne Frank* in August of 1950, when he was living with his second wife, Tereska Torres, and two children in the upstairs of a bus driver's cottage on the Côte d'Azur near Antibes. Torres, herself a writer, had heard about the stir the translation from the Dutch had made when it was published in Paris that spring, and she bought a copy for her husband at a local bookstore. Years later she recalled what she said as she handed it to him: "*Tiens, c'est un cadeau. Il paraît que c'est un livre extraordinaire. Le journal, tenu pendant la guerre, d'une petite fille morte à Bergen-Belsen, à quinze ans*"—an offering that would haunt both of them in different ways for the rest of their lives.[1] Reading Anne Frank's diary astonished and provoked Levin. Not only was the spirited young girl telling an engrossing story about herself and her family at a convulsive moment in recent European history, but her account and her fate unex-

1. *Les maisons hantées de Meyer Levin*, 42.

pectedly touched Levin's deepest feelings about his own identity as a Jew, an American, and a writer.

Levin was forty-four, and although he was reasonably well
known as a novelist and newspaper correspondent, his position
in the postwar literary world was far from secure. He was not,
by his own admission, "much of a literary master. My gifts are
basically in the urge towards honest expression and in empathy."[2] "My readership," he told a friend at this time, is "faithful
but not too numerous," and he spoke often of a constant
"scrambling for income," of doing "a bit of everything" to earn
a living: magazine articles, opinion columns, radio scripts, film
and television work, translating, and ghostwriting. Two decades
earlier, Levin had done a great deal of journalism (mainly for
the *Chicago Daily News* and *Esquire*) and published six novels
in swift succession, each a distinctive and promising accomplishment in its own right but none a financial success. *Reporter*
(1929) refashioned the brassy documentary techniques of Dos
Passos to depict and expose the speed-driven world of modern
newspapers. *Frankie and Johnny* (1930) was a spare, affecting
story of ill-fated teenage romance in an urban setting. *Yehuda*
(1931), based on Levin's own early visits to Palestine, was the
first novel in English to dramatize the clash between individual and group concerns on a modern kibbutz. Two years later,
The New Bridge offered a stark picture of the lives of an unem-
ployed construction worker and his family evicted from a tene-
ment at the beginning of the Depression. In 1937, Levin published what many readers thought (and still think) was his best
book, *The Old Bunch,* a densely textured chronicle of the inter-

---

2. Introduction to unpublished first draft of *The Fanatic* (BU).

twined lives of two dozen young Chicago-born Jews (children of immigrant West Siders), which James T. Farrell called "one of the most serious and ambitious novels yet produced by the current generation of American novelists" (*Saturday Review of Literature*, 13 March 1937). And *Citizens* (1940) was a vigorous fictional response to the 1937 strike and subsequent Memorial Day police shooting of workers at the Republic Steel Company plant outside Chicago.

Although these works had received mixed reviews and did not sell especially well, as a group they established Levin's reputation as one of the most able and enterprising young novelists of the 1930s, and *The Old Bunch* became a favorite book for many readers. The early interest in his fiction was a response in part to the energy and range of his social realism, but also to the fact that almost alone among the writers of the period, he seemed to be on the verge of shaping "a career" as an American novelist writing frequently and convincingly about the tensions of Jewish life. In the 1920s and 1930s, the commercial market for literature with any ethnic subject matter was both limited and extremely sensitive, and very few Jewish writers were able to make a living or to sustain a body of work. Elmer Rice and Clifford Odets in the New York theater might be considered exceptions, but the situation for novelists was less promising. Ludwig Lewisohn and Anzia Yezierska both gained followings in the 1920s, but either the quality or the volume of their work dropped off after that. Michael Gold's *Jews Without Money* (1930) was widely noticed, but he remained primarily an essayist. Henry Roth's *Call It Sleep* (1934), now prized as one of the splendid novels of the period, sold about four thousand copies in the thirties, and Roth did not publish another novel until 1994. The three books that make up the fresh, wryly disenchanted Williamsburg trilogy of Daniel Fuchs sold four hundred, four hundred, and twelve hundred copies between 1934 and 1938, and he abandoned fiction for screenwriting until the 1970s.[3]

At the beginning of his career, Levin himself was hesitant about using his own experiences as a Jew in his fiction. After writing some ethnic sketches and stories ("Roosevelt Road" and "A Seder") for the *Menorah Journal* and other magazines, he also worried about being labeled parochial and limiting the potential audience for his work, and he deliberately concealed the Jewish origins of the characters in his first two books. But after basing his third novel, *Yehuda,* on his formative visits to Palestine, he began writing with increasing frequency and openness about the problems of acculturation and self-definition for Jews in Chicago and elsewhere. Once he did, however, he too suffered from the timidity and the often biased, narrow, or nervous tastes of publishers and readers. One editor called on him to diversify the eth-

---

3. Daniel Fuchs, "Author's Preface," *Three Novels,* p. vii. Forty years after Levin published his first fiction, he provided a vivid description of what the marketplace had been like when he first began to write: "The magazines were cold to [Jewish] material, and book publishers avoided it with the same avidity with which they were to pursue it three decades later. It was felt that non-Jewish readers would not care to identify with Jewish fictional characters and that even Jewish readers preferred to identify with 'real Americans' in fiction. As a result, some talented writers who had begun quite naturally by writing about people with backgrounds with which they were familiar soon abandoned Jewish material or falsified it. They gave Jewish characters in their imaginative vision new, characterless names like Dick Benson or Jane Meredith, and homey Dr. Shapiro could always be endowed with a country twang and changed into Dr. Carmichael." Introduction to *The Rise of American Jewish Literature,* edited by Levin and Charles Angoff, 10–11.

nic identity of his characters in *The Old Bunch*, arguing that the book would be more typically American if it consisted of a melange of nationalities ("a few Irish, an Italian or two, and maybe a Greek") rather than a homogeneous group of Jews. The publisher of *Citizens* tried to get him to change the doctor protagonist from a Jew into a gentile to make the book more salable. Jewish readers themselves often complained of Levin's blunt treatment of the personal problems of Chicago Jews; Jews, they felt, should not be quite so obtrusive in fiction, and writers not so candid. Levin's newspaper and magazine work was also affected. In 1939, while he was writing film criticism for *Esquire*, the magazine received complaints that it was publishing too many articles by leftists and Jews. One of the awkward, if playful, editorial responses was to run Levin's film criticism under the byline of Paterson Murphy, a decision that led his friend Ernest Hemingway to quip: "The hand is the hand of Meyer but the foreskin is the foreskin of Paterson Murphy" (undated letter, circa 1939, at BU). But Levin persisted, and he was gradually able, after works as exotic as *Yehuda* and *The Golden Mountain* (a path-breaking collection of translated Hasidic tales) and as robust and absorbing as *The Old Bunch*, to create a modest audience for stories from a discerning American point of view about the way Jews lived then and in the recent past.

Just at the point when Levin seemed ready for what might be a breakthrough book, the progress of his career as a fiction writer was interrupted by America's entrance into the war against Germany and Japan. A strong-minded non-Communist progressive, Levin had always been responsive to calls for social action. As a newspaperman, he had reported firsthand on the civil war in Spain and on the mounting hostilities between

Arabs and Jews in Palestine; as a novelist, he was often praised for his sensitivity to proletarian distress in *The New Bridge* and *Citizens*. After Pearl Harbor, Levin felt a compelling need to play an active role. Getting an assignment at thirty-six was not going to be easy, but, as he liked to say, the fight against fascism could be fought without a gun, and he believed that for his writing to have currency and usefulness afterward, he would have to experience the war in an immediate way.

Levin also had strong personal reasons for wanting to get closer to the actions and passions of his time. In 1935, following a string of unsatisfactory romances and affairs, he had hastily married a twenty-year-old widow, Mable Schamp Foy, whose first husband had died of typhoid a few weeks after their wedding. She was a graduate student in chemistry at the University of Chicago; Levin had been a prize student there and was making his reputation in the city as a newspaperman and novelist. At first they seemed well matched: both very smart, good-looking, high-spirited, ambitious; but it soon became clear that each had come to the other on the rebound, and each was trying to exorcise someone else (in his case a fervently idealized teenage love who had rejected him). Although they were active in radical politics and went to Spain together to support the Loyalists in the civil war, their relationship steadily dissolved into conflict and mutual infidelity. Although they had a child in 1938, by the early forties they were estranged and soon divorced.[4]

For Levin, then, the commotion of the public sphere in

4. Mable Foy remarried after her divorce from Levin, and she committed suicide in 1951. For information about her, I am indebted to her son, Eli Levin. Meyer Levin married Tereska Torres on 25 March 1948.

1941–42 was a distraction and an escape, as well as a challenge. He went first to Washington and found work as a writer and director with a group of documentary filmmakers at the Office of War Information. Crisscrossing the country making movies in factories and housing sites to show activity on the home front, he was exhilarated by the strength of civilian commitment—and also relieved at not having to deal in imaginative work with the more difficult problems of conflicted Jewish identity in America, which had been emerging as the dominant subject matter of his fiction before the war. In 1943 Levin was assigned to London to write propaganda pamphlets for the Psychological Warfare Division, and he then worked for the Overseas News Agency and the Jewish Telegraphic Agency as a battle correspondent in France. It was in this role as reporter that Levin found the subject that was destined to shape the rest of his writing life. As he was to put it in his memoir, *In Search* (1950), "There was one story, in Europe, which I was peculiarly fitted to tell. It was the story of the fate of the Jews. Now at last as the continent was opened we would be able to discover the facts behind the gruesome rumors of mass slaughter and slavery that had been coming out of Europe" (169–70).

Assigned mainly to the Ninth Air Force and the Fourth Armored Division between September 1944 and June 1945, Levin took every opportunity to report on what the Germans had done to the Jews as more and more specific details about their already widely reported genocidal campaign were confirmed. When a concentration camp or killing center was liberated, he tried to go there, and he was among the first Americans to see the piles of dead and the devastated living at Ohrdruf, Nordhausen, Buchenwald, Dachau, and Bergen-

Belsen. Encountering the camps touched the deepest sources of horror, anguish, and fear in his personality, and changed him for good. As he was later to say, "Human beings had had it in them to do this, and we were of the same species."

His first response to the shock was to establish himself as a legman, a reporter who gathers information by being present at the event. He faithfully sent home spare dispatches: the who, what, when, where of what he described in a report from Buchenwald on 2 May 1945 as "the greatest systematic mass murder in the history of mankind." At the same time, he moved around recording the names of the dead, the deported, the survivors. Approaching emaciated inmates or refugees, he would ask them to write down their names, where they came from, and the address of one person they most urgently wanted to contact. So persistent was Levin in attempting to account for the living and dead Jews that survivors would crowd around his jeep and try to write their names on the hood, on the fenders, until the vehicle was covered with scrawls in Hebrew and Roman characters.

But despite his steady efforts to send dispatches back to America and to serve also as a kind of self-appointed, one-man social agency, tallying the names and numbers of survivors across France and Germany, Levin knew only too well that the events he was trying to register and respond to had a horror and a breadth of malignant implication that he would not be able to render. "From the beginning," he later confessed,

> I realized I would never be able to write the story of the Jews of Europe. This tragic epic cannot be written by a stranger to the experience, for the survivors have an augmented view

which we cannot attain; they lived so long so close with death that on a moral plane they are like people who have acquired ·the hearing of a whole range of tones outside normal human hearing. . . . As I groped in the first weeks, beginning to apprehend the monstrous shape of the story I would have to tell, I knew already that I would never penetrate its heart of bile, for the magnitude of this horror seemed beyond human register. My comprehension seemed to me like an electrical instrument whose needle has only a limited range, while the charge goes far beyond. Occasionally I could tell a story that gave a tangential glimpse into the hearts of the survivors. Some day a teller would arise from amongst themselves. (*In Search*, 173–74)

The belief that "some day a teller would arise from amongst themselves" became something of an idée fixe for Levin during his last weeks in Europe and in the months following his return to the United States. By this time, he had committed himself to the task of writing to help Americans realize the nature of the catastrophe inflicted by the Nazis on the Jews of Europe and to get people to reflect on its meaning for the postwar world. He also dedicated a good deal of time to assisting survivors who wanted to get to Palestine, a journey that under the British mandate was then illegal. In 1946, as a correspondent in Tel Aviv, Levin reported on the strife and terror accompanying Jewish resistance to British rule. And then in 1947–48, at considerable physical risk and financial sacrifice, he made two courageous films: *My Father's House*, the story of a child who goes to Palestine after the war, hoping to find the father from whom he had been separated in a concentration camp in Poland; and, with Tereska Torres, *The Illegals*, a documentary account of the actual clandestine voyage of a ship transporting

Jewish survivors to the Holy Land. He also translated a group diary that had been kept by inmates at Buchenwald, and he rewrote the screenplay of *My Father's House* and published it as a novel.

Throughout this period, Levin encountered some of the same difficulty getting his work to audiences that he had met in the early part of his career. The managers of the Overseas News Agency told him he could not report from the emerging state of Israel because they felt a non-Jewish byline would be more credible in America; financial backing for the two film projects was enormously difficult to obtain, and Levin worked at virtually no pay on both projects; and when the editing of *Illegals* was finished, he found it almost impossible (because of red tape, disputes, and indifference) to get the film widely distributed and shown in Europe or elsewhere. Yet despite the hazards and obstacles, Levin's determination to respond in as many ways as possible to the consequences of the German attempt to exterminate the Jews became a shaping emotional and intellectual fact of his life.

It also became something of a major personal predicament. Although he called the making of *The Illegals* his richest and most rewarding experience, he felt, too, that after having returned to ancestral Poland and having confronted Buchenwald and other camps, he had come to "the end of a stage in my journey toward self-realization. . . . I had told all I could find to tell, shown all there was to show. Now, like every Jew, I needed to come to a new understanding of myself in relation to Israel" (476). Yet after a brief return visit to Tel Aviv and to the kibbutz on which he had twice spent several months in the

late 1920s, Levin was convinced that his destiny was to remain
an American writer writing about Jews, not a citizen of the
emerging new Jewish state. His commitment was to the larger
Jewish community, Jews past and present, not to Jews in a specific physical place, however revered. He saw himself more and
more as a bicultural writer, not so much divided as enriched by
the imaginative possibilities of traditional Jewish life *and* of
contemporary experience in America.

Levin's most valuable expression of this dilemma (and of the
potential inherent in it) is his imposing work of self-inquiry,
confession, and explanation *In Search*, written in 1948–49.
Divided into three sections—"America: The Self-Accused,"
"Europe: The Witnesses," and "Israel: The Released"—the
book is nothing less than Levin's attempt to come to terms
with his identity and the condition of being a Jew in the mid
twentieth century. In Part One, he explores the consequences
of his shame and his fear of Jewishness as a boy and young
writer in Chicago. In Part Two, he depicts his life during the
war and tries to measure the impact of the Holocaust on his
sense of himself and his future. In Part Three, he describes his
major efforts (in *My Father's House* and *The Illegals*) to call
attention to the struggles of surviving European Jews to refash-
ion their lives in mandate Palestine and the new state of Israel.

Levin wrote *In Search* as if his life depended on it, and in
important ways it did. Not only was the memoir meant to be
therapeutic—an attempt to discover an emotional and intellectual equilibrium that had always eluded him—but it was also
designed to be his "big book," the magnum opus that *The Old
Bunch* and *Citizens* seemed to promise but that the war had

apparently delayed. From the moment he submitted *In Search* for publication, however, Levin's worst suspicions about his place in the literary scene in America were confirmed and intensified. Although editors found the manuscript forthright and often moving, they were put off by what they saw as Levin's relentless preoccupation with Jewish victimization and self-hatred, notably his indignation at his own difficulties getting fiction published and films distributed.

In early 1949, *In Search* was rejected by several important New York publishers. Random House found it "overburdened with resentment and a conviction of having been wronged." Viking called it verbose and self-indulgent, marred by "too much complaining about bad luck and persecution for being Jewish." Farrar, Straus turned it down for similar reasons. When Levin pressed Random House, Saxe Commins (who praised the memoir's urgency) explained that too much time was spent rehashing tedious quarrels with publishers and producers. "The reading public has little interest in the rows and grudges incidental to the production of a movie, a book, or almost anything else that they want to purchase for amusement, improvement or instruction." The manuscript, he told Levin, "leaves the impression that a particular person, yourself, had a hell of a time with everybody" (letter, 1 April 1949, BU).

Late in the year, Crown and Company accepted the book, but when Levin refused to make changes and cuts, the publishers withdrew the acceptance, fearing lawsuits and a bulky work that might not sell. At this point, frustrated and furious, Levin decided to have the manuscript printed in Paris at his own expense, "so it won't lose timeliness and die of old age" (28 January 1950, BU). Shortly after the book was printed in Paris, it was finally accepted by Horizon Press, a little-known house in New York, and it appeared in early summer 1950.

The rejections of *In Search* and the cheerless history of its publication turned out to have unfortunate, lasting consequences for Levin's writing career. Although he had earlier met with resistance from people in publishing, he usually explained his bad luck and small financial success as the result of the Depression and the inexperience or mismanagement of the people who produced and marketed his work. Now, after the disapproval of what he believed to be his most intimate, venturesome, and important book (a book about his quest for authentic identity as a Jew), he became convinced that there was something far more personal involved: an antagonism to who he was, to his view of the world and his way of expressing it. "At bottom," he concluded, "it was the same old Jewish question," and he saw himself locked in a struggle with people whose prejudices kept them from recognizing his talent and potential and prevented him from communicating with the public.[5] The editors and publishers, some of them Jewish, came to a very different conclusion, frequently describing Levin as suspicious, hypersensitive to criticism, obstinate—an increasingly difficult author with whom to work. Even friends noted his increasing outbursts of bitterness, one of them remembering "the atmosphere of palpable suffering binding you like a

---

5. In an early unpublished draft of *The Obsession*, then called *The Manipulators* (BU).

shroud." "I hope," this friend wrote in a letter to Levin, "you solve the problems, financial and emotional, which may obstruct your creative fiction."[6]

Yet despite these strains and the deteriorating situation, Levin felt entirely dedicated to his role as bicultural writer, and he turned with renewed vigor to develop two new film projects about Israel for the English and American market: the first, *The Hidden Word*, a script about the siege of Jerusalem and the opening of the emergency road to Tel Aviv, which he hoped to combine with a plot about the finding of a set of ancient scrolls like those from the Dead Sea; and the second, *Song of Israel*, a film based on *Yehuda* (his novel about a violin player on a kibbutz) that would star Yehudi Menuhin. For neither of these ventures was Levin finally able to get sufficient financial support, and his run of bad luck continued. The only book he could sell at the time was his translation of Tereska Torres's *Women's Barracks*. The Russian Boris Morros, who was supposed to have produced *Song of Israel*, turned out to be (unknown to Levin and Menuhin) a double agent for the United States and Soviet Union, who was using the film as a cover for spying on Soviet spies and had no intention of providing any money.

It was just when this string of failures and disappointments occurred and the early sales of *In Search* in Paris and New York were meager that Levin first read *Le Journal de Anne Frank*. Here, he immediately felt, was the teller he had predicted would materialize—a voice from among the dead he himself had seen at Bergen-Belsen. "As I read," he recalled, "I must

6. Undated letter from Alan Marcus (BU).

have gazed down on the body of this young girl. . . . The voice reached me from the pit."[7] As he was later to explain in a deposition for the Supreme Court of the State of New York, "It seemed to me that the girl's diary contained the elements by which the world could finally and clearly absorb the enormity of the mass murders perpetrated by the Nazis. It had a passion similar to mine in setting down truly the lives of these people and it reflected in particular the tragedy of the times as they affected the development of the young."[8] As far as Levin knew, the Dutch text had appeared in translation only in French. If he could help make the diary available to English and American readers, he might obtain some financial advantage while furthering his mission of conveying the meaning of the Nazi atrocities to people who had previously been insulated from them.

On 8 September 1950, Levin wrote of his admiration to Calmann-Lévy, the French publisher of *Le Journal de Anne Frank*, inquired about English and American rights, and asked for the address of the book's agent. Oddly, Tereska Torres, without mentioning it, had also written to praise the book. The publisher sent both letters to Otto Frank, the girl's father, who wrote back to explain the current situation regarding publication in various countries. In letters and later conversations with the Levins, Frank, who was in the process of moving to Switzerland (where his mother and other members of his family lived), recounted the early history of his dead daughter's book.

7. Introduction to unpublished first draft of *The Fanatic* (BU).

8. Deposition given by Meyer Levin, 21 February 1956, in *Levin v. Frank* (SCSNY).

On 4 August 1944, when the German and Dutch security
police had broken into the apartment behind his business on
the Prinsengracht to arrest the eight Jews who had hidden there
for more than two years, they emptied a briefcase in a search
for valuables, and the child's diary, exercise books and assorted
papers were strewn on the floor. Later that day, after the prisoners had been taken for questioning, Miep Gies and Bep
Voskuijl, the Christian women who (with Johannes Kleiman,
Victor Kugler, and Jan Gies) had kept the Jews alive in hiding,
went back upstairs into the apartment and gathered the loose
books and papers in the event that anyone should ever want
them. In the summer of 1945, following his liberation from
Auschwitz, Otto Frank (the only member of the fugitive group
to survive the death camps) returned to the house and was
eventually told of the existence of his daughter's diary. At first,
he could hardly bear to read it, but when he did he was so
stirred that he began copying out sections he thought would
interest relatives and friends. Since parts of the diary existed in
several versions, Frank served as an editor as well as a tran-
scriber. In addition to choosing between different renderings,
he omitted passages that fell generally into four categories:
those that might offend living people, those that reflected neg-
atively on his dead wife, those that were extremely intimate,
and those that he thought trivial and of little import. What he
copied he also translated into German to send to his mother in
Basel, who did not know Dutch.

When relatives and friends read the selections from the
diary, they were at once convinced of its exceptional value as
both a document of the war and an absorbing story of a lively
young girl's maturation, and they urged Frank to try to publish

it. At first, he thought the manuscript would attract little attention outside the immediate family, but he was persuaded to allow friends to make inquiries. In the winter of 1945–46, several Dutch publishers turned the book down. But in early April 1946, the Amsterdam paper *Het Parool* printed on its front page an eloquent article by the eminent historian Jan Romein, praising the unpublished diary as a strikingly graphic account of daily life in wartime and a revelation of the "real hideousness of Fascism," which had destroyed the life of a richly endowed, effervescent young girl. Publishers responded quickly, and Otto Frank signed with Uitgeverji Contact to issue *Het Achterhuis* [*The House Behind*] in a small edition the following June.

The Dutch reviews were uniformly enthusiastic, and in less than three years *Het Achterhuis* was reprinted five times, selling more than twenty-five thousand copies. Posthumously, Anne Frank had become the best-known child in Holland, and her sixty-year-old father had surprisingly found himself the busy, dedicated guardian of her expanding fame. As an experienced businessman, Otto Frank appreciated the sales potential of his daughter's remarkable book, and as a decent, compassionate man, mourning the loss of his family and friends, he hoped that her dark story but bright character might have some positive moral meaning for postwar readers. On the strength of the diary's popularity in Holland, he was able to arrange for a French edition to appear in the spring of 1950 and for a German imprint to be scheduled around Christmas, but as Frank explained to Levin in September, British and American houses had as yet shown no interest. In England, the book had been rejected by Gollanz, Heinemann, Allen and Unwin, Macmillan, and Secker and Warburg; in the United States, it had been turned down by Scribners, Viking, Vanguard, Simon and Schuster, Appleton Century, Schocken, Knopf, Harper, and Harcourt. There was no market for special-interest war books, Frank had been told, and besides, few readers in England or America could be expected to buy the prosaic diary of a teenage Dutch girl whose life ended so unhappily.

Despite these rejections, Frank explained, he had not lost confidence in the book's value and usefulness, and his Paris agent was still trying to arrange for publication in England and America. Thus he could not at this time give Levin an option on rights. Besides, Random House in New York had recently indicated that they might consider joining in a mutual arrangement with a British firm for publication in both countries, and Frank wanted to pursue this new possibility. Levin replied that his concern with the diary was not commercial but rather emotional and sympathetic, and he offered to translate it to help call attention to the book in New York. Such an opportunity, he said, would be a mitzvah, a good deed. He also told Otto Frank that he believed there was material for "a very touching play or film in the Diary," and he asked for permission to suggest this to his contacts in the field when he returned to New York in mid-October. Finally, he sent along a copy of *In Search* to give Frank some sense of his personal history and his understanding of, and commitment to, the postwar predicament of the European Jews.

Frank confessed that he did not perceive any theatrical or cinematic possibilities in his daughter's diary. For him, the appeal of the book lay in the uncommonly intimate, honest manner in which the young girl expressed her thoughts and feelings, and he worried that a filmmaker would feel compelled to emphasize the excitement and thrills of a story about people in hiding in order to entertain an audience. If Levin saw it differently, however, he should feel free to make inquiries once he was back in the States.

In New York in October, Levin did begin contacting people in theater and film, and over the next months he wrote scores of letters to agents, producers, and directors, among them Darryl Zanuck, Samuel Goldwyn, Louis de Rochemont, Stanley Kramer, Dore Schary, and Fred Zinnemann, but he could not obtain any definite commitment. In mid-November, he continued his campaign to publicize the diary itself by writing an essay called "The Restricted Market" for *Congress Weekly* (the journal of the American Jewish Congress). Here he recounted the discovery and European publication of Anne Frank's book in the context of a discussion of the attitudes among American publishers toward works prominently about Jews. He observed that the recent appearance of John Hersey's *The Wall* had led some people to believe that the resistance to books with a Jewish subject was diminishing, but he then went on to describe the success of the Anne Frank diary in Holland and France and its surprising rejection by a large number of eminent publishers in America. Following an account of his own frustrations with the many rejections of *In Search*, and of the way the memoir had been ignored by some reviewers even after its publication, he ended with a call for a continued fight for attention.

Although the primary aims of Levin's piece were to register a complaint about the treatment of his own memoir and to urge people to continue to press for the publication of Jewish books, "The Restricted Market" did have the valuable effect of calling attention to the existence of the Anne Frank diary, even mentioning the likelihood that a British and an American publisher would soon share translation and typesetting costs to bring the book out in both countries (a plan that was shortly to fall through). By coincidence, Levin's piece appeared on the same day (11 November 1950) as Janet Flanner's *New Yorker* "Letter from Paris," which described *Le Journal de Anne Frank* as one of the most widely and seriously read books in France. Given the different size of the readerships of the *New Yorker* and *Congress Weekly*, Flanner's article was likely to call more attention to Anne Frank in America than Levin's, but nonetheless his essay played a useful role in making readers aware of the worth of the book and its importance as a historical document of the Nazi assault on the Jews.

Aside from Levin's efforts, there had been several other positive developments. In September, the London firm of Vallentine, Mitchell wrote to Frank's Paris agent asking for information about English rights, and Levin helped follow this up by talking with the firm when he was in London. In November, a Dutch refugee writer, Dola de Jong, sent the editors at Little, Brown in Boston copies of the Janet Flanner *New Yorker* piece and the Levin article from *Congress Weekly*. Frank encouraged both the London and the Boston publishers, and for some weeks it looked as if a joint effort might be possible. On 22 November, Ned Bradford of Little, Brown wired Frank:

> This is definite offer to publish Anne Frank diary in US. Excellent chance simultaneous British publication. $500 advance against royalties on signing contract, additional $500 when MS delivered by translator. $1,000 trans fee charged against future royalties. Royalty rate 10% on $3 selling price, first 5,000 copies. Royalty rate 12 1/2 on next 5,000, 15% over

10,000. Prefer Dola de Jong translate. Would think eventual
sale of 25,000 not exaggerated expectation. Much enthusiasm
for book here. (BU)

Frank accepted both offers by the end of the month, but disagreements arose almost immediately about various aspects of
the proposed copublication scheme. Vallentine, Mitchell and
Frank did not like the Dola de Jong translation, and disputes
emerged over other issues of production and promotion, such
as which printing plates should be used and which firm should
get the rights to the Canadian market. But the most troublesome sticking point for Otto Frank had to do with dramatic
and film rights. Little, Brown insisted on both; Vallentine,
Mitchell cared about neither; and Frank, influenced by Levin's
urgings about the dramatic potential of the story, finally
decided to go ahead separately with the London firm (which
he did in January 1951) and, after protracted negotiations, to
cancel the contract with Little, Brown in late March. Vallentine, Mitchell did publish the British edition of the *Diary* in
May of the following year.

While all this was going on, another American firm had
come forward in the bidding for U.S. rights. In January 1950,
Francis Price, the head of Doubleday's Paris office, was shown
an advance copy of *Le Journal de Anne Frank* by the writer
Manès Sperber, who advised Calmann-Lévy. At first, Price
thought the volume of little importance—a kids' book by a
kid—and told his assistant, Judith Bailey, to send it back.
Instead, she read it with mounting enthusiasm and urged Price
to take another look. He did and eventually advised the editors
in New York to consider making an offer. The Doubleday peo-

ple came actively back into the picture just when negotiations were breaking down between Vallentine, Mitchell; Little, Brown; and Otto Frank. Even though Levin had advised Frank to stay with Little, Brown because it had the higher literary reputation, Frank decided to accept a similar offer from Doubleday and signed with that firm in late April 1951; the book was published just over a year later, in June 1952.

The details and the precise chronology here are especially important because in the subsequent dispute between Levin and Frank that led to two notorious law suits, Levin gave a different account of the events and the matters on which he and Frank had agreed. He later maintained that he was instrumental in getting the Anne Frank diary accepted for publication in the United States; and in a 1956 court deposition he claimed that in or about the summer of 1950, he and Frank had "entered into an agreement" that had four major points: (1) Levin would represent Frank's interest in the United States in regard to the *Diary*. (2) He would negotiate, as Frank's exclusive agent, with theatrical producers for a play and film to be made from the book. (3) He would attempt to obtain a producer "of prominence and capability." (4) And in sole consideration therefore, he also would have the right to write a play based on the *Diary*.[9]

Frank was subsequently to challenge the accuracy of several of the claims in Levin's account. He contended that their early arrangement was a good deal more general and vague: more like a willingness on his part to allow Levin to make inquiries about the theatrical potentiality of the material than like a

9. Ibid.

binding agreement about agency and the right to produce a dramatic adaptation of the *Diary*. Levin could counter with the point that Frank *did* sign a letter dated 31 March 1952 authorizing him to negotiate for motion picture, television, radio, and dramatic adaptation for a period of one year, but in that letter there was no mention of the right to adapt the *Diary*. Some of the acrimony that was to develop between the two men can be traced to their contentions about what was actually agreed upon in 1950 and 1951. Now, more than forty years after the events, in the absence of written contracts, it is impossible to determine precisely what in fact *was* agreed upon and when. But from existing letters, accounts, and interviews, it seems likely that many of Levin's later assertions were based more on what he had wished for than on what Otto Frank had granted or understood to be the case. Levin, for instance, was not directly responsible for getting the *Diary* published in America. Although he had written letters and made inquiries, and certainly had drawn people's attention to the book, the Doubleday contract evolved from the high praise of Judith Bailey, Francis Price, Donald Elder, Barbara Zimmerman, and others. Levin himself was not involved in those early negotiations. In fact, he wrote to Frank, in a letter dated 14 March 1952: "Should you want an agent to handle the matter at this time, I can refer you to a good one. Otherwise, I will try to do the things an agent would normally do, but without obligating you in any way—that is, I will submit the book to the various producers, story editors, etc." (BU). This letter clearly casts doubt on Levin's later claim that a formal agreement about agency and adaptation existed in 1950–51, and it supports Frank's contention that Levin confused the chance to write

with the right to write. The complex implications of Levin's
and Frank's different understanding of Levin's role, and the
consequences of their perceptions, are explored at a later stage
of this history.

In the months that followed Doubleday's acceptance of
Anne Frank: The Diary of a Young Girl, Levin continued his
unsuccessful attempts to draw the attention of producers to a
possible stage adaptation, and he spread the word about the
book's distinction at every opportunity, writing essays about it
for *Congress Weekly* and the *National Jewish Post*. He also
arranged for first serial rights to go to *Commentary*, where
excerpts from the *Diary* started appearing a month before the
book was published. Although several of the people at Doubleday (notably Frank Price, Barbara Zimmerman, Jason Epstein,
and Karen Rye) formed what came playfully to be called the
Informal Society of Advocates of Anne Frank, the prevailing
assessment at the firm was that the sales potential was small.
The first edition was set at five thousand copies, and there was
no prepublication advertising. Even an edition of five thousand
was felt by some in the company to be "something of a gamble
and assuredly large enough to meet what was expected to be
the demand for such a chronicle." Reports to the sales force
played down the grim aspects of the story and emphasized the
"beauty, humor and insight" of this "document of sensitive
adolescence."[10] Doubleday editors also managed to persuade
Eleanor Roosevelt to provide an introduction (actually written
by Barbara Zimmerman and signed by Mrs. Roosevelt), but
otherwise undertook no unusual efforts—aside from word-of-

10. June 1952 (JM).

mouth endorsement and personal letters—to promote the book in advance. It was at this point, however, that Levin made his most important contribution to the success of the *Diary* in America.

In February 1952, without declaring his interest, he had asked for and had been granted the assignment of reviewing the volume for the influential *New York Times Book Review*. At first he was told that he had about three hundred words, but when he conveyed his excitement about the *Diary*, Francis Brown, the editor, requested that he write at greater length. Levin's authoritative, dazzling review appeared on the first page of the *Times Book Review* on 15 June 1952, the day before the book went on sale. Entitled "The Girl Behind the Secret Door," this piece offered the fullest and most compelling account of the interest and distinction of the *Diary* that had yet appeared in America. Other laudatory reviews (notably those in *Time, Newsweek,* and the *Herald Tribune* over the same weekend and in the daily papers on Monday and Tuesday) also helped promote the book, but afterward nearly everyone agreed that Levin's tribute in the *Times* was what launched *Anne Frank: The Diary of a Young Girl* on its spectacular career in America.

Levin's strategy in the review is brilliant. He opens with the bold, eye-catching claim that "Anne Frank's diary is too tenderly intimate a book to be frozen with the label 'classic,' and yet no other designation serves"—a startling assertion about a work that most Sunday-morning review readers would never have heard of. Then, after reassuring his audience that this is "no lugubrious ghetto tale," no chilling "compilation of horrors," he goes on to explain why the child's journal is for now and forever. The quicksilver diarist is a born writer; her style is zestful, her observations various and unfailingly keen. Her amazing story has suspense, heartbreak, tart comedy, romance, discovery, terror, and anguish. As a fearful tale of fugitives in hiding that reveals the stirring psychological drama of a girl's sexual and moral growth, the diary has the shape and tension of a superbly constructed novel. But the historical implications of the narrative, Levin argued, give it the force of an epic, the story of a people. "Anne Frank's voice," he asserts in a sentence that was to be repeated (for better and worse) countless times, "becomes the voice of six million vanished Jewish souls." And surely, he ends, "she will be widely loved, for this wise and wonderful young girl brings back a poignant delight in the infinite human spirit."

On Monday morning 16 June booksellers across the country reported a very heavy demand for *Anne Frank: The Diary of a Young Girl,* and by early afternoon the entire first edition had sold out. Everyone at Doubleday was amazed and jubilant; a second edition of 15,000 was swiftly ordered, and a few days later a third printing of 25,000 brought the total number of copies to 45,000. A full-scale promotional campaign was ordered, with advertisements taken in major newspapers in cities across America. In the next few days, a dozen papers bought syndication rights; the Book Find Club picked the *Diary* for its August selection; and *Omnibook* chose to offer a condensation in a forthcoming issue.

People in the book trade observed that this surprising success was due almost entirely to the applause of the reviewers; one leading New York publisher told Pyke Johnson of Doubleday's publicity department, "If there were a prize for the best review of the year," Meyer Levin's piece on *Anne Frank* "would almost certainly win it."[11]

On the same morning that booksellers were receiving a rush of requests for the *Diary*, theatrical agents, producers, and people in television and film began telephoning Doubleday to inquire about dramatic rights. Although everyone at the publishing house was giddy with excitement and felt that Levin and Doubleday shared the same objectives, it quickly became clear that Levin could not be expected to handle such intricate commercial negotiations by himself. Ken McCormick, editor-in-chief at Doubleday, suggested that a cable be sent to Otto Frank in Basel, asking him to assign the task of negotiating to the firm's own subsidiary rights department, whose large and experienced staff would work closely with Levin. Levin agreed, and a cable to Otto Frank went out that same day, signed jointly by Barbara Zimmerman, the young editor assigned to the book from the beginning, and Meyer Levin: "Due to wonderful critical response Anne's Diary there is much interest from theatrical and film producers. May Doubleday have authority to handle these rights for you at usual agent's fee of 10% of proceeds. We feel strongly we could handle these rights in a way suitable to book" (16 June 1952, BU).

Although on its face the proposal made good sense, it concealed tensions between the various parties that had been developing and were about to erupt into conflict. By Monday afternoon, the people at Doubleday were aware that they had a very hot property on their hands, and they had already begun to have doubts on several counts about Levin. First, they thought

11. Doubleday in-house memo, 17 June 1952 (JM).

of him as overzealous and vague about the business of selling rights. He made odd arrangements on his own (authorizing Howard Phillips of NBC to negotiate film rights as *his* representative), appeared to be susceptible to the proposals of people with dubious credentials, and did not keep the publisher's representatives fully informed of his many consultations. Second, they perceived that Levin's own desire to write the adaptation might be an obstacle to a producer who wanted another playwright. Levin had come into the picture as Frank's informal agent; now he was forcefully putting himself forward as the preferred adapter. The ambiguity of his role was potentially troublesome. Barbara Zimmerman bluntly expressed some of the Doubleday skepticism in a letter to Frank Price: "Although Levin himself was *not* after selling the rights for base financial reasons, he seemed to be screwing the whole deal up and I think, as Ken does very strongly, that it would be best if we handled the rights and worked closely with Levin" (17 June 1952, JM).

Levin had his own misgivings about the people at Doubleday. Within hours of the time the joint cable was sent to Otto Frank in Basel, he became increasingly worried that his interests and the company's were potentially at odds. Although he had written several plays, few had been produced and none on Broadway; he was known as a novelist and journalist, not as a playwright. Now that the *Diary* was headed toward enormous success, Doubleday might want to persuade Otto Frank to aim for a glamorous sale to a powerful producer who could sign a big-name playwright, and then Levin, who wished above all to adapt the *Diary*, would be out in the cold. That night, unknown to Doubleday, Levin sent a second cable urging Frank to "Please await my letter before answering Doubleday's request for agency power." In the letter he gave a detailed account of why he had joined in the original cable and then privately sent another of his own. "As you know," he wrote to Frank, "I have from the beginning, even before there was an American publisher, had my heart in making a play and a film from this material. If I had the money, I would have offered to buy the rights from you." And then he went on to ask Frank to stipulate to Doubleday that it had the agency rights and the rights to ten percent of the value of any sale, but that "no sale shall be made unless the conditions of the agreement are approved by me, and by yourself. It would then be possible for either one of us to stipulate that I should be the writer, or at least one of the writers, in any play or film treatment. Of course, should the situation arise where a production by a famous playwright is possible only if I step aside, I would step aside. However, I should be heartbroken if the material were sold to some producer who would simply appoint any friend of his to write the play or film" (16 June 1952, BU). In his concluding paragraph, Levin proposed some wording for a cable that Frank could send to New York.

The cable that Frank did send to Doubleday on 18 June borrowed several phrases from Levin's letter and read: "Consent to give you authority to handle film and play rights with usual agent fee providing conditions of any sale of such rights be approved by Meyer Levin and myself as desire Levin as writer or collaborator in any treatment to guarantee idea of book" (BU). Although at this point, the editors at Doubleday and notably Joseph Marks, the vice-president who was handling the negotiations for dramatic rights, did not know that Levin was communicating separately with Otto Frank, they recognized that the situation was tangled and ambiguous at best. They were aware that earlier, on 31 March, Frank had authorized Levin "to negotiate for motion picture, television, radio and dramatic adaptation of *Anne Frank: The Diary of a Young Girl*, for a period of one year from this date, with the stipulation that I, as the sole owner of these rights, shall require to approve any such agreements, and any adaptations of the material in this book, before public presentation" (BU). Obviously this earlier assignment (the wording of which had been proposed by Levin himself) and the cable of 18 June conflicted at enough points to require clarification.

Proposals were coming in rapidly. Cheryl Crawford mentioned Lillian Hellman, said she might consider Levin, but mentioned other writers and directors as well; Kermit Bloomgarden, proposing Arthur Miller, promised to weigh the possibility of Levin; Norman Rose and Peter Cappell suggested Morton Wishengrad or Thornton Wilder, saying they would consider Levin as collaborator but would accept him as the sole adapter only as a last resort; Maxwell Anderson was an active bidder for the Playwrights' Company but did not wish to work with a collaborator—no reflection on Levin, he said, just a condition he felt it necessary to impose. Walter Fried suggested that Levin and Harold Clurman discuss the play, and if there was a meeting of minds, he might produce, Levin write, and Clurman direct. Among the others who came forward were Joshua Logan (who wanted to adapt and direct himself), Shepard Traube, Lemuel Ayers, Max Gordon, Robert Whitehead, the Theatre Guild, CBS-TV, and Milton Krents for the Eternal Light radio program. Although no two proposals were precisely the same, each producer reserved the right to judge whether a script (by Levin or anyone else) was acceptable. If not, he or she would have to be free to employ a collaborator or another playwright.

Given the number of people involved in the flurry of discussions and the fact that the wishes and rights of Frank, Levin, and Doubleday were still not clearly spelled out, rumors and misrepresentations spread, and distrust mounted quickly on all sides. Levin often met alone with interested parties, and his version of the prospective arrangements sometimes differed from Doubleday's. On one crucial matter—whether he would step aside for a famous playwright—he kept changing his mind, gradually becoming more resistant to the possibility. Producers and agents often gave diverging accounts of what they were offering, depending on whether they were talking with Levin or with a representative of Doubleday. If a producer thought Levin had veto power, he might encourage him and thus reinforce the impression that Doubleday was not telling the whole truth. Similarly, some bidders talking to the publisher would belittle Levin's talent in an effort to get the rights for a playwright of their own. Other producers told Levin and/or Doubleday that the division of responsibility in negotiating dramatic rights was ill-advised, but this was now the fixed condition that had evolved and had been approved by Otto Frank.

On the fourth day of the negotiations, Levin told Frank that

he had been in another lengthy discussion with several of the
Doubleday people, and they had decided on some general
guidelines:

—if definite offers were received from theatrical producers,
naming dramatists of the first rank for the task, it would be
suggested that Levin collaborate on the adaptation;

—preference would be given to whichever dramatist
accepted Levin as collaborator;

—if no first rank "name" dramatist offered to adapt the
play, Levin should have preference over other writers;

—if only one producer wanted to do the show and would
accept only a dramatist who refused to have a collaborator,
someone other than Levin himself should decide whether Levin
should step aside.

But even these revised guidelines were Levin's formulations
and hardly firm. Although he and the Doubleday representatives were entirely devoted to securing a deal that would respect
the integrity of the *Diary* and satisfy Otto Frank, there continued to be too many differences in other aims and assessments,
and too many pitfalls inherent in the decentralized negotiations, for them to work satisfactorily together. On 23 June, only
a week after the discussions had begun, Joseph Marks and others concluded that the situation had become untenable and that
further efforts would have to be made to get Otto Frank to
clarify what rights and responsibilities each party had. Frank in
Basel was still loyal to both sides and believed that a collaboration based on mutual understanding was still possible. He felt

that Levin had worked immensely hard for the book and could write a sympathetic and tasteful adaptation; he also believed that the employees at Doubleday were doing everything they could to promote the *Diary* and to effect an advantageous sale of the dramatic rights. But he understood too that if a producer bought the rights he might not want to be constrained by conditions in the choice of an adapter.

Without consulting Levin, Doubleday asked Frank if he could come to the United States to participate in the knotty discussions. When Levin learned about the invitation, he felt further confirmed in his belief that Doubleday now wanted to sign an eminent playwright and to force him out. On 2 July, he wrote a sharp letter of protest to Ken McCormick, charging Joseph Marks with actively campaigning to get rid of him as a possible adapter of the *Diary*. He had, he said, earlier suspicions, which were now corroborated by conversations with Max Gordon, Cheryl Crawford, and Norman Rose, producers who he believed were willing to work with him on the play. Marks, he claimed, gave them the impression that they would fare better in the bidding if they backed the choice of a more eminent writer, and then Marks gave him a distorted account of where he stood in each producer's favor. Expressing astonishment that Otto Frank had been called to the United States to "settle this problem," Levin indignantly concluded that "there was no problem and is no problem. . . . We have a choice of many excellent producers and could get to work at once. . . . Moreover, it seems clear to me that the only motive for having him come here to deal with 'this problem' can be the motive of talking him out of having me as adaptor, since that seems to be the problem in Mr. Marks's mind" (BU). Levin also maintained that Marks's actions had damaged his professional reputation and impeded his career.

When Joseph Marks was shown Levin's letter, he told Ken McCormick that the accusations had no basis in fact, and he declared that in all the conferences no information had been withheld from Levin, nor had he been told anything that was not absolutely true. Given the range of his charges and the intensity of his feelings, however, the negotiating situation had clearly deteriorated to the point of collapse. After consulting with their lawyers, the Doubleday representatives concluded that it was no longer advisable for the firm to continue as a party in the negotiations. Levin, they felt, had changed his mind so many times, and was now so incensed and hostile, that he had become impossible to work with; earlier he had been in love with the book, but now he seemed more eager to protect what Frank Price called "his own private gold mine."[12] Then, too, the editors remained wary of the nebulous negotiating terms and saw the threat of a lawsuit in Levin's specific claim that he was being forced out as adapter and in his general charges about professional injury. As Marks wrote to Price: "Levin, by his own statement, is a pretty fast guy with a lawsuit and from what I can learn, has not endeared himself to any of the people with whom he had worked" (9 July 1952, JM). On 7 July, the decision was made to inform Frank that Doubleday had withdrawn as co-agent in the negotiations, and a cable to that effect was sent to Basel. On the following day, in a more

12. Mentioned by Barbara Zimmerman in letter to Frank Price, 22 July 1952 (JM).

detailed letter, Marks was polite but firm. "We were acting under your instructions as partners with Mr. Levin. As you can surely understand, in a partnership there must be complete trust on both sides. Perhaps because of incompatibility of personalities, Mr. Levin and I could no longer see eye to eye on many problems which confronted us. I think it is best for the negotiations . . . for one person to handle it. We had to come to the conclusion that we must withdraw and we have given Mr. Levin detailed information of our negotiations with various people" (JM).

Otto Frank was disappointed by the news but still spoke of coming to New York to try to bring about an amicable collaboration. Despite the wording of some of his messages and his admiration for Levin, he had never intended to force him on anyone as the writer of the play, and he insisted that Doubleday still get a financial share of the proceeds for the sale of the dramatic rights. ("This is a commercial matter which has to be treated in a decent manner, so kindly do not refuse!" he wrote to Marks on 9 July.) But Doubleday remained firm in its decision to withdraw and persuaded Frank to postpone his trip and concentrate on working with Levin alone to find a suitable producer for a play based on the *Diary*.

Fortunately for Frank, Cheryl Crawford had for the past two weeks been emerging as perhaps the most promising of the bidders. She had first inquired the day after the *Diary* was published, and the editors at Doubleday knew of her reputation as an experienced and highly respected figure in the contemporary theater. In the 1930s she had been cofounder with Harold Clurman and Lee Strasberg of the progressive Group Theatre and in the following decade had worked with Eva Le Gallienne and Margaret Webster to create the American Repertory Theatre and with Elia Kazan and Robert Lewis to establish the Actors Studio. Recently she had produced several successful musicals (*One Touch of Venus, Brigadoon,* and *Paint Your Wagon*), had staged Tennessee Williams's *The Rose Tattoo,* and was planning to put on his *Camino Real.*

Although Crawford had spoken with Levin about the *Diary* before it was published, when she contacted Doubleday on 17 June she thought he was only the agent for the book and was not aware of his desire to do the adaptation. Her first suggestions for possible playwrights were Lillian Hellman and Clifford Odets, both of whom she knew and had worked with. By 25 June, when she met with Joseph Marks to explore the situation further, she understood Frank's preference for Levin and was willing to give him a chance to write a draft on speculation. She had, she explained, a high regard for Levin's talent but was aware of his inexperience as a playwright and would have to be free to use another writer if Levin's script was unacceptable. She would be willing to give him two months to present a version for her to approve or disapprove but wished first to talk with him to hear how he planned to approach the book. If his script was promising but needed work, she might select another playwright to collaborate with Levin, providing him with partial credit and a certain share of income. At this time, she also mentioned having spoken with Elia Kazan about the possibility of his directing, but although he promised to read the *Diary,* he told her that he might soon be making commitments for the fall season. For this and other reasons, she urged Doubleday to make a quick decision.

In the days following this conversation, Joseph Marks heard

reports that Levin believed Doubleday was angling for a big-name playwright and was trying to force him out. Marks talked with Levin, denied the rumor-based suspicions, explained the terms under which Crawford would permit him to write a draft version, and also mentioned other producers who were willing to consider him as the adapter. The relieved Levin swiftly provided his version of the current status of the negotiations in a letter to Otto Frank, warmly praising Crawford ("One can't go wrong with her") and explaining: "Her idea is to have me make a dramatization, while working closely with her and the director, and if the dramatization is not right, another writer would be called in for extra work. This is often done and seems reasonable to me" (11 July 1952, BU).

When Crawford phoned Doubleday on 1 July to find out how negotiations were progressing, she was told that the agents were seeing and talking with all parties, that Otto Frank had been asked to come to New York, and that no final decision would be made until he arrived. It was precisely this situation, however—the invitation to Otto Frank and the continued discussions with a dozen eager producers and playwrights—that seemed to confirm Levin's suspicion about Doubleday wanting another adapter and prompted him to write the decisive accusatory letter to Ken McCormick. The Doubleday representatives insisted that by welcoming all comers they were following Otto Frank's instructions and acting in his best interests, until they could confer with him in New York. But, not surprisingly, Levin's reading of their motives and behavior (based as it was on the conflicting testimony of many of the aspirants) was more distrustful.

After Doubleday withdrew on 7 July, Marks, Price, Zim-

merman, and Levin all urged Otto Frank to choose Cheryl
Crawford as the most sensitive, best-qualified producer for a
stage version of the *Diary*; at the same time, Crawford herself
wrote Frank spelling out her views on the prospect of Levin's
doing the adaptation:

> I have read Meyer's plays and think he has talent. I know that
> he wants very much to dramatize the Diary. I told him I
> would be willing to give him eight weeks to make a draft. If
> it turns out well, I would produce it. If, on the other hand, it
> does not seem satisfactory, I would engage another playwright
> and would compensate Meyer for his work. It would be
> splendid if Meyer could write a good dramatization as I know
> how close he feels to the book, but he is willing to take the
> chance I have suggested above. (9 July 1952, PWRW&G)

In addition to this explanation, Crawford gave Frank her general ideas about other playwrights and about possible directors,
ending, "If Meyer had the first opportunity to write it, I would
decide on one of these experienced directors so that Meyer
might have the benefit of their experience while he was writing as well as mine."

As with so many of the other formulations of conditions in
the early negotiations for dramatic rights, Crawford's statement
did not have the exactitude or the status of a formal contract
and allowed for various interpretations. Otto Frank understood
it to mean that Crawford had to decide if she liked Levin's draft
or wanted another playwright. He thought her offer a fair one
and told Barbara Zimmerman: "If a producer invests money,
risks his name, he has to know what he is doing and Miss
Crawford will certainly not accept a draft she does not like. Per-

sonally I think I should not interfere and leave it to her judgment" (18 July 1952, PWRW&G). Similarly, Frank Price told Joseph Marks that Levin was being permitted, at his own risk, to proceed with an adaptation of the play to be accepted or rejected. If Crawford felt it necessary later to bring in either a collaborator or a new writer, she would be left free to make such a choice. Price added that he advised Frank to settle this point clearly with Levin because a large part of the recent disagreement had "arisen from a duality of control and that the point must be arrived at where some one person could say 'Aye, Yea, or Nay' flatly. It seems to me, on the basis of all the various proposals, that Crawford was the best to be entrusted with this" (16 July 1952, JM).

Levin, however, seems not to have understood the agreement in the same way. He began working on the adaptation of the *Diary* in mid-July, confidently assuming that it would be stageworthy but not coming to a detailed understanding with Crawford or Frank about what would occur if she did not find it acceptable. Her letter states that she might go to another writer *or* consider calling in a collaborator. Levin appears to have thought only about a possible collaborator, not an outright rejection; this became a severe point of contention later in the year.

In late July and early August, however, Levin continued working on his script on Fire Island, while Frank in Basel and Crawford in New York exchanged letters about the forthcoming project. Frank acknowledged how much he liked and trusted Levin and how convinced he was of his sympathetic feeling for the book, but he also confessed that he had no way of judging if Levin was the right dramatist for the job. Apart from sentiment, he said, a play is a commercial matter, and a good deal of money was invested. He reassured Crawford that he did not want to interfere and was sure that he would never need to use his veto as owner of the rights. She in her turn mentioned that Levin was working on the play even though they had no contract (a delay caused by the vacation of Levin's lawyer), and she summarized her understanding of what Levin took to be the arrangement between them: if he could not write a satisfactory draft, she would have the liberty to give it to another writer or call in a collaborator. In the meantime, she told Frank, she had asked "one of our top playwrights to study the Diary with the idea of a collaboration with Meyer or taking over completely" (30 July 1952, PWRW&G).

In late August, Levin mailed Frank a draft of a proposed contract on rights and royalties. According to him, the usual procedure recommended by the Dramatists Guild was for the adapter to make a contract with the owner of the rights and then in turn make a contract with the producer of the play, who does not customarily make a contract directly with the owner of the rights. When Otto Frank received the draft from Levin in early September, he read it with surprise and some concern, for it was not in accordance with the informal terms he had worked out with Cheryl Crawford. In all their discussions, *she* was supposed to be the judge of the adaptation; thus he could not now sign a separate agreement with Levin. Since he had questions about other points as well, he suggested Levin wait until he came to New York at the end of the month so they could discuss contractual matters at that time. Frank also wrote to Crawford to explain his reservations about the proposed contract, and there the matter stood.

Although Levin's work on the adaptation was interrupted by a commission from the American Jewish Committee to do a short radio play drawn from the *Diary*, scheduled to be broadcast on CBS during the Jewish New Year, he did finish a draft of *Anne Frank* on 15 September and sent a copy to Crawford the following week. She had not seen any advance work on the play but had told Frank that she liked the way Levin in conversation described what he was planning to do. They had conferred several times during the summer, usually by phone, and had talked generally about his work and contractual arrangements. Years later, Levin claimed that at a lunch at the Algonquin, Crawford had offered him a $1,500 advance, promising $500 on submission of the first draft of a manuscript, $500 on completion, and $500 on production. He also said she spoke of Elia Kazan as a possible director and of Lillian Hellman as a possible collaborator (the "top playwright" she had referred to in an earlier letter). But there seems to be no record of any such conversation from the period itself.

By the end of September, Levin's confidence was high. The half-hour radio broadcast had received very favorable reviews in *Billboard* and *Variety*; Crawford had phoned to say that the first draft was "promising, good enough to proceed," and Otto Frank had arrived in New York to begin consultations about contracts and a production. But then on 2 October, at a meeting with Levin at her office, Crawford said that she had just reread the play and had lost touch with the characters: they no longer moved her; they seemed stated rather than explored. The scenic construction worked against both progressive development and dramatic tension. She now thought the script did not have enough theatrical potential for Levin to continue working on it, nor did she think there would be any use engaging a collaborator. She wanted to start afresh with a new writer.

Given her earlier encouragement and the depth of his own commitment, Levin was stunned by so sudden and negative a reaction. He reminded her of previous praise and of Otto Frank's observation that the characters were truly represented. But Crawford, while admitting that her response was a subjective one, said she had given the play a painstaking reading and had to trust her own judgment about what would or would not move an audience in the theater. (Later evidence suggests that she had also been influenced by the responses of Lillian Hellman and other friends with whom she had discussed Levin's draft.) Stricken at the unexpected prospect that he would lose what he believed to be the creative and financial opportunity of his life, Levin asked for more time to make revisions and for someone else to read the script. Crawford said she would think about these requests.

The following day, however, Crawford wrote to Otto Frank at his Manhattan hotel, reporting on the meeting with Levin and explaining the reasons for her unfavorable assessment. Although she again admitted that her response was entirely subjective, her tone and emphasis in the letter suggest that her decision was very close to being final. Levin, she told Frank, was a man of integrity who had to write what he felt, and although he would try to respond to her criticisms, the job would not be easy; and she gave no indication that she thought he could succeed in revising the script to her satisfaction. On 7 October, she told Levin, "I can't say yes as much as I would like to," but she did agree to let someone else read the play and proposed Kermit Bloomgarden, with whom Levin had already been in contact. Bloomgarden, like Crawford, had produced a number of major plays on Broadway (notably several of Hellman's and Arthur Miller's *Death of a Salesman*), and had also inquired in July (although later than others) about getting dramatic rights to the *Diary*. At that time, Levin opposed his selection on the grounds that Bloomgarden's left-wing political sympathies made him a risky choice, since the House Un-American Activities Committee was likely soon to investigate Communist influence on Broadway. Now, however, Levin accepted the suggestion and sent a copy of the draft to Bloomgarden, who read it and had an extremely negative response, telling Crawford and Frank that no reputable producer would consider putting on a play of so little theatrical promise. (Later, Bloomgarden was quoted as having said "a producer would have to be crazy" to stage Levin's work [*Obsession*, 83].)

In the meantime, the dismayed Levin was talking with theater people who knew something about his adaptation, and he asked several of them to read the draft, hoping for positive reactions and support. The well-known director and critic Harold Clurman and the producer Herman Shumlin found the early version promising (as did the younger Norman Rose and Peter Cappell), and the agent Miriam Howell agreed to represent Levin in his efforts to get the play accepted. They all lent support to Levin's contention that to reject the script at this time as unstageworthy was premature. This encouragement led Levin to think he might be able to convince Crawford to allow him to continue working on the draft alone or with a collaborator, or to persuade Frank to cancel the arrangement with her and to stage the play with another backer. But Crawford had been further confirmed in her decision by Bloomgarden's unqualified rejection, and she now offered to compensate Levin for the writing he had already done, if he would quit the project. Levin refused, on the grounds that he had never agreed to withdraw completely and that Crawford was bound by the earlier agreement to engage a collaborator to work with him.

Frank, extraordinarily distressed by the turn of events, found himself torn by conflicting loyalties and obligations. Although he was genuinely grateful to Levin for his invaluable work on behalf of the *Diary*, he also felt morally and even legally committed to Crawford. Some weeks earlier, he had been persuaded by Joseph Marks and others to get a lawyer to handle the upcoming contract negotiations for the play, and after consulting with his boyhood friend Nathan Straus, Frank approached John F. Wharton of Paul, Weiss, Rifkind, Wharton and Garrison. When it became clear that the disagreement between Levin and Crawford was unlikely to be resolved, Frank decided to turn the matter over to Myer Mermin, a respected attorney at Paul, Weiss with considerable experience in handling theatrical cases. Mermin first learned the details of the dispute on 23 October and in the next few days conferred with all parties to determine if there was any likelihood of resolution or compromise. Frank maintained (as he had from the start) that he was unable to assess the dramatic value of a script based on his own anguished history and had to rely on the expert judgment of experienced theater people, in this instance Cheryl Crawford. He was, however, troubled by the negative reactions of producers as prominent as Crawford and Bloomgarden.

Crawford continued to argue that Levin's script was unacceptable, but she agreed to talk with Harold Clurman about the possibility of allowing Levin time for further revision. Levin repeated his belief that the original understanding between himself, Crawford, and Frank called for the engagement of a collaborator if his script was not wholly satisfactory. He also insisted that there were other producers (Norman Rose, Peter Cappell, Herman Shumlin, and Walter Fried) who had expressed genuine interest in the prospect of putting it on, and thus he would not submit the fate of his play and his reputation to Crawford's "unsteady opinion." As the controversy continued, Levin's doubts multiplied: he now maintained that Crawford had never intended to produce his play but had agreed to let him draft a script only in order to secure the dramatic rights from Frank in the first place. On 28 October, Levin wrote to Crawford restating his case for having his play produced and asked her to release Frank from his obligation to her. The next day Mermin wrote to Levin asserting that Crawford and Frank's interpretation of the original agreement was correct and that Levin—since he had no legal right—should withdraw his play. Crawford rejected Levin's request and Levin rejected Mermin's, and the discussions appeared again to be deadlocked.

Mermin perceived the major difficulty in resolving the conflict to be the absence of a contract; although he believed the informal agreement—woven through letters and conversations—supported Crawford and Frank, it nonetheless remained open to interpretation and perhaps even legal challenge. He also recognized the mix of emotions involved: despite their convictions about being in the right, both Frank and Crawford were in different ways indebted to Levin and were troubled by the possibility of being unjust to him. In this strained atmosphere, Miriam Howell, Levin's agent, and Mermin, Frank's lawyer, eventually came up with a new proposal. Would the three parties accept an arrangement in which Levin could submit his script to a limited group of producers within a set time period to see if any of them was willing to produce the play? If a commitment was made within the time allowed, Crawford would step aside and the play would be staged by a new producer; if not, Levin would renounce his claim as the preferred adapter, and Crawford and Frank could proceed uncontested to negotiate with another writer. Although Crawford, who believed the original agreement was clear and unconditional, considered this new proposal inadvisable, she agreed to go along with it out of personal deference to Otto Frank's feelings of obligation to Levin, and because there may have been some injustice done to Levin at an earlier stage. No one underestimated the problems inherent in the proposition: drawing up a list agreeable to both sides and settling on a reasonable number of names, a satisfactory time frame, conditions of production, and so on. Frank and Crawford would want a limited list of notable producers who they believed could deliver a successful play, a list that might exclude some people acceptable to Levin. Levin and Howell would want a longer list with the names of some people already favorably inclined toward Levin; this list would no doubt include producers unacceptable to Frank. Mermin, doubtful of Levin's claims and playwriting abilities, seemed to want most of all to get a clear-cut contractual agreement that would clarify the rights of all parties and allow his client to proceed with a successful adaptation of his daughter's diary.

At the start, Mermin pressed Miriam Howell to submit the initial list of names to be considered, for he knew if he made the selection, Levin would object to its being stacked against him. Howell and Levin submitted twenty-eight names; Mermin and Frank argued that this list was too long and included producers with whom for various reasons they refused to deal. They proposed the number fourteen. After protracted, contentious negotiations in which each side continued to raise objections to names offered by the other, Mermin and Howell agreed on the following list of producers: Richard Aldrich and Richard Myers, Alfred de Liagre, Maurice Evans, José Ferrer, Walter Fried, Oscar Hammerstein, Leland Hayward, Theresa Helburn (the Theatre Guild), Gertrude Macy, Guthrie McClintic, Gilbert Miller, the Playwrights' Company, Irene Selznick, and Robert Whitehead. In the last stage of the talks, Levin asked for the opportunity to make additional suggestions and also for the right to have his play performed in Hebrew in Israel if it should be refused for New York. Mermin objected to the first request as contrary to the original ground rules of the negotiations, but he agreed to add the point about Israeli rights. Then Levin, angry at the final restriction of his options and at an earlier elimination of Herman Shumlin (who he had reason to think would consider producing his script), said the agreement was unfair and he would sign only "under protest," which he did on 21 November.

The contract stipulated that Levin had one month to get a signed production agreement from one of the fourteen producers on the approved list. If one of the group agreed to stage his version within a year, in accordance with the specified terms covering royalties, advances, subsidiary rights, and other matters, the play would be accepted, and Crawford would give up her claim. If, however, such a commitment was not obtained by 21 December, Levin would withdraw his work and would agree not to use it in the future "in any manner whatsoever." Frank would then have the right, free of objections by Levin, to engage any other dramatist to adapt the *Diary* and any other producer to produce it. Levin would also renounce any claims for infringement of his play unless another writer willfully made use of a new character, plot, or situation created by him and not found in the book. A supplement dated 25 November added two points: (1) if Levin's script was ultimately to be withdrawn, Crawford would pay him a sum of $500 for work already done; and (2) Levin would have the opportunity to make arrangements for the production of a Hebrew version of his *Anne Frank* in Israel subsequent to the New York opening of another play based on the book.

The concerns and tactics of each party were obviously complex. Mermin believed that the history of the dispute and the rejections of Levin's script by Crawford and Bloomgarden were so well known in the theater world that no producer would likely come forward to stage the play, and Otto Frank would then have an incontrovertible legal document denying Levin his rights to the Anne Frank story. Admittedly, some producer *might* sign on, but this was a small risk worth taking. Levin believed the opportunity of having his play submitted to a large number of producers was more "normal" than having it judged only by Crawford; and since she had already said no, at least he now had a set of live options. His risks were the bad publicity of the controversy, the very short trial period, and the fact that the list reflected many more of Mermin's choices than his own. Indeed, one reason he signed "under protest" was his belief that Mermin deliberately barred all those producers who had previously shown an interest and might have done his play (most notably Herman Shumlin).

Although Levin submitted copies to all the named producers and received a few favorable comments about his work, he was unable within the month to get any written pledge to produce it. Some readers found the material unsuitable for drama or doubted its commercial potential; others praised the script but said they were already committed; others just did not care for the play. Whatever the assessment, the result was clear: on 21 December Levin lost whatever rights (however contested) he previously had.

Yet even before the outcome was known, Levin had begun a campaign to demonstrate the inequity of the agreement and to try to reinstate what he claimed to be his rights. To publicize his case, on 9 December he wrote a letter to Brooks Atkinson, drama critic of the *New York Times*, maintaining that he was fighting for the life of his play against adversaries who, through threats, pressure, and deceit, had gotten him to sign an agreement that deprived him of his rights. Atkinson replied that the quarrel between Levin, Crawford, and Frank was private and not a matter to be aired in the columns of the *Times*; he suggested that a more fitting platform might be the trade journal *Variety*. Following Atkinson's suggestion, Levin in February did send a similar letter to Hobe Morrison, *Variety*'s editor, which subsequently provoked an irate denial from Cheryl Crawford and was not printed.

In December, however, Levin wrote of the approaching deadline to Elia Kazan, asking for an account of the director's conversation with Crawford and asking too if Kazan might read his script. Kazan replied that he did tell Crawford he liked the

Diary and would welcome a chance to read a play based on it, but because of heavy commitments could not consider direct- ing it or even looking at Levin's version now. All this, he remarked, had been said in casual conversation and meant nothing more definite than that he would like someday to see a play based on the book and would be happy to look at Levin's version next spring.

Then, the day after the deadline for selling the play, his claim lost, Levin harshly attacked Crawford and Mermin in a letter to Otto Frank, who had returned to Basel in mid- November. Both the producer and the lawyer, he charged, had deceived him through a series of bluffs and dishonest state- ments: Crawford had never intended to stage his play but had used him and Kazan to insinuate her way into Frank's favor; Mermin had gone far beyond a lawyer's prerogative, making autocratic aesthetic judgments about who was fit to handle a production of Levin's play and then rigging the "acceptable producers" list against him. Infuriated by his forfeiture, Levin further accused Crawford of trying to castrate him, of being "the kind of homosexual" who felt a deep compulsion to destroy people not like himself. Not content merely to take his play away from him, she needed to destroy his confidence in himself as a writer, "for she objected not to anything specific but to the deepest part of a man's creative ability, the emotional sense of the work itself" (22 December 1952, BU).

Levin acknowledged the extravagance of his passion and, in the last part of the letter, he tried to separate his hostility toward Crawford and Mermin from his feelings for Frank:

> You will feel this is an angry letter. My anger is not against
> you. It is against people who use deception and manipulation.

It is against lawyers who pretend they know more about art than artists, who take the incredible responsibility of destroying creative work. It is against the sort of people who have all my life stood between myself and my audience, and who have proven wrong every time. . . . You may feel that I stood in the way of your plan. I can only regret that you did not have more faith in what I wrote.

I do not associate you, as a personality, with all that is written above. We all feel that you were absolutely straight and generous with us, and that there were simply professional things in the background which you could not understand. We hope for every happiness for you in your new life. (BU)

But before this letter reached Frank in Basel, Levin learned of still another development in the dramatic rights negotiations that aroused him even more. He read a newspaper report that Carson McCullers, who had recently turned her novel *Member of the Wedding* into a prize-winning play, was being considered as the new adapter of the *Diary*. A month earlier in Paris, Frank Price, at Crawford's suggestion, had met with McCullers to explore the possibility of her adapting the *Diary* if Levin's version was to be withdrawn. McCullers found the idea appealing, read the book, and soon afterward sent a rapturous letter to Otto Frank:

I don't know how to write you, during the three days I have been reading Anne's Diary I have been crying, and now I need to write to you—and I don't know what to say. I think I have never felt such love and wonder and grief. There is no consolation to know that a Mozart, a Keats, a Chekhov is murdered in their years of childhood. But dear, dear Mr. Frank, Anne, who has that dual gift of genius and humanity has through her roots of unspeakable misery, given the world an enduring and incomparable flower. Mr. Frank, I know there is no consolation but I want you to know that I grieve with you—as millions of others now and in the future grieve. Over and over in these days I have played a gramophone record of one of the posthumous sonatas of Schubert. To me it has become Anne's music. (28 November 1952, PWRW&G)

McCullers's astonishing outpouring led quickly to a meeting with Frank, who found her frail, walking with a cane, "unlucky to look at," but "a sensitive and lovable creature . . . very, very sympathetic." The prospect of adapting the *Diary* excited her, conversations continued, and her possible involvement was public knowledge in New York by the third week of December. Again Levin vented his feelings in a letter to Frank:

I am disgusted and enraged at the thought that a non-Jew has been selected to write the play. I should think Miss Crawford would have had more tact. You may say it does not matter and all the rest of it, but after the way my work was treated to bring in a Gentile writer over the dozens of excellent Jewish writers that are here, to have it produced by a Gentile when important Jewish producers who were eager to do it were ruled off the list, is scandalous beyond measure. I will not stand for this. I will write about it wherever I can. It is adding insult to injury. I will tell the whole story of Cheryl Crawford's double-dealing, in the press, and I will protest the way in which Mr. Mermin saw to it that my play would be killed. (25 December 1952, BU)

› 2

The Old Jewish Question

LEVIN'S INDIGNATION AT THE PROSPECT that Carson McCullers, or indeed any gentile, would adapt Anne Frank's book for the theater brought the subject of Jewishness to the forefront of the dispute, where it was to remain. Levin and Otto Frank had discussed the issue before. Six months earlier, just after the publication of *Diary of a Young Girl*, when producers and agents were soliciting Doubleday for the dramatic rights, Levin sent Frank in Basel a summary of the various applicants. The publisher, he said, may well favor Maxwell Anderson, one of the most prolific and highly regarded of contemporary playwrights, but Levin was against him for several reasons. Anderson's recent plays were not popular, and his grand style, Levin felt, was wrong for the intimate subject matter of the child's book. Besides, Anderson would not work with a collaborator, and he wasn't Jewish. The Anne Frank story, Levin insisted, required an identification with the persecuted that only a Jew was likely to have. As he put it in a subsequent letter: "All literature, all art, is an expression of the soul; no stranger can as well express the soul of a people as someone from that people" (31 December 1952, BU).

Frank's answer was swift and equally heartfelt. Although he was not "pro Anderson" (he was not familiar enough with the American theater to have a decisive opinion), he felt Anderson to be at least a defensible choice. He was not Jewish, but he had certainly written often about discrimination. And Frank went on:

> As to the Jewish [issue] you are right that I do not feel the same way you do. I always said, that Anne's book is not a warbook. War is the background. It is not a Jewish book either, though Jewish sphere, sentiment and surrounding is the background. I never wanted a Jew writing an introduction for it. It is (at least here) read and understood more by gentiles than in Jewish circles. I do not know, how that will be in USA, it is the case in Europe. So do not make a Jewish play out of it! In some way of course it must be Jewish, even so that it works against anti-Semitism. I do not know if I can express what I mean and only hope that you won't misunderstand.[1]

Frank's reply boldly highlights fundamental differences between the two men. He himself came from a cultivated, well-to-do Frankfurt banking family that had assimilated into middle-class German society in the nineteenth century. Following his graduation from Lessing Gymnasium in 1908, he had enrolled briefly at the University of Heidelberg but cut short his studies to go to New York with a fellow student,

---

1. Quoted in Judith Doneson, "The American History of Anne Frank's Diary," 152, and Levin papers, 28 June 1952 (BU).

Nathan Straus, whose family owned R. H. Macy's, where Frank hoped to learn about business practices. When his father died in 1909, he returned to Germany to work for a metal engineering company in Düsseldorf. As a young man, he thought of himself essentially as a German businessman, not as a marginal Jew; and he moved in a liberal circle of Jewish and non-Jewish acquaintants. He did not attend Hebrew school, nor was he bar mitzvahed.

During World War I, Frank rose to the rank of lieutenant in a German artillery regiment, served during the major tank battles at Cambrai, and afterward observed that he could not recall ever encountering an anti-Semite in the army or as a youth in Frankfurt. During the 1920s he was very active in the family's banking business at a time when inflation and then the depression caused devastating losses. After the Nazis gained power in Frankfurt in March 1933 and intensified their persecution of Jews, Frank decided to protect himself, his wife, his two children, and his livelihood by moving to Amsterdam, a city he knew and one where he had friends and business connections. He was soon able to open an agency of Opekta-Werke, which manufactured and distributed pectin, a powdered fruit extract used to make jam. Although he became a member of a liberal synagogue in the city and was proud of his later activity in Reform Jewish organizations, he thought of his identity mainly in racial rather than in religious terms. Hiding during the war, he read Goethe and Schiller in German and Dickens in English to his two daughters, and the family celebrated the feast of St. Nicholas more eagerly than Hanukkah. He once proposed giving Anne a children's Bible for Hanukkah, so she could learn something about the New Testament, but he responded to her sister Margot's perturbation by backing off: "Yes—er, I think St. Nicholas Day is a better occasion. Jesus just doesn't go with Hanukkah" (*Diary*, 3 November 1943).

After Auschwitz and the phenomenal fame of his daughter's book, Frank devoted much of his life to memorializing Anne by interpreting the "message" of her diary in affirmative, universalist terms. For him, the most effective way to fulfill her desire "to live after my death" and "to do good" was to construe her book as the work of a young idealist expressing horror at the cruelties of bigotry and war and voicing hope for a more peaceful, tolerant world in the future. To further this image, he helped found the Anne Frank Foundation in 1957 and participated regularly in its many activities during the last years of his life. He also kept up a large correspondence with people around the world who wrote to him about their reactions to his daughter's book. He often ended his reply to a young person who had written to him with words such as these: "I hope that Anne's book will have an effect on the rest of your life so that insofar as it is possible in your circumstances, you will work for unity and peace."[2]

The original purpose of the foundation was to maintain the premises at Prinsengracht 263 (the Anne Frank House) and eventually to operate an international youth center nearby. The center would conduct educational and philanthropic programs designed to promote among young people "the ideals bequeathed to the world in the diary of Anne Frank." These ideals were at first deliberately defined very generally, as can be

2. Rian Verhoeven and Ruud van der Rol, *Anne Frank: Beyond the Diary*, 105.

seen from the formulation in an early planning document: "The principal purpose of the International Foundation would be to use the name Anne Frank as a symbol for all constructive activity, relating in any way to adolescents (young people from 12 to 20 years old), which furthers inter-group understanding in an atmosphere of freedom and of hope." Although the aims of the Anne Frank Foundation were soon expressed much more concretely and have evolved over the years to respond to contemporary events, the initial intentions were to promote democratic ideals among the young and to combat prejudice, discrimination, and repression in every form.[3] That Anne Frank's diary was also an indelibly affecting account of the outer and inner worlds of a keenly observant, life-affirming girl who wished to be a writer ensured its appeal and immense influence.

Before he had read his daughter's diary, Otto Frank thought of her as a high-spirited, occasionally feisty child, whose energy had to be channeled as she moved toward adolescence. After reading the entries, he confessed that in important ways he had not really known her. Although they were very close, he hardly suspected "anything about her innermost thoughts, her high

3. The following statement of the goals of the Anne Frank Foundation in the late 1980s reveals some of the ways in which aims and activities have evolved over three decades: "Seeks to educate the public on events of World War II, particularly the Holocaust, and to make known the current prejudices, discrimination, and persecution affecting Jews today. Supports efforts to pressure governments in countries where human rights violations occur. Maintains the home of Anne Frank as a museum and memorial for the victims of Nazi repression. Documents research and education programs in racism, anti-Semitism and neo-Fascism. Holds courses for teachers, social workers and others dealing with minority problems and discrimination. Maintains collection of anti-Semitic and neo-Fascist material."

ideals, her belief in God and her progressive ideas."[4] Anne, her father once told an interviewer, cared for God, but "she didn't show any feeling for religion. Margot showed an interest, but Anne never did. She never had a real Jewish education" (*Times*, London, 16 April 1977, 12).

But even after reading and editing his daughter's diary in 1945, Otto Frank was inclined to discount the significance of her many revealing observations about Jews and Jewishness. Not only does the diary contain chillingly matter-of-fact descriptions of anti-Jewish laws enacted in occupied Holland— how "the gaudy yellow star spoke for itself"—but it is also filled with terse, graphic reports of Jews dragged from houses, loaded into cattle trucks, and sent to the transit camp at Westerbork and then to Poland, where according to radio reports many were being gassed or murdered in other ways. Furthermore, as the child matures, she ponders the meaning and implication of being a Jew at a time of previously unimagined evil. Some of these reflections reveal Anne's extreme sensitivity to the fates of friends and acquaintances directly exposed to Nazi vicious-ness; others express her anguish at having betrayed the less fortunate by being "safely" secluded in the secret annex. "I feel wicked sleeping in a warm bed," she confides to Kitty, "while my dearest friends have been knocked down or have fallen into a gutter somewhere out in the cold night. I get frightened when I think of close friends who have been delivered into the hands of the cruelest brutes that walk the earth. And all because they are Jews!"

4. Reported by Frank's second wife, Elfriede Frank-Markovits, *McCall's*, January 1986, 108.

Anne Frank's specific identification with the misfortunes of other Jews deepens as the months in hiding pass. Recording a frightening dream about her recently deported friend Lies, she insists that Lies is "a symbol to me of the suffering of all my girl friends and all Jews. When I pray for her, I pray for all Jews and all those in need." In the second half of the diary she occasionally asks questions of a kind that suggest a rapidly expanding moral and philosophical nature and a need to inquire about ultimate human mysteries. One instance is especially striking and has often been cited as illustrative of her rapid growth in a time of peril. Describing an attempted break-in at the warehouse, Anne reports that the concealed Jews were reproached by their gentile protectors:

> We have been pointedly reminded that we are in hiding, that we are Jews in chains, chained to one spot, without any rights, but with a thousand duties. We Jews mustn't show our feelings, must be brave and strong, must accept all inconveniences and not grumble, must do what is within our power and trust in God. Sometime this terrible war will be over. Surely the time will come when we are people again, and not just Jews.
>
> Who has inflicted this upon us? Who has made us Jews different from all other people? Who has allowed us to suffer so terribly up till now? It is God that has made us as we are, but it will be God, too, who will raise us up again. If we bear all this suffering and if there are still Jews left, when it is over, then Jews, instead of being doomed, will be held up as an example. Who knows, it might even be our religion from which the world and all peoples learn good, and for that reason and that reason only do we have to suffer now. We can never become just Netherlanders, or just English, or represen-

tatives of any country for that matter, we will always remain Jews, but we want to, too.

Be brave! Let us remain aware of our task and not grumble, a solution will come, God has never deserted our people. Right through the ages there have been Jews, through all the ages they have had to suffer, but it has made them strong too; the weak fall, but the strong will remain and never go under!
(11 April 1944)

Part of what makes this passage so remarkable (aside from its having been written by a fourteen-year-old) is its status as an impassioned compendium of topics that have absorbed the Jewish people for more than two millennia: the origin and meaning of persecution and the possibility that suffering may be morally redemptive; the nature of the Jews' special relationship to a severe but faithful God; the role of the Jew as "different" among the world's peoples; the perplexing, often paradoxical, relationship between rights, duties, and obligations; and the dogged assertion of the value of Jewish life in the face of affliction and uncertainty. And all these subjects are expressed in a fervid tone that moves in a rush from resentment to challenge, wonderment, doubt, incipient rebellion, and finally to faith, acceptance, and proud affirmation of Jewish identity—an extraordinary range of feelings about essential ethical and historical issues the child is now first beginning to articulate.

That Otto Frank tended to minimize utterances such as these is, of course, understandable. He himself was a modest, reserved man who did not often verbalize his innermost thoughts and concerns. Having survived Auschwitz and the devastating loss of his wife, daughters, and friends, he felt compelled at fifty-six to repress the horrors he had lived through in order to rebuild a shattered life. Furthermore, when Anne's *Diary* was so favorably reviewed in Holland and France, he wanted to help create an atmosphere in which the book would be bought, read, and appreciated more widely. For this he felt it imperative to sound a healing note, and he felt confirmed in his constructive instinct by daily letters from readers all over the world (the vast majority of them not Jewish) who testified that his daughter's rare book was an inspiring celebration of life in the face of hostile forces. Few correspondents or friends spoke of the specific crime of Germans murdering Jews or of the more general human capacity for abusing people of different beliefs and appearances. Otto Frank, then, would be inclined by temperament and upbringing to continue to see his daughter's book as most admiring first readers around the world saw it.

Levin's background and view of life differed from Frank's in vital ways. Descended from eastern European shtetl Jews, Levin was born on Chicago's Sangamon Street in 1905, after his parents, Joseph and Golda Bassise, had come separately to America from Lithuania. (The family name had been changed to Levin in the commotion of passing through immigration at Ellis Island.) His father ran a small shop called "Joe the Tailor," near the old Dearborn Station, where he did pressing and mending and sold secondhand clothes. He also dabbled in real estate, and by the time Meyer was an adolescent he owned several apartment houses on Independence Boulevard, a respectable street on the west side of the city. By the 1920s, the family was becoming fairly well-to-do (they had a car and a baby grand piano and eventually lived in a good-sized house with two bathrooms), and

Joseph Levin was able to close his shop (although after losing his investments in the Depression, he opened another).[5] Like many Jewish immigrant parents, the Levins greatly valued family ties and education. Joseph scrimped and saved to bring his widowed mother, brother, and sister to America, and to educate all his children. Meyer graduated from the University of Chicago before he was nineteen; his sisters, Bess and Bertha, also went to college, and both became teachers; Bess married a doctor and Bertha a high school teacher.

When the novelist Levin later wrote about his childhood, however, he remembered most vividly not the parental sacrifice and emerging opportunities for the children, but the apprehensions of his earlier years on Racine Avenue in the notorious "Bloody" Nineteenth Ward, when the family "seemed always on the edge of catastrophe" and he was often threatened by Italian kids yelling "kike," "Jewsonofabitch," or "I'll cut your nuts off, you lousy little sheeny." Although he was a timid boy who avoided confrontation, he often recalled one fight when two Italian kids ordered him to kiss a cross of sticks. In a sudden rage, he knocked one of them down and, astonished at his own prowess, ran away.

His parents, though, always treated him as the gifted son, indulging most of his whims and ambitions. Even though they would have preferred him to study medicine or law, they went

5. Levin's cousin, Judith Klausner, remembers this shop as "a small place. There were three pressing machines and a sign in the window 'Pants Pressed While You Wait.' The old men sat in cubicles, curtains hung from a sagging string for semi-privacy. I recall watching the men sitting inside the cubicles in their underwear reading the daily *Forward*" (letter to author, 2 May 1994).

along with his decision (announced dramatically at the age of nine) to be a writer. They tearfully accepted his marriage to the gentile Mable Foy; but when they learned that she had entered the University of Chicago at fifteen, his mother said, "Like you!" and expressed relief that "our prodigy affinity somehow balanced the shikseh part: a brilliant girl."[6] After he established himself as a writer, his parents accepted his being different and expressed great pride in his many accomplishments.

Despite his affection for his parents and his gratitude for their sustenance, the young Levin often had confused, conflicted feelings about their Jewishness and his own. In his autobiography, he confessed that "my dominant childhood memory is of fear and shame at being a Jew" (13). As an adolescent succeeding at school, he was especially sensitive about his parents' coming from "ordinary village folks, *proster Yidden*, plain Jews"; and he once remarked that "ours was perhaps the only old country Jewish family in which I never heard a claim to being descended from some important line of rabbis." He was also embarrassed by some of the ways his mother and father behaved. They spoke Yiddish at home and when he was a child did not make much of an effort to become Americanized. Early on in Chicago, their Jewishness was a source of concern. "All through childhood," Levin once told an interviewer, "I sensed, and resented, this terrible shame and inferiority in my elders; they considered themselves as nothing, greenhorns, Jews."[7] From their son's point of view, there was little notably positive

---

6. The quotations in this paragraph are from the unpublished memoir *In Love* (BU).

7. Ira Berkow, *Maxwell Street*, 272.

or inspirational about the way they led their lives. "Like so many immigrants," Levin later wrote, "my parents were observant in a deteriorating way, as it seemed only by habit." Although his mother went to a kosher butcher, she rarely objected to milk in the coffee during a meat meal. His father had to keep the shop open on Saturday, his busiest day; and though he observed the Sabbath eve meal, he attended the synagogue only on the High Holidays. For a while, the son went along, but disliking the crowds, the noise, and the talk of business, he gradually stopped going. Like Otto Frank, he was never bar mitzvahed, though he did attend an after-school Hebrew class; the class was more like a social than a religious event, run by a college student rather than "a traditional knuckle-rapping melamed." After he left school and traveled in Europe, young Levin became emotionally detached and increasingly distant from his parents.

Predictably, the son's ambivalence about his mother and father, and his fear of harassment in the alien urban world around him, were reflected in his many apprehensions about himself. As an adolescent, he tended to make the family version of Jewishness his scapegoat, and he later spoke of his boyhood environment as "a prison." His earliest stories were full of images of severing and amputation that can be seen to reflect his guilt at being Jewish and lower-class and suggest a longing for self-punishment. At fifteen, he published a ghetto tale about a boy who was ashamed to have his gentile girlfriend meet his parents. When he and the girl happened to stop at his father's clothing stand on Maxwell Street (the busy market center for Jews), the boy pretended not to know him. At the University of Chicago, despite his achievements as a student and journalist,

Levin was nagged by a sense of unworthiness and of not belonging; soon after graduation, his trips to Europe and Palestine—although motivated by a desire for adventure—were also (as he well knew) efforts to escape a feeling of Jewish inferiority and to discover a more secure place in the world. But as he once explained, the old apprehensions would sometimes resurface and then, for all his "labor . . . to fit myself into the world pattern," he would still feel "a little member of my clan, overanxious, self-centered, insecure, the eternal bright and troublesome Jew. As soon as I got into the world among the goyim, I messed up" (*In Search*, 169). At the same time, however, his early writing often embodied a father-and-son search theme, reflecting his sharp regret that the American-born children of immigrants had lost touch with their parents.[8]

In later years, Levin's relationship to his Jewishness went through many other stages and modifications: from nervous avoidance in his early twenties, to the excited discovery of Zionism and kibbutz life, to worries about whether he could be both American and Jew, to an ultimate acceptance of his problematic identity and condition as a Jew (and as a writer about the predicament of being a Jew) in such books as *The Old Bunch* and *In Search*. It was, however, only after he had encountered the death camps and tried to write about them

---

8. Levin's ambivalent feelings about his parents lasted all his life. Tereska Torres recalls him "almost never speaking of them," and his judgmental unpublished memoir, quoted above, was written when he was past seventy. On the other hand, after Joseph Levin's death, his son wrote lovingly about him in public print and private letters. And Judith Klausner reports that he regularly consulted his sisters by telephone and mail about his parents' welfare.

that he identified himself in a positive way with the Jewish people, if not the religious beliefs of Judaism. As he once wrote: "My Jewishness was a jumble. Under religion, if I had to fill out a form with such a line, I would usually put, 'None.'"[9] But despite his perpetual doubts and questioning, he came in his maturity to a powerful, almost mystical, faith in his membership in the larger Jewish family—a family with whom he shared a common history and a passion for the pursuit of truth and justice. To promote in his writing the renewal and continuity of this entity—the Jewish people as a dynamic spiritual being—became one of the commanding principles of his life.

Levin could, as he revealed in his memorable review for the *New York Times*, see *Anne Frank: The Diary of a Young Girl* as a various, fascinating, and uplifting book; but most tellingly for him, it was a specifically representative book: the story of one innocent girl who symbolized the six million Jews slaughtered by the Nazis simply for being Jewish. This was the particular story that in 1952 he so eagerly wished to bring alive on the stage.

So when the disagreements between Levin and Frank continued and intensified in January of 1953, the question of contracts and assignment of rights became inextricably tangled with profound convictions and beliefs, and with the two men's feelings for each other. At the start of their relationship Levin admired and identified in complex ways with Frank. The dignified elder man was cooperative, evenhanded, and kind. Since he owned the rights to the *Diary*, he held the key to Levin's golden opportunity, but he also became an emblematic char-

9. Unpublished memoir, *In Love* (BU).

acter for the American writer. As the dead child's father, he was already playing the role Levin himself now so ardently wished to play: the man who helps the teller get the story told and disseminated to a large audience. As a survivor of Auschwitz, Frank was himself a kind of teller—a man who had lived through hell and whose struggles to rebuild his life demonstrated the great challenges faced by postwar Jewry. People who knew him spoke often of his compassion and generosity. At sixty-three, he was sixteen years older than Levin, and given his background and personal history, he was a kind of father figure for the younger man. Yet at the same time, certain things about Frank unnerved Levin. He had the high-toned reserve of many cosmopolitan German Jews, and the two men's emerging disagreements about the Jewish content of the *Diary* clearly threatened Levin's own confidence and position.

As Levin continued to insist that he was the victim of deception and that "at bottom it was still the old Jewish question," Frank tried on several counts to be sympathetically responsive to his claims and frustrations. Although he kept denying Levin's charges that Crawford and Mermin were duplicitous, Frank always acknowledged his gratitude: Levin had contributed a great deal to the fortunes of the *Diary* in America and he *was* the first person to recognize its dramatic potential. Frank was also willing to seek advice from others on how closely tied to a concrete Jewish situation and atmosphere a stage adaptation of his daughter's book ought to be. To get more information, he earnestly informed Levin, he had written to seven American liberal Jews and had gotten answers that supported his position. As one correspondent wrote: "The theme of Anne's diary seems to be a universal one. The fact

that it was written by a Jewish girl is a very fine thing for any
Jew. But, so far as the world is concerned it would seem to me
a distinct advantage, if the play were written by a non-Jew. In
the first place, that would emphasize the universality of the
theme. In the second place, there is, to my mind, little doubt
but that the play would be much more readily accepted on its
merits if it were written by a non-Jew" (19 January 1953, BU).

But Levin was not satisfied with Frank's attempts at consolation. Appreciating the gratitude, he nonetheless took the
arguments about universality from American liberals as an all-
too-familiar effort to evade the horrific implications of the German program of mass murder of the Jews. He continued to
press his claims to Frank and others. He wrote to *Variety* hoping that his account of the history of his script might get people
to support him, or at least might serve as a cautionary tale for
other dramatists considering the writing of a new adaptation.
Hobe Morrison, the editor of *Variety*, checked Levin's letter
with some of the parties involved and, after receiving an indignant response from Crawford dismissing Levin's charges as
unfounded and slanderous, decided not to print it. Levin then
protested to the Dramatists Guild, only to be chided by Mills
Ten Eyck, the general secretary, for setting out to write without
a contract and for thinking that the signed agreement of 21
November might be disavowed. He again threatened to sue
Cheryl Crawford and came finally to conclude that he was not
morally bound by an agreement based on what he believed to
be false representations. He therefore repudiated the contract
and refused, he told Frank and Mermin in January, to consider
his play withdrawn. Indeed, he announced that he was thinking
of staging a performance of his script to test an audience's reac-

tion, and he continued to talk to theater people about the possibility of mounting it on Broadway.

Levin's behavior in the early months of 1953 had several nerve-racking consequences for Otto Frank. Cheryl Crawford, who had just lost a substantial sum after the failure of *Camino Real*, decided that she could not bear the strain of a possible Levin lawsuit and the risk of backing another serious drama, and she decided in April to cancel plans to produce the Anne Frank play. Carson McCullers, who had been considering adapting the *Diary* for either Crawford or Robert Whitehead, felt her health could support neither the test nor the controversy. By late spring, Otto Frank's nine-month effort to contract with a producer to adapt the *Diary* remained obstructed.

Throughout this period, Frank's letters to Levin (whose activities continued to cause him so much trouble) were marked by a desire to be friendly and fair. He would argue each of Levin's contentions about tricks and deceitful maneuvers and try to demonstrate how he believed it to be factually wrong, or—if seen in another light—a matter of honest disagreement. When he discovered that Levin had decided to make the controversy public by writing to the newspapers and was threatening to sue Cheryl Crawford, Frank was wounded, lost his composure, and angrily accused Levin of grasping self-interest and cruelty. Yet as they argued by mail, Frank kept trying to separate the disagreement from his personal feelings for Levin, repeating his gratitude, expressing regret for the failure of Levin's script to win a backer, and saying he wished they could resolve their conflict and remain friends. He also corresponded separately with Tereska Torres (who did not think her husband had been cheated of his rights and was distressed by his tactics)

and invited her and the children to visit him. Levin, too, tried
to convince Frank that his anger was directed not against him
but against powerful editors, theater people, and lawyers, who
had disregarded his rights and the quality of his work.

While exchanging urgent letters with Levin, Frank was also
in close contact with other people in New York, notably Barbara Zimmerman, the young editor, and Myer Mermin, his
lawyer. Since Zimmerman had been involved with every stage
of the publication of the American edition of the *Diary* and the
snarled negotiations for dramatic rights, she and Frank were in
constant touch by mail and quickly grew to be exceptionally
fond of each other. Zimmerman was twenty-four (the age that
Anne Frank would have been had she lived) and was thrilled
about the *Diary* and its prospects. She was also, for Frank in
Basel, an ideal correspondent: very bright, attentive, and eager
to pass on colorful accounts of the book's unanticipated triumph. Frank complimented her often for devotion and relia-
bility, sent her small gifts, and was soon addressing her affec-
tionately as "dearest little one" and "little Barbara." She told
colleagues and friends that Mr. Frank was "absolutely charming, a self-contained, thoroughly *good* person. . . . amazing" (3
October 1952, BE). He soon came to rely on her not only for
editorial advice but also for judgments about personalities and
business decisions. At the start, she also liked Levin ("a very
pleasant guy") and was convinced he loved the book as much as
she did. But in the early days of the flurried negotiations with
agents and producers, she began to have misgivings about his
motives and actions, no matter what his original intentions
might have been. After 7 July 1952, when Doubleday withdrew,
she felt (as others at Doubleday did) that Levin was increas-

ingly rash and untrustworthy, absorbed only in getting his own play staged in New York, no matter what that might mean for the entire venture. Following Cheryl Crawford's rejection of Levin's script and her reluctant agreement to go along with the plan to allow him to submit it to fourteen additional producers, Zimmerman felt that Levin had been given every chance to make the case for his play, and she was steadfast in advising Frank not to give in to any impulse to reconsider the rejection.

"Levin's bitterness has no basis in fact," she told Frank in January 1953, and when he sent her copies of the accusatory letters Levin was writing, she kept reassuring him that he and Crawford had been perfectly ethical and honest, and that Levin was unscrupulously twisting every fact for his own advantage. When Frank asked her whether a Jew or a non-Jew should write the play, she admitted that a Jew would feel in certain ways more intensely about the book, but in other ways this might be a disadvantage. "I don't believe that a non-Jew will not feel as strongly in other ways about Anne's book, and at the same time they will not have the danger (which a Jew might have) of limiting the play to simply Jewish experience. The wonderful thing about Anne's book is that it is really universal, that it is a book, an experience, for everyone. And I think that just a little objectivity would, on the part of the writer, ensure this very broad appeal" (7 January 1953, PWRW&G).

A week later, in another discussion of the same subject, she argued that Carson McCullers (who at the time was still considering the adaptation) would be a superb choice because she was a woman writer with uncommon understanding of adolescent girls, and her religious background was less important than the nature of her talent.

I am a Jew and I've thought about it deeply and I do feel
honestly that the problem of whether a Jew writes this or not
makes no difference at all. I thought Meyer's radio adaptation
false to the book because it did not at all give any credit to
Miep and others, yet purported to be a Religious Adaptation.
(15 January 1953, PWRW&G)

In response to Frank's question about the advisability of getting a Jewish director for the adaptation (to help guarantee "the
atmosphere"), Zimmerman replied: "There seems to be no
danger about whether the director chosen is a Jew since all of
them are! Daniel Mann, Kazan, etc. But that too makes no difference." When Frank expressed compassion for Levin and
questioned whether he was treating him fairly, Zimmerman
reacted by apologizing for not "sounding particularly charitable
. . . but I shall try to be certainly. I *understand* how he must
have felt, but I could never agree with him. Sympathy comes
after understanding and I expect that this is what I feel for
Levin." But Levin's intensification of his campaign of writing
to the papers, spreading derogatory stories about Crawford, and
threatening to sue her finally eroded the sympathy Zimmerman was trying to have for him. "He is impossible to deal with
in any terms, officially, legally, morally, personally." She maintained that he was "a compulsive neurotic who was destroying
both himself and Anne's play" (15 January 1953, PWRW&G).
Although Frank clearly valued Zimmerman's assessments, he
told her that he was not as angry as she was with Levin, for he
tried to keep in mind his love for the *Diary* and his personal
disappointment. "I agree," he told Zimmerman, that his
actions were wrong and ugly, but in his innermost [nature] he

is not a bad man. Difficult, not 100% normal, oversensitive" (14 February 1953, JM).

Similarly, Myer Mermin, as Otto Frank's lawyer, was altogether devoted to protecting his client's property and advancing his interests, and he also admired "that unusually gentle and sensitive man," who had suffered such catastrophic personal loss. Mermin had come on the scene in the third week of October 1952, soon after Levin began entreating Frank to intercede with Crawford to allow him to offer his rejected script to other producers, several of whom had recently given him some encouragement. Although there were no contracts, Mermin believed the summer letters between Frank, Crawford, and Levin had made the agreements about time, assessment, and consequences clear to everyone. Levin had been given two months to submit an adaptation of the *Diary*, and when Crawford judged it unsatisfactory, she was free either to call in a collaborator or turn to another writer and compensate Levin for his work. According to Mermin, Levin had no legal rights, and his multiplying, unreasonable appeals were causing Frank a great deal of bother and distress. But Mermin also recognized that his interpretation of the situation might not be entirely shared by others. Frank was still nagged by the possibility that Levin was being treated unjustly, and though he felt fully committed to Crawford, he could conceivably be swayed by Levin's persistent arguments and pleas. Besides, other people might find some of Levin's claims of priority convincing.

In his protracted, often antagonistic negotiations with Levin, Mermin came to some of the same conclusions about his character and motives as had Zimmerman and others at Doubleday. In the lawyer's view, Levin's original idealistic zeal for promoting the success of the *Diary* had become subsumed in his desperation at the prospect of not getting his own adaptation produced on Broadway. As his chances diminished, his obstructionist tactics and the unpredictability of his shifting claims increased.

During much of 1953, Zimmerman and Mermin worked to discredit Levin's case even further. In February, when Levin reported that Harold Clurman and Robert Whitehead wished to stage his *Anne Frank*, Zimmerman assisted Mermin in correctly proving to Frank that Levin was exaggerating their commitment. In April, after Crawford withdrew, Kermit Bloomgarden (whom Levin had opposed the year before) again indicated his desire to take an option on the dramatic rights to the *Diary*, and both Zimmerman and Mermin strongly supported his petition. They tried to reassure him that Levin's allegations were legally groundless, but they remained worried that Bloomgarden, like others before him, might be deterred by the controversy. When another producer, Teresa Hayden, came forward in August with a clear bid to stage Levin's version, Mermin said, "Absolutely no," on the grounds that he was negotiating with a leading theatrical figure whose name (Bloomgarden) he could not disclose. Zimmerman responded to Frank's inquiries about Hayden's qualifications by reporting that from everything she had heard the new applicant was difficult to work with, not especially accomplished, and not very smart. Moreover, she had recently been associated with a string of failures. When Bloomgarden finally signed a production agreement on

1 October 1953, Mermin arranged to have him indemnified against any possible claim Levin might make.

Once Bloomgarden had signed a contract to arrange for and then stage an adaptation of the *Diary*, Levin's script was effectively shelved, but his campaign to rectify what he believed to be the wrongs against him continued unabated. A short time before, when he had been invited to take part in a conference on moral and ethical values at the Jewish Theological Seminary, he had hoped to discuss his case with Simon Rifkind, a partner at Paul, Weiss, who was also participating in the conference. But Rifkind disregarded him. At this same period, Levin was also conferring with a rabbi from the Society for the Advancement of Judaism and frequently seeking advice from friends and acquaintances about his options. He now spoke often about artistic and moral values superseding questions of mere legality, if the legitimacy of an agreement could be persuasively challenged.

In October, when he learned that Bloomgarden was going to do the play, Levin offered the producer, who had been so critical of his first script, a revised version, expressing a willingness to work with a collaborator and to assign all his royalties to an Anne Frank memorial. Bloomgarden showed no interest. Levin also began to speak more aggressively in his letters to Frank. He would not, he said, bring a legal action against Anne's father, but he wanted him to know that he felt about his work exactly as Frank felt about his daughter. He had created his play out of love and would continue to insist on its right to have a normal life and a normal death, and that was why he intended to stage it before an audience. Frank was quick to point out the inappropriateness of comparing the creation and rejection of a theatrical adaptation to the conception, life, and death of his daughter, and he dismissed Levin's assertion that his creative work was being "suppressed."

In his continued attempt to get Levin to cease his efforts to have his dramatization produced, Mermin wrote him a detailed assessment of the case, stressing again the insubstantiality of his claims and the pain he was causing Otto Frank. He also warned him of the consequences he and others would face were he to infringe the copyright by staging his play before an audience. In a postscript, Mermin moved out of his role as Frank's lawyer to add a personal note. Having recently read *In Search,* he expressed admiration for Levin as a person and a writer, especially for his instinct and capacity to share the "actions and passions of our time," but he now felt that Levin's emotional attachments had led him to behave completely out of character, and he was in danger of doing damage to Frank and himself. This plea to get Levin to live up to his part of the agreement was clearly a rhetorical calculation, for a week earlier, summarizing the situation for Otto Frank, Mermin described Levin as irrational and unpredictable, and saw him as indulging a fantasy that he was discharging the solemn duty of an artist to his creation (letter, 20 October 1953, PWRW&G). Responding to Frank's suggestion that they might postpone signing the contract with Bloomgarden until the situation with Levin was cleared up, Mermin remarked that any such delay "would be a postponement forever." Even if they decided to institute litigation against Levin and were to obtain a court judgment, the procedure would be costly and there was no guarantee that even a court judgment would silence him.

Any hope that Levin might be placated vanished in December, when he learned that Bloomgarden, after abortive talks with John Van Druten, George Tabori, and again Carson McCullers, had engaged Frances Goodrich and Albert Hackett, the married team of Hollywood screenwriters, to do a new stage version of the *Diary*. Working mainly for MGM and Paramount, Goodrich and Hackett had since the early 1930s contributed to dozens of popular musicals and comedies, most of which were adaptations. They refashioned Victor Herbert's *Naughty Marietta* for Nelson Eddy and Jeanette MacDonald, Dashiell Hammett's *Thin Man* for William Powell and Myrna Loy, Irving Berlin's *Easter Parade* for Judy Garland and Fred Astaire, and Edward Streeter's *Father of the Bride* for Spencer Tracy and Elizabeth Taylor. After scripts by Marc Connelly, Clifford Odets, and Dalton Trumbo failed to satisfy Frank Capra, he called in Goodrich and Hackett to help rescue *It's a Wonderful Life*, and they were two of the four writers to earn credit for a film that has remained very popular. Several of their screenplays were nominated for Academy Awards, and throughout the studio era they were widely admired for their debonair dialogue and ability to craft plots that had box-office appeal. Although they rarely worked on material as somber as the Anne Frank story, they had been warmly recommended to Bloomgarden by a mutual friend, Lillian Hellman, who described them as versatile professionals able to make something winningly stageworthy of the young girl's diary.

After initial reservations about the fit between their talents and the Anne Frank text, Goodrich and Hackett responded enthusiastically to Bloomgarden's inquiry. The project was a fine opportunity, they said, because the story offered tense drama, a possibility of intimacy, and "moments of lovely comedy which heighten the desperate, tragic situation of the people" (November 1953, GH). Introducing themselves to Otto Frank, they expressed a desire to catch "the spirit and indomitable courage of your daughter." Although Frank himself had qualms about Hollywood screenwriters going to work on the *Diary*, he was reassured by the seriousness of their intentions and commitment. The project, they told him, was "a tremendous challenge." They had already begun reading books about Holland, Judaism, and modern European history and were consulting with Jewish friends and even with a rabbi about the ritual for celebrating Hanukkah (27 December 1953, GH).

Frank saw the exchange of letters with Goodrich and Hackett as an opportunity to impress upon them his own conceptions of the direction he hoped the project would take. Again, as in his discussions with Levin, he emphasized his belief that the play should not be focused on a distinctively Jewish situation but should emphasize the universal appeal of the girl's personality and growth, and "propagate Anne's ideas and ideals in every manner" in order "to show to mankind whereto discrimination, hatred and persecution are leading." When the writers queried him about the religious orientation of the people in hiding, he observed that the dentist Dussel "had a rather orthodox education whereas my wife was progressive and had a deep religious feeling." Margot "followed more or less my wife." He himself was "not educated in a religious sphere," but after his marriage and "all the experiences of the Hitler regime," he had become more conscious as a Jew. Anne was more inscrutable. Religious forms and ceremonies did not seem to impress her very much, but she did stand "next to me while the candles were lighted and joined in singing the 'Maoz Tzur' [Rock of Ages], the well-known Hanukkah song" (2 February 1954, GH).

Frank's comments had a considerable impact on the way Goodrich and Hackett conceived of their adaptation. They had heard Bloomgarden's opinion that Levin's first version was weakened by lots of "breast-beating," which they took to mean solemn didacticism about the wretched fate of the Jews at the hands of the Nazis. Following Frank's lead, they wanted to tell an intimate story that would above all emphasize the positive, so as to have an inspiring effect on a wide audience, an ambition that governed their thoughts and choices throughout the drafting process.

For Levin, the selection of the team he called "the Hacketts of Hollywood" was another in a series of insults and blunders. He protested to Frank that the screenwriters were merely "hired hands," not playwrights of any particular distinction, who had no connection to the Jewish subject matter. Given their backgrounds and experience, they would probably try to engage a general audience at the expense of the inner truth of the diary, and the result would be a conventional Broadway play. Levin also wrote to Goodrich and Hackett themselves, explaining his engagement with the project and his bitter sense of grievance at the stifling of his work. At first, Frances Goodrich was sympathetic to the writer who had lost a creative opportunity, and she admitted that if what Levin said was true, he had gotten "a pushing around." But she and her husband were reassured by Bloomgarden that "an understanding had been reached with Levin," and they embarked on their exacting new assignment (5 January 1954, GH).

On 13 January, however, Levin took a step that instantly

turned the simmering private conflict into a public scandal. He placed an ad on the theater page of the *New York Post* that read:

A CHALLENGE TO KERMIT BLOOMGARDEN

Is it right for you to kill a play that others find deeply moving, and are eager to produce?

When you secured the stage rights to Anne Frank's "Diary of a Young Girl" you knew I had already dramatized the book, but you appointed new adaptors. Anne's father, Otto Frank, said of my play, "I can't imagine how anyone could more truly recreate the characters."

Cheryl Crawford was to produce it but had a change of plan, common in the theater. Thereafter, three good producers made offers for my play. One said, "I'm in love with it." Mr. Frank was influenced to reject these offers. A powerful theatrical law firm gave me just thirty days to secure an acceptable producer from a restricted list. Barred from this list were the producers of *Life With Father, Junior Miss, The Time of Your Life, The Watch on the Rhine* and many of like stature. Is such manipulation fair to my play, to the public, to the theater itself? You thereafter acquired the rights to the Diary, and shoved my play aside. The Diary is dear to many hearts, yours, mine, and the public's. There is a responsibility to see that what may be the right adaptation is not cast away.

I challenge you to hold a test reading of my play before an audience.

A PLEA TO MY READERS

If you ever read anything of mine, *The Old Bunch, In Search, The Young Lovers*, my war reports from Europe and Palestine, if you saw my films, *My Father's House* or *The Illegals*, if you read my sequel to Anne Frank's Diary in this paper, if you have faith in me as a writer, I ask your help. Write to Mr. Frank and request this test.

My work has been with the Jewish story. I tried to dramatize the Diary as Anne would have, in her own words. The
test I ask cannot hurt any eventual production from her book.
To refuse shows only a fear my play may prove right. To kill
it in such a case would be unjust to the Diary itself.

This question is basic: who shall judge? I feel my work has
earned the right to be judged by you, the public.

Write or send this ad to Otto Frank c/o Doubleday, 575
Madison Avenue, N.Y., as a vote for a fair hearing before my
play is killed.

Meyer Levin

The immediate effect of Levin's extraordinary action was to
rally nearly everyone involved in the affair in disdainful alliance
against him, but it also had an unexpected and different impact
on the broader public and on some people in the Jewish community. When Bloomgarden read the notice, he mockingly
told Goodrich and Hackett that he would "decline the challenge" because it was beneath his dignity to reply. "The truth of
the matter," he continued

is that there isn't a person in the theater who has not found
him ridiculous and laughable by his unethical attachment to
the book originally. *The New York Times*, for instance, was
furious that he had written a glowing book review for the
book and was acting as the agent at the same time. It is also
well known that any producer wanting to have a dramatization made of the book originally would have had to take Mr.
Levin as the dramatist or there would have been no sale. This
was the position that Cheryl Crawford found herself in when
she bought the rights to have the book dramatized. (18 January
1954, KB)

And he concluded that the best response would be simply to ignore Levin's attacks and to get on with plans for the play.

In a letter to Basel, Frank Price (who, since Barbara Zimmerman's marriage to Jason Epstein and departure from Doubleday, was in charge of the book) condemned Levin's advertisement as preposterous and his meddlesome behavior as blackmail. Nothing was being served by all this commotion, he told Otto Frank, "but the personal vanity of a paranoic man." Price was so indignant at Levin's tactics that he could not resist mildly rebuking Anne's father for "your own gentleness of spirit," which in many ways "has allowed this matter to go on to the point where it has reached this impasse" (19 January 1954, PWRW&G).

Frank himself was clearly coming to the end of whatever sympathy and patience he had for Levin. Responding to an inquiry from Goodrich and Hackett, he told them that the persistent attacks no longer touched him, and he offered a brief account of the history of the controversy that emphasized the distortions and omissions in Levin's newspaper challenge to Bloomgarden. "He has no legal and no moral right to act as he does," Frank concluded. "I have the impression that he formed an 'idée fixe' in his mind and tries to make trouble without any real base. I think he will stop if he sees that his attempts have no result" (24 January 1954, GH).

Otto Frank's hope that Levin would end his protest and that the clamor might die down was wishful thinking, for some of the *Post*'s readers felt sympathy for Levin, seeing him as the intrepid writer, defending the life of his art against censorship, or as the Jewish underdog, standing up against power brokers and mighty institutions. Levin's appeal to have his play read in public seemed modest and reasonable, even if another version were eventually to be preferred to his. Why couldn't two renderings of the same story exist in the public domain? Why couldn't the audience be given a more active role in determining what they might see and read? As a columnist in *Publishers Weekly* put it: "The notion of the public deciding in advance what is going to be worth seeing, instead of waiting for the critics' verdict, is unusual and provocative. Maybe it's just what the theater's been needing!" (23 January 1954). Several dozen people wrote Frank urging him to allow Levin to give his work the hearing he asked for, and others (among them Norman Mailer and James T. Farrell) responded to the protest by signing petitions and writing letters of support.

Although at first the number of written responses was small, Levin saw them as a conspicuous endorsement of his cause, and he intensified a public campaign to enlist backers that was to go on for many years, and was to become one of the most notorious aspects of his ongoing quarrel with Otto Frank. In the early months of 1954, however, the supportive responses could not relieve the enormous frustration Levin felt at the silence of Bloomgarden and Frank (who was beginning to ignore his letters or return them unopened). The previous autumn, Levin had approached Ephraim London about the grounds for a possible suit against Crawford, Frank, and Bloomgarden, but the lawyer discouraged him. Now, angrier than ever, he consulted others, and by the spring, he was able to arrange terms by which a young attorney, Samuel G. Fredman, of Weinstein and Fredman in Manhattan, agreed to determine if he had a case.

Through much of April and May of 1954, Levin continued discussions with Fredman about prospects for a lawsuit, but he was also busy at the various creative activities by which he supported himself and his family. He worked on a documentary film about Frank Lloyd Wright; wrote a regular column, called "Candid Commentator," for the *New Jersey Star-Ledger* and Long Island newspapers; did some reviewing and ghostwriting; and continued to do research for a novel on the infamous Leopold and Loeb murder case, the early part of which he had covered as a young reporter in Chicago—a project that would result in his powerful, best-selling book, *Compulsion*, in 1956. This subject attracted Levin for many reasons: Leopold and Loeb had been high-powered intellectuals at the University of Chicago; they were self-hating wealthy German Jews revolting against their fathers; and they claimed to be motivated by Nietzsche's ideas of the Superman (which linked them forward to the Nazis). "It was inevitable," Levin had written, that their "'crimes of decadence' should appear to me as a symbol. I, the west-side boy, had turned my precocious energy into accomplishment; they, the rich south-siders, turned the same qualities into destruction" (*In Search*, 27). That the victim's name was Franks has been noted by many commentators.

Meanwhile, Goodrich and Hackett were writing successive versions of their adaptation of the *Diary*. At first they stayed especially close to the entries themselves, quoting many passages directly and at length, basing their scenes on events that Anne herself recorded. Much of what they selected seemed designed to illustrate Anne's quip that she was "on vacation in a very peculiar boarding house"—a place where sequestered people got on one another's nerves but tensions were amusingly relieved by the mischievous high spirits of a thirteen-year-old girl who kept a diary. The grim historical specificity of the story—Jews in hiding from Nazi persecution during World War II—was clear enough (each character's behavior was shaped by fear of the fatal knock on the door), but its implications were far less important than the immediate domestic situation and the life-affirming personality of the protagonist. Many of the notable theatrical features of the final play are not present in the earliest drafts, where, for example, Otto Frank, not Anne's voice-over, reads the narrative passages from the *Diary*. And several now-famous scenes—Anne's nightmare, the Hanukkah celebration, Van Daan's stealing bread, and the security police hammering on the door at the end—are absent. Frances Goodrich later admitted that at the start she and her husband were constrained by their deference to the seriousness of the project and their concern for how the already revered book would be faithfully presented on the stage. "We were," she said, "so afraid of making people unsympathetic that we have not made them human."

When they finished the fourth version, Goodrich and Hackett sent copies to Bloomgarden, Hellman, and their agent, Leah Salisbury, and then flew from Los Angeles to confer with the readers. They also mailed a copy to Otto Frank in Switzerland. In New York they were greeted with a barrage of negative criticism. Bloomgarden and Hellman complained that the writers were still excessively close to the *Diary*; the play had too much direct narration and not enough dramatized action. By accentuating dailiness, comedy, and Anne's playful charm, moreover, they were turning a unique, electrifying experience into something mundane and episodic—a kind of "Scenes from Life in Hiding." The abnormality of the situation and the effects of confinement were being softened, Bloomgarden told them, and their preoccupation with the endearing personality of Anne led them to neglect the characterization of Otto, Edith, and Margot, and to forgo the theatrical potentialities of the intricate family dynamics.

Otto Frank also objected to the script, but he was so worried about hurting the playwrights' feelings that he kept his letter in his pocket for three days before mailing it. His critique paralleled but extended Bloomgarden's: the portrait of Anne was superficial; the writers were neglecting her interiority and maturation. Having read thousands of reviews and letters about the *Diary*, Frank was certain that audiences reacted most powerfully to Anne's struggles during puberty (especially her relationship with her mother and with Peter), to her revulsion at war and discrimination, and to her inextinguishable idealism. The present draft, with its emphasis on adolescent hijinks and domestic humor, did not do justice to these elements.

Taking these criticisms to heart, Goodrich and Hackett went back to revise again. When stories about their difficulties were reported in newspaper theatrical columns, Levin wrote them to say that *his* play conveyed the inner lives of the characters, and he offered his services as collaborator, but they ignored him. Two other people did, however, have decisive influence on the shape the play was eventually to take: Lillian Hellman and the well-known playwright, screenwriter, and director Garson Kanin. In early September, Goodrich and Hackett met with Hellman on Martha's Vineyard to continue discussing her reactions to their work. "She was amazing," they later reported, and gave the writers "brilliant advice on construction," particularly about reducing narration and intensifying dramatic impact in

the scenes of Dussel's arrival, Anne's nightmare, and the
Hanukkah celebration.[10] Exactly what else Hellman told them
is not known, but a look at the consecutive drafts of the later
summer and fall allows a few conjectures. Version six (on which
Hellman had the most influence) was markedly better than the
fourth draft the writers had submitted in late May. Now, the
play was less static and episodic: suspense was more successfully
sustained, and scene divisions (marked more clearly here) were
beginning to hint at what was to be the work's most pro-
nounced and affecting emotional rhythm. In the final version,
each scene varies and develops a tension that had been established at the end of the previous scene or at the beginning of
the current one—the tension between, on one hand, the rigor
of confinement and the dread of discovery and, on the other,
the main characters' unquenchable desire for freedom and their
affirmation of life. Although this is a familiar and perhaps even
a hackneyed theatrical device, it is ultimately used to great
effect by Goodrich and Hackett. Bloomgarden had earlier
remarked that the script was not taut enough and lacked spiritual inspiration. After Hellman worked with the playwrights,
melodrama and uplift were fused in ways that were eventually
to exercise a legendary hold on audiences around the world.

More than a year later, after *The Diary of Anne Frank* had
opened in New York and Levin learned of Hellman's role in
advising both Cheryl Crawford and the Hacketts, he charged
that because of her German-Jewish assimilationist background
and her Stalinist and anti-Zionist sympathies, she had

---

10. Frances and Albert Hackett, "Diary of *The Diary of Anne Frank*,"
New York Times, Sunday, 30 September 1956, sec. 2, p. 1, col. 3.

prompted Crawford to reject his play for being "too Jewish" and had altered the Goodrich and Hackett version to tone down the accent on Jewish issues and make the play more international. This idea of a Hellman-inspired attempt to de-Judaize and universalize the text became the core of a conspiracy theory Levin espoused in different forms for the next twenty-five years (it will be examined in later chapters). But unpublished documents from the period now make it clear that the person who had the greatest influence in universalizing the play was not Hellman but Garson Kanin, who joined the team as director in late October. Enthusiastic about the project and certain the script "would not need masterminding or doctoring," Kanin did have specific suggestions designed to heighten intimacy, suspense, and audience identification. His recommendation that Anne's voice-over read the diary entries as orchestrated bridges between scenes gave the final play one of its most compelling features. He also had dozens of valuable proposals about pacing, momentum, sound effects, and ways of intensifying the atmosphere of alarm on stage. But it was in his determination to make the stark story more accessible and pleasing to a wide audience that Kanin had his most telling influence.

The director declared that the *Diary* was not a gloomy or depressing book about the persecution of the Jews but rather "an exalting comment on the human spirit," a play about what G. B. Shaw called "the life force"; and he urged the writers (and later Boris Aronson, the designer) not to emphasize a bleak, tragic tone that might put theatergoers off. When, in reading the closing moments of the sixth version of the play, he came upon a vital exchange between Anne and Peter, he pressed

Goodrich and Hackett to revise it to broaden its appeal. Anne has just spoken of the strength she has gotten from religious belief, and Peter answers ironically: "That's fine! That's wonderful! But when I begin to think, I get mad. Look at us, hiding out for two years! . . . Caught here, like rabbits in a trap, waiting for them to come and get us! And all for what? Because we're Jews! Because we're Jews!" And Anne replies: "We're not the only Jews that've had to suffer. Right down through the ages there have been Jews and they've had to suffer."

Kanin found this "an embarrassing piece of special pleading." Throughout history, he told the writers:

> people have suffered because of being English, French, German, Italian, Ethiopian, Mohammedan, Negro, and so on. I don't know how this can be indicated, but it seems to me of utmost importance.
>
> The fact that in this play the symbols of persecution and oppression are Jews is incidental, and Anne, in stating the argument so, reduces her magnificent stature. It is Peter here who should be the young one, outraged at being persecuted because he is a Jew, and Anne, wiser, pointing out that through the ages, people in minorities have been oppressed. In other words, at this moment, the play has an opportunity to spread its theme into the infinite. (8 November 1954, GH)

In a subsequent version of the script—developed after a three-week collaboration with Kanin in London—Peter's reference to the persecution of the fugitives "Because we're Jews! Because we're Jews!" disappears; and Anne says: "We're not the only people that've had to suffer. Right down through the ages there have been people that've had to suffer. Sometimes one race . . . Sometimes another . . ."—which is very close to what she says in the final rendering. At other points, too, Kanin urged changes that de-emphasized the connection of the annex inhabitants to their Jewishness. Noting a reference to Anne, Margot, and Peter's attending the Jewish Secondary School, he asked if it would be possible to convey that this was not from choice but because they were *forced* to do so by the authorities. And in the very last stages of revision, he urged that the sober "Rock of Ages," the traditional hymn in the Hanukkah scene, be replaced (as it was) by a more light-hearted, joyful melody, to prevent the close of Act I from becoming "as flat as a latke."[11]

Following their three-week working session in London, Goodrich, Hackett, and Kanin spent ten days in Amsterdam, where Otto Frank gave them information about the backgrounds and characters of all the people who figured in the diary. He took them through the house, walked about the city, answered endless questions, and provided a density of personal context that they found both indispensable and emotionally

---

11. In later years, although he did not know of Kanin's role, Levin often deplored the omission of the specific reference to Jews in Anne Frank's lines in the play. In 1976, he told Ira Berkow that "the actual psychological effect of omitting such a passionate Jewish speech from the stage . . . who can imagine it? The attitude is that the Jew would assimilate and disappear. To take out 'Jewish suffering' and put in 'all people suffer' is to equalize the Holocaust with any kind of disaster. If you do this, you unhook the search for meaning, you unhook the wrong to the Jews. Then you go on over the years with statements like 'There weren't six million. There were four million. There were two million. There were a lot of Russians and Poles who were killed in the camps. So the Jews are just exaggerating.' And you end up with what they're using now. The bottom line reads: 'The Jews did worse to the Arabs in Palestine than the Nazis ever did to the Jews.' It's been stated that way by any number of leaders in the United Nations" (*Maxwell Street*, 276).

chastening. Frances Goodrich later spoke of the experience as "harrowing," and she told a friend, "I thought I could not cry more than I had. But I have had a week of tears." For Frank the meeting was also exhausting, but it confirmed his belief that the writers and director were sensitive people who had caught the spirit of Anne's book and were working with the utmost sincerity and devotion. "I have," he told Bloomgarden, "every possible confidence in their work" (letter, 12 January 1955, KB).

Toward the end of 1954, Goodrich and Hackett were completing the play, which was scheduled to open in the next two months. But events did not proceed as smoothly as everyone associated with the production had hoped. Personal problems forced Kanin to ask for a delay, and since he was seen to be an indispensable member of the team, the opening was postponed until autumn. Coincidentally, as this decision was being made in the last days of December, Levin began litigation against Cheryl Crawford and Otto Frank. In a verified complaint filed by Samuel Fredman in the Supreme Court of the State of New York, Levin alleged that the producer and the owner of the rights to the *Diary* breached agreements made between 1950 and 1952 to allow him to write or collaborate on a stage adaptation of the book. From Crawford he was seeking $76,500 for fraudulently inducing Frank to break the contract of March 1952. From Frank he was asking that the agreement of November 1952 be set aside because it was obtained by fraud, and that he now be given the right to either write or work with someone else on a dramatic adaptation of the play.

In the weeks following the filing of the complaint, Levin continued his efforts to explain and gather support for his actions. He went to court, he said, because he had exhausted

every other avenue for settling the dispute. After rational dis-
course broke down, he had suggested arbitration, a hearing
before a committee of theatrical professionals or even mediation by a panel of rabbis, but all these proposals were rejected.
Now, he was suing Otto Frank, not for money, but for the
right to have his adaptation performed, since Frank had authorized and approved it; and he was suing Crawford for the loss
of several years of time and for damage to his reputation. In
an article in the *National Jewish Post*, in letters to "friends of
the theater" and to members of the rabbinate, in public statements distributed to other groups, Levin reviewed the history
of the controversy and urged that the matter be seen as a subject of serious concern to the larger community, not as a mere
personal quarrel. Anne Frank's *Diary*, he wrote, was not a
mere commercial property but folk material and a legacy to
humanity, and his play was a contribution to its correct understanding.

For Otto Frank's attorneys and people involved in the production of the play, Levin's litigation and subsequent publicity
campaign provided only new evidence of what they believed to
be the absurdity of his claims and behavior. The suit, Bloomgarden reassured Goodrich and Hackett, was "the ridiculous
act" of "a wacky and unethical character" and would certainly
be thrown out of court. Levin, he said, was a disappointed
writer who had tried his hand at the dramatization of a great
book and failed to write a good enough play (14 January 1955,
KB). Myer Mermin saw little point in wasting time and money
contesting an action he considered vexatious, and he advised
Frank to move to vacate the summons on the grounds that he
was not a New York resident doing business in the state, a

motion that the court upheld at the end of March. But in the meanwhile the lawyers exchanged affidavits, attended hearings, and conferred among themselves to determine if there was any basis on which the dispute might be resolved.

As if the situation were not tangled enough, another unexpected difficulty arose early in 1955, when the Ohel Theater in Israel wrote Levin to ask if they could produce his version of the Anne Frank *Diary*. As the agreement of November 1952 stipulated, Levin *did* have the option to stage his play in Hebrew in Israel, but now a disagreement developed about terms and duration. Levin claimed the original contract gave him the unconditional right to permit such a production at any time; Mermin pointed out that if Levin insisted on the invalidity of that contract (as his suit contended), he could not assert that his right was protected by it. But Mermin briefly considered using authorization of a possible Israeli production as a negotiating tool on the chance that Levin might withdraw his lawsuit and stop interfering with plans for the New York staging. Such an arrangement, however, required the consent of Bloomgarden, Goodrich, and Hackett, who, stung by Levin's threats and obstructive behavior, had little faith in Levin's willingness to uphold an agreement if he later felt his interest was not served by it.

For much of 1955, lawyers on both sides explored possible resolutions of this particular disagreement (as well as other conflicts) between the parties. In the fall, however, these talks were eclipsed by the opening of *The Diary of Anne Frank* in preview at the Walnut Theater in Philadelphia and then, on 5 October 1955, at the Cort in New York. Greeted with nearly unanimous acclaim, the Goodrich and Hackett play was praised the next day for just those qualities that the writers and director worked so painstakingly to embody in the script. "The genius of this play is that there is nothing grim or sensational about it," William Hawkins reported in the *New York World-Telegram and The Sun*. "Instead it relates the flowering of a youngster who was pure in heart, whose faith bloomed with her mind and body, under the terrible scourge of history." That terrible scourge of history and the budding faith, though, were for most reviewers rather abstract. In the *Daily News*, John Chapman announced that "*The Diary of Anne Frank* is not in any important sense a Jewish play. . . . It is a story of the gallant human spirit." Richard Watts in the *Post* applauded its understatement and quiet conviction. "There isn't a Nazi in it," he wrote. For Brooks Atkinson in the *Times*, it was "a lovely, tender drama" about "the shining spirit of a young girl," enchantingly played by Susan Strasberg. The words "glow" and "warm" appeared in five of the seven next-day reviews, and every critic testified to seeing something magical, iridescent, or mesmerizing happen on stage at the Cort. Even the set of the hiding place, Walter Kerr marveled in the *Herald Tribune*, "is brilliantly drawn, a stunning background for a play that is—for all its pathos—as bright and shining as a banner."

These ecstatic reviews defined the terms by which *The Diary of Anne Frank* was to be discussed by the millions of Americans who would see it on stage in New York and around the country in subsequent years (as well as on film in the pious 1959 version directed by George Stevens from a screenplay by Goodrich and Hackett). Not only was the play a phenomenal popular and critical success (playing to capacity houses, moving audiences to tears, and winning the Antoinette Perry "Tony"

Award, the New York Critics' Circle Award, and The Pulitzer Prize in the spring of 1956), but it became a staple of community and school stages as well. Most theatergoers adored the Goodrich and Hackett *Diary* because they felt it transformed horror into something consolatory, inspirational, and even purgatorial: the characters may have been doomed, but the play was full of hope, energy, humor, lyricism, and "ineradicable life." People came out of the theater thinking not of all the eradicated lives and the monstrous implications of the German attempt at genocide, but rather of a smiling young girl who affirmed that "In spite of everything, I still believe that people are really good at heart." In her diary, Anne Frank followed that sentence with an apocalyptic vision of "the ever approaching thunder," destruction, and "the suffering of millions." But in the play one is left as the curtain falls with the sanguine, reassuring observation about human goodness—a repeated utterance so mindfully placed and so resonant that it soon became a tag line summing up the message of the *Diary* for countless people around the world. Indeed, so famous is the closing scene of the play that many people—including the editors of the *Oxford Companion to American Theater* (1992) and the *Cambridge Guide to American Theater* (1993)—mistakenly believe the line affirming human goodness is actually the last line of Anne's own diary.

Of the dozens of reviews that appeared in the fall of 1955, only a handful raised objections to the way Goodrich and Hackett had adapted the book for the stage. In the November *Commentary*, Algene Ballif shrewdly argued that the Broadway Anne Frank was a stereotypic American teenager, more like a Jewish Corliss Archer, the adolescent girl in *Kiss and Tell*, than the singular Dutch girl in the *Diary*. In its desire to entertain, Ballif suggested, the play told the audience mostly what they already knew and what they wanted to hear. Similarly, Richard Hayes in *Commonweal* protested that the writers and director offered "only their stagey counterfeits, fragile shells of emotion," and failed to translate the recorded facts of the Anne Frank story into "another kind of truth—dramatic, poetic" (28 October 1955). Eric Bentley, writing in the *New Republic*, noted that the play ended "weakly with Anne reflecting on the goodness of human nature—a principle which her story is far from confirming." But even Bentley seemed pleased that "contrary to most people's expectations, including mine, the *Diary* proves to be a touching, charming and not at all harrowing piece of theater" (2 January 1956).

When Levin saw the preview in Philadelphia, he had some of these same sound criticisms, but his immediate response was far more personal and impassioned. Writing to Otto Frank at the time of the Jewish High Holidays, he began by speaking of "a final effort at reconciliation," but he then went on to express again his anger and profound sense of grievance. "I have seen the play," he told Frank," and "need hardly tell you that it is very much like the play I wrote; you can read." The three years of "delays, of torment, of difficulty" were all unnecessary. His finished play, he argued, would have been the same in tone, "except for the fact which you too must be able to recognize, that in my play the characters are more fully and truly developed." The rest of Levin's letter consisted of his habitual attack on the people in positions of power who had persuaded Frank to reject his original dramatization, and he ended with this plea about justice and ethics:

I have urged you always to make it possible for me to find
justice without recourse to the long, costly, and sometimes
unpleasant processes of the law. I urge it again, I urge you to
recognize the highest belief of our people in ethical conduct,
and to place it above commerce, and above commercial
loyalty, and above even the forms of legality, though for my
own part I am quite confident that I could receive justice
within these forms. (24 September 1955, BU)

Given Levin's passionate dedication to getting the story of
the Jews of Europe told, his great contribution to the original
success of the *Diary*, his enormous disappointment at the rejection of his play, and the chance that he may have been badly
treated, it is difficult not to wonder at this point (and at many
other points in the protracted controversy) if there might have
been ways in which he could have been accommodated and
even satisfied: some effort made to allow his play to be performed by community groups or small theaters (now that the
Goodrich and Hackett *Diary* was such a tremendous success);
some compensation given for his setbacks and loss of time. But
in fact the situation had by this time taken on a kind of fatedness, of inexorability, with everyone holding views that became
harder and harder to reconcile, and each disputant becoming
further enclosed in positions from which he or she seemed
unable to withdraw.

Frank was now convinced that Levin was a sick man in the
clutches of "a persecutional mania," and he spoke frequently in
his letters to Mermin and Tereska Torres about feeling utterly
helpless and full of pity at the tragedy in his former friend's life.
But he was also deeply wounded by Levin's repudiation of their
written agreement and by his accusations of fraud and deceit.

Yet even when Frank thought of trying to alleviate Levin's pain
and to rescue them both from the distressing situation, he was
hemmed in not only by temperament and morality but by
prior commitments and legal constraints. During this period,
he sometimes asked Mermin about the prospects of a settlement with Levin, but he was opposed for different reasons by
everyone involved in the dispute. Bloomgarden, Goodrich and
Hackett were now interested primarily in protecting their valuable property, and given Levin's previous behavior, they saw no
justification for being responsive to him. They continually
blocked any effort to give him even amateur rights to his play,
arguing that royalties from such rights were often considerable
and that an extension could jeopardize touring-company pre-
sentations of their work. They opposed allowing his *Anne
Frank* to be done in Israel on the grounds that a staging there
(whether it succeeded or failed) would depress interest in European productions of their version. Mermin, after the Goodrich
and Hackett play was successfully launched, was becoming less
and less inclined to negotiate with a man whose case he
believed to be groundless and whose demands were often vague
and constantly changing. Furthermore, the spectacular reception of the play on Broadway and the far-reaching talk of how
"good it would be for the Jews" confirmed Frank's belief that
Goodrich and Hackett had given him the adaptation he wished
for and that he was right to have refused Levin's. Similarly, the
more often the play was praised for eliciting pity and concern
for the Jews and for stimulating contributions to Jewish charities, the less patience people were likely to have with Levin's
campaign against it, especially his claim that Goodrich and
Hackett had diminished the Jewish content of the story. Yet

despite the determined opposition to responding at all to Levin, lawyers on both sides did conduct many conversations and negotiations in an effort to resolve the conflict, but to no avail.

In the weeks following the premiere of the play, stories about its stunning impact appeared daily in publications around the world. Susan Strasberg was featured on the cover of *Life*, *Newsweek*, and many Sunday newspaper supplements; inquiries about production rights came in from scores of foreign theaters; and discussions with film producers were intense. In reaction, Levin's protest took new and increasingly belligerent forms. In his letters to Frank and others, he often drew on analogies to Nazi genocide to express what he felt had been done to him and his work. To Brooks Atkinson, he declared that his play had been "killed by the same arbitrary disregard that brought an end to Anne and six million others. There is, among the survivors, a compulsion to visit on others something of the evil that was visited on them" (27 September 1954, BU). To Otto Frank himself Levin compared the way his play was dealt with to "the arbitrary way in which the Germans took away some business that a Jew had created, and simply handed it to one of their own onhangers." And he went on: "When you were shut in the Annex, and later when you were in the barracks in Auschwitz, there must have been night after night, year after year, night after night, when you could not get to sleep because over and over in your mind the question kept asking itself, why, why, why have they done this to me?" Similarly, he concluded, he has had the same sleepless nights asking, "Why has Mr. Frank done this to me?" (19 October 1955, BU).

The cutting extravagance of Levin's language understandably deepened the resistance of Frank and others to responding in any positive way to his accusations and claims. It also exposed a great deal about the depth and nature of his own disillusionment. Not only was Levin voicing his anger at the loss of an opportunity to adapt the *Diary*, but he was expressing the shock of his perception that he was now in potentially destructive conflict with the man who for several years had meant so much to him: the dead child's father, the esteemed survivor, the holder of "the rights," a justice figure, and in insinuating ways his own surrogate father. But Levin continued his public and private campaign. He tried to organize writers to protest in his behalf by signing a petition urging that Anne Frank's *Diary* be considered a legacy to humanity, a literary work rather than a commercial property, and that qualified productions of his original play be permitted. Although Norman Mailer, James T. Farrell, and others supported him, the petition was dismissed by Frank and Bloomgarden as just another tactic. Through much of the fall, Levin also continued to gather material for his lawsuit, interviewing people who had been involved in the negotiations with publishers and producers in the summer and fall of 1952.

One prickly point of contention in those early negotiations had concerned the role of Herman Shumlin, the well-known Broadway producer and director, who had among his credits several of Lillian Hellman's most successful plays, as well as *Grand Hotel* (1930) and *The Male Animal* (1940). In April 1952, Levin had asked Shumlin to read Doubleday galleys of *Diary of a Young Girl* to see if he might be willing to produce a play based on the book. Although initially skeptical about the prospects of a play on such a grim subject—audiences, he said,

would not come to see people they know have ended in the cre-
matorium—Shumlin had admired the work and said that he
wanted to see Levin's adaptation before considering an option
on the material. Six months later, after Crawford had rejected
his draft, Levin had asked Shumlin to read it, and the producer
told him that he had done a remarkable job so far and
expressed an interest in seeing the script again after he had
completed further revisions. At about the same time, two
young producers, Norman Rose and Peter Cappell, contacted
Shumlin and said that they had been and still were interested in
producing the Levin dramatization, but that Frank and his
associates would not grant them the rights because they did not
have sufficient prestige. They were approaching Shumlin now
because they believed that if he, an established producer, would
join them, their opportunity to do the show would be
improved.

Shumlin agreed to explore the matter further, but when
Cappell and Rose's lawyer phoned Mermin, he was told that
Shumlin was not among the fourteen acceptable producers and
their inquiry could not be considered. Afterward, Levin said
that he had tried desperately to get Shumlin's name on the
original list of producers but was opposed by Mermin, who
blocked him because he wanted at any cost to keep Levin's play
from being produced. Mermin and Frank later maintained that
Shumlin was rejected not because he favored Levin's play but
because he had had no box-office hits in recent years, his reputation had fallen, and he was not of the caliber of Cheryl Crawford. They added that Shumlin wanted to coproduce with Rose
and Cappell, who Levin himself had earlier agreed were too

young and inexperienced; and Frank continued to assert that Shumlin never actually made an offer but only expressed an interest.

In an affidavit prepared for Samuel Fredman in October 1955, Shumlin stated unequivocally that had he received an opportunity to produce Levin's play in association with Rose and Cappell, he "was ready, willing and able to accept that opportunity. I found the Levin adaptation satisfactory at that time as a first draft for a production and I affirm that I made an effort to acquire production rights prior to the 21st day of November 1952." Although this clearly supports Levin's contention about Shumlin's positive interest, it does not decide the arguments about Mermin and Frank's motives. As owner of the rights to the *Diary*, Frank had the prerogative to rule against Shumlin on any grounds, whereas Mermin could be defended on the basis of his belief (after the testimony of Crawford, Bloomgarden, and others) that Levin's script was a poor bet for success on Broadway. In later years, Shumlin voiced regret on several occasions about having gotten involved on Levin's side and said that Levin was making "a scandal of something that was not."[12]

But noting all this, one can still see why Mermin's handling of Shumlin's interest in producing the play—like so much else in the controversy—could justifiably have inflamed Levin. Not only was he angered at the exclusion of a reputable producer who saw promise in his script, but he could never accept his having been given so little time to work on the project before

12. Letter from Rabbi Samuel Silver, editor of *American Judaism*, to Meyer Levin, 27 September 1957 (BU).

Crawford and others turned it down. Goodrich and Hackett
had more than a year to shape their play through at least eight
versions, and they benefited from the criticism of many sea-
soned Broadway talents. Levin had no such good fortune; his
first draft—despite the promise first seen in it by Frank, Crawford, Shumlin, Harold Clurman, and others—was rejected
before he had any sustained opportunity to revise it.

But Levin's most significant new charges—and the ones that
were to resonate for a decade and more—concerned not Shumlin but rather the relationship of the Goodrich and Hackett
Broadway version to his original unproduced script. Once he
saw the play in Philadelphia, Levin began arguing in print and
privately that the adapters had plagiarized material from his
work and that they had misrepresented the meaning of Anne
Frank's *Diary* by eliminating vital material about Jewish identity, which was in his view the most important aspect of her
life and book. As he put it in an article for the *National Jewish
Post* in mid-October, Anne's diary was "the representative document . . . of all who perished in the great catastrophe," and it
"was an adaptor's duty to find in it and to project the basic
themes, the basic meaning of the ghastly experience." Of all
Levin's charges, these were the two that were to prove hardest
for his adversaries to counter, and they became dominant subjects of the controversy from this point on.

> **3**

Levin's *Anne Frank*

LEVIN'S CHARGE OF PLAGIARISM against Goodrich and Hackett has proved to be one of the most persistent and difficult-to-assess aspects of the long controversy. When he first made the claim after the premiere of their *Diary*, it was immediately ridiculed and dismissed as wholly unfounded by everyone associated with the production, but two years later at the trial before the Supreme Court of the State of New York, it was the only allegation on which the jury found in Levin's favor, and he was awarded $50,000 in damages. Frank and Bloomgarden's lawyers called this result "a gross and shocking miscarriage of justice" and submitted motions to have the verdict dismissed and a new trial ordered. Even though the judge did subsequently set aside the jury's decision, he ruled on a technicality about unproven damages, and a later out-of-court settlement left the matter of "wrongful appropriation of ideas" hanging in the air. Levin, deprived of damages, still felt vindicated; Frank, Bloomgarden, and the Hacketts (who were not defendants in the suit) remained incredulous at the allegations and the verdict; but as late as the 1980s, a critic looking back at the history declared that "Levin has a strong case."[1]

Now, more than forty years after the argument about plagiarism erupted, a review of the circumstances under which the *Diary* was first dramatized, the ambiguity of the textual evidence, and the conflicting claims of the parties involved suggests that the case is unlikely to be settled conclusively. The first problem in weighing Levin's accusation is that since he and the Hacketts fashioned dramatic texts from an identical source, many of the same situations, scenes, and pieces of dialogue in their plays have their origins in Anne Frank's book itself. Second, although the Broadway writers said they never saw Levin's rendering and had no idea he had written a radio script as well, the radio play was broadcast twice on CBS, and several of the key figures involved in the process of revising their play—notably Kermit Bloomgarden and Lillian Hellman—had heard or read Levin's work. Whether and precisely how their knowledge of these two texts influenced Goodrich and Hackett is impossible to determine. Third, Levin's play exists in several versions, and no one can be sure which one Bloomgarden and Hellman had seen. The version most widely available now (the text that was performed by the Soldiers Theatre in Tel Aviv in 1966 and privately printed by Levin a year later) was substantially revised for the Israeli production and is not the script of contention in the 1950s. The versions seen in 1957 by the lawyers and the jury have never been published, and even though they exist in various archives, they are difficult

1. Stephen Fife, "Meyer Levin's Obsession," *New Republic* (2 August 1982), 26–30.

to date and order with certainty. To complicate matters further, Bloomgarden and others claimed that the Levin text submitted at the trial had been revised *after* the Goodrich and Hackett play had opened in New York and reflected his acquaintance with it (although this claim, too, is debatable).

Looking closely now at the various versions of Levin's *Anne Frank* will not settle the argument about plagiarism beyond reasonable doubt, but it can shed valuable light on what Levin was trying to do (and actually did accomplish) in his adaptations of the *Diary*; it also helps clarify some of the most important issues involved in the thirty-year Levin-Frank dispute. Three different texts are relevant: Levin's radio script of 1952; the draft for the stage play that he submitted to Cheryl Crawford (and several lightly revised versions of it); and the play performed in Israel in 1966 and "privately published by the author for literary discussion" in an expanded edition the following year.

The radio script, Levin's first completed adaptation of the *Diary*, was written in response to a request from the American Jewish Committee to provide a twenty-five-minute dramatization for broadcast on CBS the night before the beginning of Rosh Hashanah, the Jewish New Year. Although Levin had trouble producing a draft that satisfied the coordinator, Milton Krents, the final version was aired on 18 September 1952 and was praised by listeners and reviewers. Levin's approach was simple but effective and revealing. Since he could not in less than half-an-hour offer anything resembling a complete dramatic version of the *Diary*, he chose and connected passages that highlighted some of the main features of the book and demonstrated why it was relevant to Rosh Hashanah, the Ten Days of Penítance, and Yom Kippur, the time at which for

Jews God judges humanity, and individuals examine their virtues, sins, and hopes for the future.

After the announcer establishes the didactic significance of the occasion, Levin blends three distinct patterns of sound: the filtered voice of Otto Frank narrating the history of his family in hiding, their fates in the death camps, and the survival of his daughter's book; the filtered voice of Anne, over the sound of a scratching pen, addressing her diary; and several dramatized scenes in which the inhabitants are heard talking with one another in the annex. Frank's later reportorial narratives are concerned primarily with events in and outside the house—deprivation, bickering, roundups, deportations, accounts of Jews being gassed, the progress of the war. Anne's voice records the pulsations of her inner being—the desires, preoccupations, ideals, and changing convictions of the quicksilver girl. The enacted scenes offer slices of immediate life—Anne receiving the diary or sparring with her algebra teacher; the two families arriving at the secret apartment; the strains of caged existence; and Anne's emerging romance with Peter.

The dominant impression of Anne that comes across from this tightly knit, though very brief, scenario is of a sensitive, reflective girl who broods alternately about sacred and mundane things. Her first speech reveals the lonely child looking for consolation in nature and celebrating God through His creation. But the adolescent Anne is also there, speaking of friends, clothes, boys, movie stars, and of herself as "simply a young girl in need of some rollicking fun." More dominant, though, is the grave, meditative Anne, the child for whom "memories mean more . . . than dresses." Her most vivid moments are speculations about the plight of people during war and the meaning of present and past suffering. "The whole earth waits. Jews and Christians wait, and there are many who wait for death"—this haunting sentence from the *Diary* (and several others like it) are given pride of place. Although Levin inevitably uses "In spite of everything, I still believe that people are really good at heart," he also includes the dark vision of wilderness and destruction. Dramatizing Anne's guilt about deserting Lies Goosens, Levin carefully links the episode to her emerging perceptions of the need for Jewish continuity. Indeed, the climax to the radio play is the passionate dialogue between Anne and Peter in which he denies and she proudly confirms their Jewish identity against a backdrop of air raid sirens, shouts of "Open, Jews!" and the terror of imminent seizure. The drama closes with Anne expressing faith in religion and love, and hoping— now that she is "a woman with inward strength"—to "work for the world, and for mankind," if "God lets me live." Frank, as narrator, then discloses Anne's death and links it to the question raised in a prayer on the Jewish New Year: "Who shall live and who shall die?" Anne lives, he asserts, in her book, and he wonders if he has been spared so that he might return "to receive her diary, to give my little daughter's words to the world, and all mankind."

On the basis of listener response, Levin's radio adaptation looked like an auspicious trial run for the forthcoming Broadway show. Reviewers in *Billboard* and *Variety* particularly liked the blend of suspense, character study, and homily, one noting that "the script retained all the sensitivity and moving qualities of the original," while the other observed that "it holds interest for Jew and Gentile alike." But Levin knew well enough that writing a twenty-five-minute sermonic scenario for broadcasting at Rosh Hashanah was far less of a challenge than writing a play that would appeal to a Broadway audience and turn a profit. For that purpose he created a work of notably different tone and structure.

The three-act play written for Cheryl Crawford begins with a good deal more daring. The opening scene, which takes place in the street outside the Franks' apartment on Anne's thirteenth birthday, is designed to be both an alluring sketch of ordinary life and a suggestive ritual about a girl on the verge of becoming a young woman. Anne and some friends talk effusively about school, flirtations, and bodily changes; her mother appears in an upstairs window and the conversation turns variously to plants, puberty, periods, babies, and other subjects unusually explicit for the stage in 1952. Levin even includes the detail from the *Diary* about Anne's desire that she and Lies touch one another's breasts as a pledge of eternal friendship. The animated, at times comically ardent, birthday mood is suddenly modified by the entrance of Mr. Frank carrying a package and remarking: "We don't want the Nazis to get their clutches on our possessions." He explains the plans for concealment, and minutes later, when Margot receives a letter ordering her to report for service with a labor battalion, Mrs. Frank instructs the family to disappear into the secret annex. The scene ends with the ironical flourish of an errand boy delivering a bouquet of flowers from Harry Goldberg, Anne's admirer, who has tried on occasion to interest her in Zionism.

The discordant notes in this ambitious first scene have considerable dramatic promise. Levin quickly establishes the tensions that will emerge as the major motifs and themes of the story as a whole: the conflict between youthful avidity and adult concern, between the desire to grow up, and the encircling threat of anti-Semitic persecution. His initial characterization of Anne is appealingly gritty. Although recognizable as an exuberant teenager, she also displays a candid interest in the physical facts of life that makes her more like the realistic author of the *Diary* (who writes easily of "talk, whispers, fear, stink, flatulation, and always someone on the pot") than the sanitized heroine created by Goodrich and Hackett.

The second scene, in the hiding place itself, efficiently develops these subjects. As the families arrive, talk turns to the conditions of incarceration and the strict regulations for daily behavior in the sealed rooms. Here, the dramatic tensions relate to security, health, and to impending conflict between the occupants over the use of sheets, silverware, and the w.c. The Franks and Van Daans all know the political realities: Anne quizzes her father about the chance of their being taken to a concentration camp or shot; Van Daan mentions Westerbork, and his wife the SS. Anne, though, is still portrayed as the figure associated with expansiveness and growth. She laughs a lot, moves to open a window, compares herself to a caterpillar making its cocoon, and continues to unsettle others with a pert remark about daughters inevitably going through a phase of infatuation for their fathers. Sexual currents are on the surface: Mrs. Van Daan flirts outrageously with Mr. Frank; and Koophuis, jesting about an upstairs harem, calls the Frank sisters his secret loves. At two notable points, characters behave in ways that have marked parallels in the Broadway version and would figure largely in the arguments about plagiarism at the 1957 trial. When they enter the vacant apartment, Koophuis removes the yellow star from Margot's coat, and Margot puts her finger to her lips and then touches the emblem (because it also is the Star of David) before he puts it away; and soon after, the hunted Jews peel off layers of clothes and a joke is made about Anne "revealing" herself. Levin was later to claim that both these scenes were copied from his play by the authorized adapters, but Goodrich and Hackett maintained that one of these scenes is derived from the *Diary* itself and the other, although not in the book, was different enough in their version to be accounted for by creative coincidence.

Levin ends this second scene with an exchange designed to mix anxiety and comedy. As the gentile protectors leave the Jews to their confinement, Mrs. Van Daan speaks of feeling as if "we were being sealed in a tomb," and her husband gloomily replies, "In Poland . . . people are actually hiding in holes in the earth." This solemnity is lightened by Anne's burst of laughter at the sight of Peter stumbling under the weight of a sack of beans that snags on a nail and bursts; but the mood immediately darkens again when Anne is chided for making a noise that could jeopardize them all.

Levin's technique here is similar to what was to become the very successful governing strategy of the Goodrich and Hackett play. He too establishes a rhythm of fear followed by relaxation followed by a reminder of danger—a familiar but effective means of shaping the audience's response by accenting both the frightful suspense of the situation and the capacity of the fugitives to respond positively to it. This pattern continues to dominate the third and closing scene of Act I, which takes place six months later, in November 1942, when the Germans are holding much of Europe. At the start, everyone is dejected, bickering about exercise routines and food, quarreling about

books fit for teenagers to read and where the expected new resident, Dr. Dussel, should sleep. When Miep enters to
announce that the Allies have landed in Africa, spirits soar; but
when Dussel arrives and reports on the arrests and deportations of local Jews they all know, spirits again plunge. Then
Levin concludes Act I with his most powerful piece of writing
in the play so far. The sleepy Anne overhears Dussel's account
of Nazi atrocities, and she at first cries out, "Oh why do we
have to be Jews?" But then in bed she has a vision of her tat-
tered friend Lies crying for help. Responding to the shock,
Anne expresses guilt at having previously hurt Lies's feelings
and shame now at having deserted her, and she prays to God
for her own forgiveness and for protection for her friend. The
scene is pivotal because it reveals Anne questioning and then,
through the power of her maturing imagination, beginning to
affirm her identity as a Jew.

On the basis of Act I of Levin's *Anne Frank*, it is easy to see
why Cheryl Crawford had encouraged him in the late summer
of 1952, and why other theater people later thought the draft
had promise. But reading the second act, one can also begin to
understand why Crawford grew skeptical about the play's
potential for a New York production. At this point, Levin
makes a set of reasonable artistic choices that are faithful to
the inner truth of the *Diary* but that would likely provoke
doubts in the minds of a producer who had to consider the
exigencies of commercial theater. Instead of trying to inten-
sify dramatic suspense by spotlighting the outside threat to the
caged Jews, or to develop the external tensions embedded in
the adolescent's relationship with her parents, Levin chooses
to explore the interior implications of the material. As he was

to explain years later, he wanted to create a play that was Chekhovian in atmosphere and balletic in form—a work that captured the "probing of a young girl" who was "thwarted at each impulsive moment while she strives for self-realization" but who is ultimately able to express her independent identity as a Jew and as a writer in the face of discouragement and persecution (*The Obsession*, 68).[2]

Levin's Act II, which opens on a hot summer afternoon in 1943, does move convincingly in this direction. The inhabitants of the annex, a year after their arrival, are further sunk in despondency and inertia. Peter toys with a magnet; his father sprays his sore throat; his mother reflexively wipes a table; Dussel won't come out of the toilet; and Frank tinkers with an ailing watch. Against this deftly depicted stagnant background,

---

2. In the archives at Boston University, there is an undated letter written by Levin (probably in the mid-fifties), addressed "Dear Anne," in which he explains his intentions to the subject of his play: "We agreed that the play should not strive for emphasis of the melodramatic situation. Dramatic tension existed through the awareness of the audience that the fatal knock on the door might come at any moment. The power and the beauty in your diary is in the insistence of life itself to continue its natural development, even in such tension. . . . The task then was to find a dramatic form that could hold together the material of the loosely woven diary. I felt I had found it; in the stages of adolescent emotional development, there was the same dramatic suspense as in watching a child learn how to walk. The reaching first toward the father, toward the mother for support. The effort to attain a chosen object, the boy and the thrusting away of the anxious arms of mother, of father, as they reach out to prevent your fall. And in the third stage, the standing free, in self-realization—the attainment at the very tragic moment of the knock on the door. The form appeared to me as something close to ballet, with the girl in the climax achieving her first sense of maturity, recognizing the separate existence of mother, father, sister, boy."

Levin presents Anne the diarist, the hopeful writer eager to put everything down in her private journal and to publish the book when she is free. Margot, seeming to understand her sister's passion, observes, "I suppose it could be exciting. All the times we've nearly been caught, the robbery in the front office, and that nosey plumber." But Anne answers: "Not only things like that. I want to remember exactly how I felt." To externalize Anne's rich inner life, Levin has her read brief sentences from the daily entries: "Now it is suddenly clear to me what Mommy lacks," or "Yesterday I read an article by Sis Heyster about female bodily change . . ." This effort to represent Anne's growing commitment to record her feelings in language is certainly true to the original *Diary*; indeed, that devotion can be said to be the girl's most profound and moving personal affirmation. But it does pose problems for someone writing for the theater. With the other characters becoming increasingly passive and shadowy, Anne's assertion of the vitality of her "written" life only makes the play seem increasingly more internalized and untheatrical, prompting the thought that it is in danger of becoming a staged reading of a diary rather than a journal transformed into a stirring dramatic action, or even an engrossing Chekhovian mood piece.

At the beginning of the second act, Levin's heavy reliance on *Diary* entries and his difficulty in finding stage equivalents for the life that exists so memorably in the pages of Anne's book are apparent in his handling of the people around her. As he concentrates on the complex inward process of Anne becoming a young woman, a writer, and a Jew, her parents and the Van Daans fade from the play. Otto Frank, who had only a minor role in Act I, is hardly noticeable in the first scene of Act

II; and Edith Frank, who is named as her daughter's adversary, is at this point close to being a cipher. Similarly, the intense focus on Anne's inner development detracts from the overt drama of the plot. The Nazis are barely mentioned in Act II, Scene I, and the palpable suspense that is essential for theatrical effect appears to be draining from the play.

Some of the earlier dramatic energy is recovered again in the concluding scene of Act II, set on the first night of Hanukkah, 1943. Here the physical and spiritual hardships of the characters and their markedly different ways of responding to them are forcefully presented. The Van Daans, running out of money, engage in an electrifying quarrel about the selling of her fur coat. Edith and Otto Frank are brought to center stage in a compelling episode in which they talk anxiously about their insufficiencies as Jews and as parents. Against this background of parental apprehension, Anne and Peter express their deepening affection for each other and provide a touching, if temporary, defense against the disturbing world outside. The scene closes with a suspenseful sequence in which the audience sees two thieves just outside the annex threatening to enter as the families begin to light candles for Hanukkah.

Levin's ceremony is very different from the long, cheerful scene that is similarly placed for climactic effect at the end of Act I of the Goodrich and Hackett *Diary*. Far more realistic and sober, his ritual is performed by Jews whose tentativeness about their own religious beliefs and fright about the future mute their observance of the festival commemorating one of the great victories of their people. At first Anne balks at reading the prayers for blessing the candles, insisting that all prayers should be private, and she recites only when Margot nudges her into compliance. Otto and the Van Daans can't recall the words to "Rock of Ages," and Edith has to get the song going on her own. At the curtain, the eight inhabitants huddle close to one another as if they were seeking protection from furies they do not have the resources to combat. Levin's brief, unadorned rendering of Hanukkah in the hiding place seems closer to what most likely went on there than the excessively romantic version in the Goodrich and Hackett play. But again, one can see why a prospective producer might think Levin's quietly authentic scene not quite what was needed to absorb and entertain a large public on Broadway.

The third and final act of Levin's 1952 *Anne Frank* further highlights both the potential and the problems of the play. Surprisingly, the first of its two scenes opens with a surreal dream sequence: Anne's recorded voice-over is heard reading from the *Diary* about her crush on a boy named Peter Wessel; and as the curtain rises, she is sitting opposite him as he says, "If I had only known, I would have come." The lights fade, and we are back in the annex with Anne, dressed in a ballet costume, practicing movements and talking with Margot about their hopes for the future. The sequence with Peter Wessel is clearly meant to reveal Anne's preference for him over Peter Van Daan and to prepare for her subsequent disillusionment with her new boyfriend; but given the realism of the rest of the play, the dream vignette strikes a jarring note, and Levin eliminated it in later versions.

The conversation with Margot, though, is essential, for it allows us to see Anne exploring and modifying her sense of her own identity as a Jew. After she hears Margot confirm an earlier decision to be a nurse in Palestine, Anne remarks: "Perhaps I'd go there, just to see the places in the Bible. I'd adore to go to Paris for a year, and London, and learn the languages. I want to be a journalist, to be something in the world, I can't imagine a life like Mummy's or Mrs. Van Daan's. And just being a nurse in Palestine, Margot—you could do much more." A revealing exchange follows in which each girl tries to define her particular idea of Jewish destiny: Margot sees it as making a free life for herself and doing something for her own people; Anne's desire is more expansive—to do something "for all mankind," without losing her own firm sense of being Jewish.

This striking episode is interrupted by the appearance first of Peter and then of the adults (including Miep and Henk), who bring the idealistic girls back to the tangible reality of black-market rations and threatened arrests, but back also to reports of Allied troop successes and the imminence of a German defeat. Immediately after Miep and Henk leave, Anne and Peter go off to his room to continue their blossoming romance. Impatient for kisses, Anne is also eager for more talk about beliefs and values, but her avid questioning of Peter leads to a disenchantment that soon inspires another affirmation. At this point, Levin skillfully turns the now-famous *Diary* entry about the meaning of Jewish suffering into an incisive dialogue in which, by interrogating Peter, Anne comes to recognize his shallow evasiveness and her own basic need for commitment— a revelation that ends with a vision: of the war-torn world becoming a wilderness, and of tranquility perhaps returning again.

In the last scene of the play, Anne remains a struggling, often balked aspirant, a figure much closer to the three-dimensional writer of the *Diary* than to the smiling paragon created

by Goodrich and Hackett. At one moment, she is asserting a
new-found inner strength, while at another she tearfully admits
being insensitive to her parents' feelings when she wrote them a
resounding "declaration of independence." Talking with Otto,
she calls herself "a bundle of contradictions" and astutely
defines her dilemma as being mercurial and self-divided in ways
she is now still groping to understand. As she says this, three
men in SS uniforms come up from the pit, pistols in hand.
Anne cries out, "And I keep on trying to find a way of becoming what I would so like to be, and what I could be if—if. . . ."
When the pounding on the door starts, Otto walks quietly to a
hidden safe and puts Anne's manuscript inside, saying at the
curtain, "They'll never touch you. . . . Something of us must
live." Except for the awkward posturing in this last line, Levin's
concluding scene draws from the most memorable and affecting of Anne's last *Diary* entries and succeeds in faithfully portraying her as the figure who has captured the world's attention as a vibrant girl, a victim, and an unforgettable emblem of
lost possibility.

Levin, then, wrote a play in the fall of 1952 that—for all its
first-draft deficiencies—was closer to Anne Frank's book, more
successful in capturing the singularity of the young girl and the
political and religious issues raised by her predicament, than
the Goodrich and Hackett version produced to great acclaim
three years later. But, unhappily for him, the fidelity and
roughness of his script were considered to be untheatrical and
risky by people whose taste and judgment were formed by the
more conventional, streamlined products of the popular stage,
and by the constrained political atmosphere of post–World
War II America. Their view of his play was so negative that

despite his having been told by Cheryl Crawford in the summer of 1952 to "write long," he was never given the chance to revise the script in consultation with a producer and director. Levin had hoped Crawford and others would read with a stage eye and allow for what still had to be done; but this did not happen until the director Peter Frye produced the script in Israel in 1966. The most valuable qualities of Levin's play became apparent only after that production, and others in Boston in 1983 and 1991 and elsewhere. But this afterlife and its implications will be considered in Chapters 4 and 5.

At the beginning of 1956, after Levin had charged Goodrich and Hackett with plagiarizing from his script and diminishing the Jewish content of the *Diary*, attorneys on both sides continued to explore ways in which the overall dispute might possibly be resolved. Levin himself had approached Ephraim London again in the hope of getting "a fresh start toward a settlement that might preclude a public airing of the whole issue." London, an expert in constitutional law, was especially well known for his work against censorship. In 1950, defending Roberto Rossellini's *The Miracle*, he had successfully argued that the First Amendment's protection of speech and the press extended to films as well, and he was later to win a similar case for the movie of *Lady Chatterley's Lover*. Early in February, London telephoned Myer Mermin offering to serve, not as an advocate, but as an impartial mediator, and on the twenty-third the men met for several hours of candid talk about viewpoints and proposals.

London invited Mermin to advance a proposal of settlement, but Mermin said that he did not think it appropriate for any such offer to be made by Otto Frank or his counsel. Any suggestion for a resolution should come, he said, either from Levin himself or from London, if he thought he could work out a compromise. Mermin contended that the greatest deterrent to a settlement was Levin's practice of regarding agreements as binding only so long as they served his purpose. From Paul, Weiss's point of view, a proposal from Levin, or from London as mediator, would have to meet this problem of fidelity before it could be considered. London agreed to try to frame some compromise in the light of the discussions with both parties.

To their mutual surprise, however, the next day Weinstein and Fredman began a second lawsuit by having Kermit Bloomgarden served in an action brought against him and Otto Frank. Charging fraud, breach of contract, and wrongful appropriation of ideas, Levin as plaintiff asked damages of $150,000 against Frank and $100,000 against Bloomgarden. The producer was also served with a warrant attaching Frank's right to royalties from the Broadway production. The earlier litigation against Cheryl Crawford for damages of $76,500 remained pending.

Mermin canceled further conferences with London, and a new round of accusations began. Mermin claimed that the litigation and the attachment of royalties were begun to put pressure on the mediation discussions, but Fredman argued that preliminary steps for legal action had been taken long before, and the dates were a coincidence. Levin continued soliciting rabbis to sign a petition defending his right to have his play performed in public. In his cover letter, he claimed that there were two ways to destroy Jewish life: "One is physical extinction as practiced by the Nazis. The other is extinction of Jewish identification. In some countries this is practiced through the extermination of Jewish culture." The suppression of his play was, to his mind, an obvious illustration of the process. Informed by Levin that he had nearly 250 signatures from members of the rabbinate, Frank responded irately, maintaining that Levin was now motivated by wounded pride, envy, and a desire for money (having earlier pledged to waive all fees and royalties or contribute them to charity). He labeled the claim of fraud and deceit "detestable" and charged Levin with abusing his reputation as a writer on Jewish life to influence the Jewish community unjustly. Frank also wrote to several prominent figures in Jewish organizations expressing his disappointment at the large number of rabbis who would sign petitions without knowing anything about the background of the feud and without asking him or Bloomgarden for their side of the story. The producer, too, was active in explaining his view of the quarrel. Responding to Rabbi Samuel M. Silver, director of public relations at the Union of American Hebrew Congregations (who had written for a clarification), Bloomgarden declared that Levin was trying to convert his private disappointment into a public moral issue. As for his claim that the Broadway version of the *Diary* fails to do justice to the spirit of the book, Bloomgarden proudly announced that only two weeks earlier the Hebrew Immigrant Aid Society had awarded him their highest award for his production of the drama. And he concluded:

> obviously one cannot hope for 100% unanimity in appraising any play—but the response to this play from people in all

walks of life and of all religious faiths has been such as to
make me feel that it is not only good theater but that it is also
an inspiriting communication which carries forward the spirit
and the message of Anne Frank's diary. I feel that anyone who
takes steps to injure this production is doing a disservice to
the spirit of Anne Frank. (24 February 1957, KB)

Meanwhile, the expanding fame and financial success of the
play further confirmed Bloomgarden and many others in their
assessment of the beneficial influence of this version of Anne
Frank's story and in their strong opposition to Levin's behavior
and petitions. In New York the play was grossing nearly
$30,000 a week; during the spring of 1956, it won all the major
critics' prizes; offers to stage foreign productions were coming
in from around the world; and several large film studios and
independent producers were considering bids of close to half a
million dollars for motion picture rights. Enthusiasm for the
play and the anticipated film served also to increase sales and
new translations of the *Diary* in book form. Ironically (and
painfully for Levin), his 1952 prophecy in the *New York Times
Book Review* that this "wise and wonderful young girl . . . surely
will be widely loved" was being fulfilled in ways beyond even
his most extravagant imaginings.

Despite their mounting antagonism, however, Frank and
Levin both had reasons for wanting an out-of-court settlement.
Frank wished to end the continual disturbances of the ongoing dispute and to free the attached royalties for use in restoring
the house on the Prinsengracht and starting the work of the
Anne Frank Foundation; Levin felt he might be able to get
amateur rights for his play (which Fredman had told him he
could never get by suing), and he was also finding the legal fees

and the emotional cost draining. Conscientious efforts to locate grounds for a settlement continued during the late spring and summer, but old obstacles remained and new ones emerged. Mermin insisted that Levin would have to withdraw the charges of fraud, breach of contract, and wrongful appropriation of ideas, and that Fredman needed to provide a satisfactory guarantee of finality. Levin demanded nonprofessional rights for his script, an exclusive period for production of his work in Israel, a substantial percentage of royalties from the Broadway play, and payment of five thousand dollars for legal expenses. Goodrich, Hackett, and Bloomgarden refused to go along with the first three demands, and Otto Frank objected especially to the third and the fourth.

Through much of the summer of 1956, the attorneys were also engaged in submitting to the court affidavits and procedural motions about technical matters: notably bills of particulars and the possibility of consolidating the two lawsuits. They also jousted with each other. Edward Costikyan of Paul, Weiss maintained that for years the plaintiff had been conducting a campaign of harassment of the defendants and had repeatedly changed and revised his version of the facts, asserting new claims, repudiating written agreements, and conducting a rancorous public relations campaign in the press. Fredman countered by objecting to the vituperative language and challenging all Costikyan's claims about the alteration of facts. If it was harassment, he said, for the plaintiff to insist on his day in court, then the long delays in the process demonstrated that the defendants, through the earning power achieved from the play that was the cause of the litigation, have harassed the plaintiff. At one point, Costikyan—increasingly skeptical about

chances of negotiation when positions were so far apart—
remarked to Fredman that the tone of his letter suggested "that
the controversy between our clients might, unless you and I are
careful, extend to a controversy between us as attorneys" (16
April 1956, PWRW&G).

Through all the charges and countercharges, talks about settlement possibilities continued. Attorneys for Paul, Weiss
repeatedly declared that Levin's claims were entirely without
merit, but they hoped to buy Otto Frank freedom from harassment and from a lawsuit that could last for years. For a short
time in September, one new offer seemed promising. Frank
would be willing to pay Levin five thousand dollars upon the
release of the attached royalties, and another five thousand dollars contingent on the movie rights being sold; Levin would
have the right to produce a Hebrew version of his adaptation in
Israel for a designated period of time (if the other parties
agreed); all of Levin's causes of legal action would be dismissed
with prejudice, and counterclaims protecting Frank's rights and
enjoining Levin from issuing further statements or taking additional action disparaging Frank's rights would be stipulated and
entered as a judgment in the case; Frank would pay ten thousand dollars jointly in his name and Levin's to the Women's
International Zionist Organization; and statements would be
released to the press and interested parties detailing the terms of
the final settlement.

When Samuel Fredman read the proposal from Paul, Weiss,
he immediately wrote to Levin (who was then in Paris), urging
him to accept it. After expressing his fond personal regard,
Fredman said that he and all Levin's friends agreed "that it
would be to your best interest to achieve a reasonable settle-

ment, with honor, which would free you from the drudgery of what is to follow in the lawsuit, and would at the same time, preserve your position." After explaining why he believed the terms, with some revision, were sensible, the attorney ended by beseeching Levin: "On the eve of Yom Kippur—with all that this day connotes to a person like yourself—[take] the glorious opportunity to achieve a reasonable compromise" (12 September 1956, BU). When Levin read the settlement document, however, he found it both disrespectful and inadequate. His case, he said, was not a "nuisance claim," and given the amount of money Frank and the others were earning from the play and would earn from the film, the sums mentioned were trifling. He recommended that the entire matter be left open until he returned to the States in October.

Between the time Paul, Weiss had made the proposal and the time Levin arrived back in New York, three events occurred that shattered any possibility that settlement deliberations would continue. Levin's novel, *Compulsion*—the fascinating story of Leopold and Loeb's calculated murder of Bobby Franks—was being set for publication by Simon and Schuster and promoted as a sure-fire bestseller, which, before the end of the year, it was. Then, on 30 September, Frances Goodrich published in the Arts section of the *New York Times* her "Diary of *The Diary of Anne Frank*," excerpts from the journal she had kept during the composition and production of the prize-winning play. Unintentionally, the piece was a bombshell. When Levin read it, he found substantiated nearly everything he had suspected about the role of Lillian Hellman (who had recommended the Hacketts to Bloomgarden and critiqued the script at a critical point) and about the favored treatment given to the playwrights (who had nearly a year to rework eight versions). Providing a symbolic capstone to the entire affair was the entry for 6 December 1954: "Took plane to Amsterdam. Presents from Mr. Frank waiting in the room. This is St. Nicholas Day." The lawyers at Paul, Weiss were also attentive to some of the same details, but for their own reasons. They protested to Frances Goodrich that the week-by-week report of assistance given the Hacketts might heighten Levin's sense of grievance, exacerbate his bitterness, dampen his readiness to settle, and affect the sympathy of jurors should the case go to court. On each count they proved correct.

But it was the third event that was the most spectacular and had the widest reverberations. On 1 October, *Das Tagebuch der Anne Frank* opened simultaneously at major theaters in seven German cities and provoked astonishing, unprecedented responses. In Düsseldorf playgoers sat silently in the grip of overwhelming emotion, and at intermission they remained in their seats, "as if afraid of the lights outside, ashamed to face each other." When the play ended, there was neither applause nor curtain calls as the audience, many in tears, filed out of the auditorium. In Berlin, nearly two minutes of quiet followed the ending; then, after the beginning of applause was stifled by hisses, everyone walked out drained, staring straight ahead "as if at a funeral." The impact and reactions were similar in Karlsruhe, Hamburg, Constanz, Aachen, and Dresden (the one venue in the Soviet zone).

The English critic Kenneth Tynan, who had complained that the New York production "smacked of exploitation," was overwhelmed at the premiere in Berlin. "At the Schlosspark," he wrote in the *Observer*, "I survived the most drastic emotional experience the theatre has ever given me. It had little to do with art, for the play was not a great one; yet its effect, in Berlin, at that moment in history, transcended anything that art has yet learned to achieve. It invaded the privacy of the whole audience: I tried to stay detached, but the general catharsis engulfed me." And Tynan concluded with the admission that his comments were obviously not drama criticism. "Yet in the shadow of an event so desperate and traumatic, criticism would be an irrelevance. I can only record an emotion that I felt, would not have missed, and pray never to feel again" (7 October 1956).

The day after the opening, newspapers all over Germany reported the impact of the play less as a theatrical event than as a notable chapter in the social history of the country. Within the week, media around the world were describing the seven-city phenomenon as the Germans' "facing up to history"—a mass response to twelve Nazi years of degradation that now included guilt, shame, grief, and perhaps penance and purgation. The experience in a playhouse was continually compared to a religious ritual: The *Diary*, one reviewer said, had the effect of "a present-day requiem"; the audience seemed to be engaged in an act of contrition.

Within the next few months, *Das Tagebuch der Anne Frank*, performed 1,984 times in fifty-eight other German cities, was seen by more than a million people. Attending this particular play quickly became a national ritual. Theater playbills often contained extracts of comments from President Heuss discussing the subject of collective guilt, and these quotations were accompanied by photographs, statements from Otto Frank and other notables, and eyewitness accounts of his daughter's anguish in Bergen-Belsen. At most of these performances, the behavior of each audience differed only slightly. Early on, a Hamburg rabbi had protested that the absence of applause transfigured a theatrical performance into a sacred act; but he also felt that it would be inappropriate for the audience to clap loudly as though the play were just another absorbing entertainment. He suggested a compromise: one single, brief burst of applause—a suggestion later adopted in many places.

Anne's diary in book form, which in Germany had only modest sales between 1951 and 1956, became an instant (and continuing) bestseller, and the child herself became a national heroine and myth. Young people especially were obsessed with the book and its protagonist. Early in 1957, for instance, two thousand youths, mostly from Hamburg (in a demonstration initiated by the Society for Christian-Jewish Cooperation), walked and bicycled in the rain carrying flowers to the mass graves at the former concentration camp at Bergen-Belsen, where Anne Frank had died—a ritual that was reported in the international media and imitated elsewhere and in later years.

Commentators at the time argued that the staging of the Goodrich and Hackett play marked a milestone in the history of Germany's reaction to its own Nazi past. In 1945, they said, when Germans had first been confronted with pictures and reports of the millions slaughtered in death camps, many responded with disbelief and derision. In the fall of 1956, after seeing or reading about the play, people appeared to be reacting with shock, dismay, shame, and concern. Kuno Epple, the chief producer of the Düsseldorf Schauspielhaus, said that *The Diary of Anne Frank* succeeded "because it enables the audience to come to grips with history, personally and without denunciation. We watch it as an indictment, in the most humble, pitiful terms, of inhumanity to fellow men. No one accuses us as Germans. We accuse ourselves" (*New York Times Magazine*, 17 February 1957). Other commentators, however, were far more skeptical. They pointedly remarked that the play let the Germans off easily; it did not show the SS or the ghastly fate of the hunted; it ended with the hammering on the door, not with scenes at Auschwitz or Bergen-Belsen. Other critics argued that the nationwide purging at a play about a teenage girl was a form of maudlin self-pity and not likely to get people thinking about the historic meaning or the political and cultural implications of state-sponsored genocide and their own relationship to it. Telford Taylor, U.S. chief counsel for the prosecution of war crimes at Nuremberg in 1946, once asked Goodrich and Hackett why they thought their play was such a remarkable success in Germany. When they answered that it was a heart-rending work about a lovable young girl and her family, he replied that he believed the audiences liked it because the play never pointed an accusing finger at anyone and because it took place in Holland, not Germany.[3]

Norbert Muhlen, a journalist who spoke with scores of Germans soon after they saw the play in 1956, observed that "the scale of reaction ranges all the way from genuine shock to total rejection of the book's theme." Fairly typical of one extreme was an old Protestant nurse who said: "I was more than shocked. . . . I feel guilty. Yet we had no idea what happened to the individual Jew. Please tell me how to help the survivors." But at another point on the scale was a spectator who confessed to

3. Handwritten by one of the Hacketts in their copy of the German translation of their play (GH).

being profoundly touched "because the play reminds us of our own fate. . . . After all, we too lost so much during the war." And finally, close to the other end was a man recently back from a Russian prison camp who complained that too much fuss was being made about the Jews. "It was better to be gassed to death," he said, "than to rot slowly in a Russian prison camp." Muhlen found the responses of young Germans more encouraging than those of their elders, yet even they usually linked Anne Frank's fate to their own adolescent anxieties and rarely asked about the relevance of the play to the Jews who once lived among them, or to the roots of the catastrophe in their country's political and social history (*Anti-Defamation League Bulletin*, June 1957).

Now, forty years after the premiere of the Goodrich and Hackett play, there is no denying the enormous emotional impact it had on audiences all over Germany. Although one can say that its sentimentality and evasiveness—its minimizing the Jewish subject in an effort to achieve an all-embracing, consoling universality—contributed to the tendency of many German playgoers to identify with the victims rather than to see themselves among the perpetrators, a fair claim can also be made that by not confronting the audience with the horrific historical actuality, the Goodrich and Hackett play, however ironically, helped accelerate the long-delayed process of response to the Nazi past, especially among the young. But even this claim is sometimes challenged. In 1962, Hannah Arendt called the admiration for Anne Frank, especially in Germany, a form of "cheap sentimentality at the expense of great catastrophe"; more recently, Saul Friedlander, comparing the opening of *The Diary of Anne Frank* in Germany with the telecast of "Holocaust" in 1979, has wondered whether "such shock-like confrontations" do not quickly become for the majority of the population, "a set mechanism . . . a near automatic process."[4]

On a smaller stage, the repercussions for the Levin and Frank quarrel were also considerable. In New York in October, newspapers and magazines—from the *New York Times* to *Life* and *Variety*—ran lengthy articles about the extraordinary impact *The Diary of Anne Frank* had on German theatergoers. The flood of publicity only served again to support all the antagonists in positions they already held. Having read the "Diary of *The Diary*," Levin was now absolutely convinced that a left-wing clique in the Broadway theater (spearheaded by Hellman) had schemed to strip him of his rights and opportunities in order to profit from a uniquely valuable and important property. The excitement in Germany reminded him how the inner truth of the *Diary* had been distorted and how much he had lost. But now that *Compulsion* was a bestseller, he could afford to conduct his fight in the courts. Frank, Bloomgarden, Goodrich, and Hackett were more certain than ever that their play was both a powerful force for moral good and a huge moneymaker, and thus there was no reason on any grounds to be responsive to requests and demands they believed to be

4. Arendt, letter to the editor, *Midstream*, September 1962, 85–87; Friedlander, *Memory, History, and the Extermination of the Jews of Europe*, 7–8. For a brief, thoughtful discussion of the complexities of German responses to Anne Frank's *Diary* and to the Goodrich and Hackett play, see Alvin H. Rosenfeld, "Popularization and Memory: The Case of Anne Frank," in *Lessons and Legacies*, 260–70.

wrong. Indeed, they all thought they had been uncommonly generous in their attempts to work out a settlement agreement, and when Levin rejected the September 1956 Paul, Weiss proposal, they assumed that the case was headed for court. As Myer Mermin icily explained to Fredman in November, they were not prepared to make settlement offers indefinitely just "to satisfy your client's overblown notions of what this litigation is worth." The rejection of Frank's "fair, generous and well-considered proposals must terminate these discussions. We will proceed to litigation" (SCSNY).

Although everyone believed the trial would be held early in 1957, another incident occurred that caused more turmoil and consternation. In the third week of January, news reached New York that the Habimah Theatre in Tel Aviv had opened a major Hebrew production of Goodrich and Hackett's *Diary*. First-night applause had been lavish; unlike the Germans and Dutch, the Israelis summoned the performers and director for repeated curtain calls. Afterward, the managers announced that to honor Anne Frank a forest was being planted in the Jerusalem hills. Simultaneously, the establishment by the American-Israel Cultural Fund of an Anne Frank Memorial to support Israeli writers (endowed by the American adapters of the *Diary*) was also disclosed.

Samuel Fredman wrote immediately to Paul, Weiss, protesting the staging as a violation of his client's rights established in the agreement of November 1952. Otto Frank was shocked and chagrined; he had regularly declined offers to have the play performed in Israel on the grounds that the question of Levin's rights still had to be clarified, and he had never consented to a production by Habimah. His attorneys, however, saw no dilemma. According to Mermin, Levin's chance to have his script done in Israel had long passed; Habimah was in violation of copyright; and besides, if Levin was suing on the grounds that the 1952 agreement was obtained by fraud, he could hardly now claim to be protected by it. But in response to Mermin's telegrams to Habimah asking that they desist immediately, the company held off, suggested paying royalties, and kept performing. Frank, who had been increasingly upset by the effect of Levin's many accusations on his reputation in the Jewish community, now felt in another distressing bind. He did not want to sue an Israeli theater company, but on the other hand he did not want to seem to be authorizing the forbidden production.

Interpreting the events in Tel Aviv as a calculated move by Frank, Bloomgarden, Goodrich, and Hackett to further block his rights and suppress his play, Levin escalated his campaign to publicize the charges. In the next few weeks, he appeared on Mike Wallace's *Nightbeat* television show, on the radio with Barry Gray and then with Tex and Jinx McCrary, and on the lecture platform at several New York synagogues. Invited to discuss the interest in his best-selling *Compulsion*, he would eventually turn the conversation to an account of how his original adaptation of the *Diary* was rejected and suppressed by a clique on Broadway who believed it to be too Jewish and not commercial enough. His play was a literary work, he said, not a mercantile property, and it should be given its right to life on the stage. At the Park East Synagogue, for instance, he opened his lecture with an analysis of how the Leopold and Loeb murder of Bobby Franks in the novel was motivated by Jewish self-hatred, a sense of shame leading the killers to wish to destroy themselves, or at least to obliterate their sense of religious identity. Then he explained how Jewish self-hatred motivated the left-wing, anti-Zionist coterie of Bloomgarden, Hellman, and others to silence him as an adapter of the *Diary*. He urged all his listeners to help persuade his adversaries to avoid a nasty, protracted lawsuit and agree to settle the matter by arbitration.

The lawyers at Paul, Weiss (who represented both Frank and Bloomgarden) sought without success to convince the broadcasters not to try a forthcoming lawsuit in the media. They also explored the possibility of charging Levin with defamation but rejected the move on the grounds that his attorneys might succeed in getting such a suit consolidated with the pending action, thus broadening the case and giving Levin a chance to make more personal attacks under the privilege of litigation. Furthermore, they continued to oppose Levin's call for arbitration because he wanted a group representing the rabbinate and professionals in the arts, who would consider the issues without being bound by the rules of legal evidence. Paul, Weiss did, however, work with Kermit Bloomgarden to prepare a press release explaining his role in the contentious history and to answer a pro-Levin article titled "The Betrayal of Anne Frank," by Rabbi Jacob Weinstein in *Congress Weekly*. Similarly, they supported Otto Frank when he expressed a desire to write to prominent Jewish figures. In letters to leaders of B'nai B'rith and other organizations, Frank protested Levin's one-sided representations, personal attacks, and irresponsible behavior. Describing how hurt he was that Jewish community groups and temples were allowing Levin to use their facilities to influence the public through the presentation of misleading and incorrect statements, he asked that they bar his access.

Levin was also meeting resistance to his activities from those closest to him: mainly his lawyer, wife, and editor. Samuel Fredman had urged his client to be more responsive to settlement proposals and now threatened to resign if Levin continued to discuss the legal aspects of the disagreement on radio and television. He also chided Levin for angrily protesting his reputation as belligerent and litigious while continuing to advertise and perpetuate his quarrels. Tereska Torres had often said that her husband's vehement fight for his rejected script was futile and self-destructive—a waste of time, money, and energy that was harmful to his writing and family life. Speaking of the recent past as "wasted years, sick years, dreadful years," she told him "it is yourself you should be suing for damages." Although she acknowledged he had been shabbily treated and hurt by others, she declared, "I am not speaking now about your rights at all, nor about the truth of your case, nor about its justice—all I am speaking about is your reaction to this injustice." And as she had done before, she urged him to forget about a battle he was destined to lose and turn to other creative work.[5]

But Levin was not convinced, and he kept up his defiant efforts to win the right to have his views acknowledged and his play performed. He wrote Eleanor Roosevelt, asking her to talk with him about "a complex and rather tragic matter" connected with the adaptation of Anne Frank's *Diary*. Mrs. Roosevelt had been closely associated with the original book ever since she allowed her name to be used as author of the preface, and she had often written and spoken about the importance of the

5. All quotations are from undated letters written by Tereska Torres to her husband (BU).

work's humanitarian message. Months before, in discussions
with attorneys, Levin had proposed her as a possible neutral
party. At their meeting in April, he recounted his long struggle
with the adaptation and asked her to intervene to bring about a
peaceful settlement and to avoid the upsetting consequences of
a court proceeding.

Agreeing to help, Mrs. Roosevelt wrote to Frank describing
her talk with Levin and his desire to avoid a trial that would
bring out disagreeable things, such as Frank's motives for moving to Switzerland, which according to Levin had to do with
evading high Dutch taxes. She hoped Frank would now be
willing to submit the dispute to arbitration. Instead, he was
troubled by the letter. His previous correspondence with Mrs.
Roosevelt had been amicable, but he felt this most recent letter
was formal and cold. Obviously impressed by Levin's impassioned account, she did not seem to him to realize she was lis-
tening to an especially partisan view of the history. Responding
to Mrs. Roosevelt, Frank admitted his distress and offered an
account of the affair from his side. He said that Levin's view
was slanted and incorrect, and he expressed particular disappointment that she did not perceive the account of his motives
for moving to Basel as both erroneous and a form of blackmail.
He could not now act differently, he said, in response to a man
who accused him of fraud and who had repudiated a contractual agreement he had earlier signed. Only a court trial would
establish the facts of the case.

Having been informed of the exchange between Frank and
Mrs. Roosevelt, the attorneys at Paul, Weiss asked one of the
partners, Lloyd Garrison, and one of their clients, the public
official Nathan Straus (both longtime friends of the Roosevelts)

to intercede. In his letter to Mrs. Roosevelt, Garrison said that
Levin had elicited a sympathetic response to his cause that the
facts did not warrant; and Nathan Straus similarly supported
Frank, his friend from college days in Heidelberg. By early June
1957, Mrs. Roosevelt had decided to back off, and she wrote to
Tereska Torres (who had also asked her help with arbitration):

> I do not feel it is possible to really be a judge between Mr.
> Otto Frank and your husband. I have no doubt that both of
> them think they are right. Mr. Straus, whose opinion I re-
> spect and the firm of lawyers whom they employ, and whom
> I deeply respect, think your husband is wrong. I don't think
> Mr. Frank moved to Switzerland to escape taxation, as your
> husband told me, nor do I think he was moved to refuse your
> husband's version of the play by any but the best advice which
> was given to him as to the success of the production. . . . It
> would be well if the case could be settled by arbitration but
> you would probably not be satisfied with the people they
> suggested just as they would not be satisfied with the people
> you would suggest. . . . (5 June 1957, TT)

When Levin found out about the participation of Straus and
Garrison, he was perturbed and told Mrs. Roosevelt that he
knew Straus was an old friend of Frank's, "but it never struck
me that he could have taken the most active part in the entire
affair, as it would now seem. It must, then, have been embarrassing for you for me to bring a complaint that turned out to
be against someone who had been so close to Mr. Roosevelt" (7
June 1957, BU). From Levin's own point of view, however, the
episode was another instance of people with great power moving in consort against him.

Although the court trial had originally been set for March

1957, schedule conflicts and procedural motions kept delaying it throughout the year, and in the meantime the renown of the *Diary* and its commercial value kept growing phenomenally. Film rights had been sold to Twentieth Century Fox, and the eminent director George Stevens began a much-publicized, worldwide talent search to find a girl to play Anne in what was being heralded as the most anticipated picture of the decade. (The search resulted in the selection of Millie Perkins, an eighteen-year-old, non-Jewish model.) Throughout the summer, reports appeared about the establishment of the Anne Frank Foundation in Amsterdam and about the remarkable impact of the play in Europe and Asia. A long article in *Variety* noted that Anne Frank was now for young people the most famous figure in Germany and an inspiring symbol of the continuing fight against Nazism. To celebrate her birthday on June 12, Georg Solti conducted the Frankfurt Opera House orchestra; there was also a special religious observance in Paul's Church and commemorations elsewhere.

Levin's fortunes on the other hand were worsening, and his mood was becoming more desperate. When people labeled him a crackpot and a troublemaker, he charged a deliberate character-assassination plot that had had calamitous effects on his writing career. In response, he tried to gather discrediting information about Otto Frank's behavior in Auschwitz, and he wrote several syndicated columns questioning the background of Gusti Huber, who had been praised for her role as Edith Frank on Broadway. In the Cort Theatre *Playbill*, Huber's career was said to have been "abruptly terminated when the Germans over-ran Austria," but Levin produced evidence to show that she appeared in films made in Berlin and Munich during the war.

When he turned to his own creative work—an adaptation of *Compulsion* for the stage—Levin unhappily became involved in yet another ferocious quarrel. The producer, Michael Myerberg, thought the first script needed work and convinced the playwright to accept a collaborator, Robert Thom; but when the two men could not see eye to eye on revisions, Myerberg proposed that Alex Segal, stager of the show, serve as final judge. After accepting, Levin came to suspect that Segal and Thom were in league against him, making changes that vulgarized the play. Levin applied to the Dramatists Guild for arbitration; Myerberg obtained a court order requiring Levin to show cause why the arbitration should not be enjoined; and Levin countered by instructing Samuel Fredman to get an injunction to halt the premiere of the production.

Although the play eventually opened despite Levin's strong disapproval, the widely publicized argument had distressing consequences for him. Not only was he being branded again as uncooperative, litigious, and a bad playwright, but his decision to take Myerberg to court just before the suit against Frank and Bloomgarden was to be tried caused a crisis in his marriage. After years of differing with her husband about his response to the rejection of his play, Tereska Torres felt overwhelmed by the atmosphere of constant contention. When she learned about the threat of a second suit just as everyone was preparing for the trial of the first one, she left an impassioned note expressing her desperation and came close to committing suicide—a trauma that is depicted in Levin's novel *The Fanatic*

and his memoir *The Obsession*, and in Torres's own autobiographical work, *Les maisons hantées de Meyer Levin*. Torres took
the children and planned not to return, but then Levin himself came close to a breakdown and pleaded with his wife to
come back and help him get through the difficult weeks of the
trial. She did, but the court proceedings were nonetheless a tax-
ing ordeal.

The trial opened before New York Supreme Court Justice
Samuel Coleman and an all-male jury on 13 December 1957
and ran for twenty-one days. Levin contended that after he had
adapted *The Diary of a Young Girl* for the stage, a change of
producer and writer resulted in his being defrauded of his
rights. Otto Frank, he claimed, breached the original oral agreement that gave him the right to do the play, and Crawford and
Frank used deceit and misrepresentation to obtain the agreement of November 1952, by which he surrendered those rights.
He also maintained that ideas and material from his *Anne
Frank* were borrowed by Goodrich and Hackett for their
Broadway version. From Otto Frank and Kermit Bloomgarden, producers of the play, he sought $600,000; and from
Cheryl Crawford, in a consolidated suit, $450,000. He
declared, however, that any money over expenses he might
receive from the lawsuit would be donated to Jewish charities.

On January 6, after more than two weeks of frequently challenged, inconclusive testimony and hostile questioning, Judge
Coleman dismissed all the charges related to fraud and breach
of contract on the grounds that there was no legal cause for the
action. However, he ordered the jury to decide the one remaining issue: whether the Hacketts in their adaptation had used
any new character, situation, or plot originally created by Levin

in his version. Two days later, after deliberating for ten hours, the jury returned a ten-to-two verdict in Levin's favor, calling for damages of $43,750 and twenty-five percent of future movie rights and/or royalties. The judge rejected the monetary finding, contending that he had instructed the jury to arrive at a definite, fixed amount which would dispose of the value of any claim Levin might have, and he ordered them to continue deliberations. They soon returned with an award of $50,000.

Reactions to the jury decision were swift and passionate. Levin felt vindicated but indignant at the continued suppression of his work and at the failure of the media to publicize his triumph and expose the authors and producers of a Pulitzer Prize play. The defendants were shocked by a judgment they believed to be totally unjust. The trial, they felt, was a charade: the jury was not qualified to judge a matter as intricate as wrongful appropriation of ideas, and the judge had mishandled this part of the proceeding.

In the days following the jury's award of damages to Levin, the attorneys at Paul, Weiss submitted briefs moving to dismiss the judgment and asking for a new trial. The evidence, they argued, was inadequate to warrant submitting the case to a jury, the verdict was against the weight of the evidence, and there were errors in the charge of the court. In late February, Judge Coleman set the decision aside, but not on the grounds argued by Paul, Weiss. Citing the absence of testimony as to the value of what was taken, Coleman concluded that there was "a complete failure of proof as to damages" and ordered a new trial. Howard Spellman, Levin's trial attorney, claimed a victory for the plaintiff: "There is nothing in the judge's decision indicating that the verdict of the jury to the effect that Mr. Levin's literary efforts were appropriated was wrong. We intend to press the issue to a conclusion either by a new trial or an appeal" (February 1958, BU).

In fact, nearly all the participants were fed up with the harsh, prolonged confrontation, and both sides hoped to avoid a costly, unpredictable new trial by investigating yet again the possibility of an out-of-court solution. Frank, past seventy, found the affair increasingly burdensome, and he wished to focus his energies elsewhere. Not only was he busy with the Anne Frank Foundation, but he was also having to deal with the disturbing repercussions of another conflict that had erupted the year before: proceedings against a Lübeck school-teacher, Lothar Stielau, whose article claiming *The Diary of Anne Frank* was a forgery stimulated a series of neo-Nazi attacks on the book and on the old man himself. Most bizarre, perhaps, was the chronic rumor that the fabricated diary was coauthored by the child's father and the American writer Meyer Levin. Moreover, Frank had been wanting, after several delays, to visit Israel, and he did not wish to go empty-handed. Levin, too, was weary and depressed by the long, fruitless controversy; he had settled in Israel, just published a new novel, *Eva*, and hoped to free himself for other writing.

However, many of the old barriers to settlement still remained, and although talks started, they stalled, started up again, and dragged on for more than a year. Frank's main goal was to end both the lawsuit and the controversy: to get Levin to give up all his alleged rights to the book, play, and movie of the *Diary*, and to stop airing the subject in public. But because of his feeling of having been injured, Frank strongly objected to paying any money to Levin himself, either for expenses or for his own benefit. He would, however, consider a payment to charity, though not directly to his adversary. Although Levin also wanted to settle out of court, he was incensed at being deprived of the award for damages and was determined to get authorization to perform his play in Israel and with nonprofessional groups in the United States. The question of production rights continued to be a source of disagreement, as was the matter of "buying Levin off." Goodrich and Hackett were opposed not only for financial reasons but also because they had now been vilified as plagiarists. Frank resisted because he felt that granting permission to stage the rejected play would generate more arguments, not eliminate them. If license were given and an audience liked the work, Levin would assert that his adaptation was better than the Broadway version and might instigate a lawsuit claiming he had been defrauded when Crawford in 1952 told him his script was unstageworthy.

Although Levin was now living mostly in Israel and had given his lawyers carte blanche to work out terms of settlement, he remained in constant touch during the convoluted negotiations. In May 1958, Fredman submitted a proposal with five main points: (1) Levin would be paid $37,500 plus Frank's share of funds held in Israel as royalties for the unauthorized Habimah production; (2) Levin would give up his rights, title, and interest to the play and anything related to the play or *Diary*; (3) a public statement would be issued absolving the Hacketts of deliberately copying Levin's material; (4) all the parties would sign a general release; and (5) if the defendants insisted, everyone would agree to make no public statements unless the text was approved by both sides.

Paul, Weiss responded that the sum was too high and the

claim to Israeli rights unsubstantiated and unjustified. In July, their counterproposal (Frank would pay $15,000, perhaps $20,000, as a donation to Jewish charities, with no payment of attorney's fees) was turned down by Fredman as insufficient, and Judge Coleman was informed that the parties were unable to agree on terms for a settlement. Nonetheless, despite the deadlock, conversations continued about levels of payment, who would contribute and to whom, what general-release statements might be accepted, and what finally was being resolved.

Meanwhile, Levin kept up his protest in public. In early June, an article by Moshe Kohn supporting some of his claims appeared in the *Jerusalem Post*, with information the reporter could only have gotten from the plaintiff himself. Fredman accused his client of wanting to sabotage the settlement efforts. "You will just have to learn," he told Levin, "that your only comment with regard to Anne Frank is 'No comment'" (13 June 1958, BU). But Levin said he would continue to speak out until the matter was fairly concluded. In September, at the time of the Jewish High Holidays, he published an open letter to Otto Frank in the Israeli paper *Maariv*. At the trial, he wrote, he had realized for the first time that Frank hated him and that this hatred was based on fantastic misinterpretations of a few lines in letters written in the summer of 1952. Reviewing the history of the case—its "deep and dreadful consequences" and "incalculable human costs" (two heart attacks [Bloomgarden's and his own], an attempted suicide [his wife's], financial loss, and harm to his career)—Levin asked Frank to set aside all animosity and submit the quarrel to mediation. In response, Frank said Levin was mistaken in believing he hated him, and he maintained that Levin was responsible for the "deplorable" damage because he had started and perpetuated the quarrel by distortions and lies. The only terms Frank could accept would be for each man to pay his own lawyer and give a certain amount to Jewish charity. Mediation was out of the question.

The correspondence between the two men—which had been suspended in the year before the trial—resumed briefly and showed more graphically than ever the gulf between them. Levin continued to accuse his opponents of having used Anne Frank's diary "as a shield for a bitter political vendetta against a Jewish writer." Frank dismissed these accusations as nonsensical and repeated his opposition to an arrangement that he believed would benefit a person whose behavior had been so reckless.

Through much of the fall and early winter of 1958–59, efforts to settle the refractory case continued. Frank and his attorneys were further exasperated by Levin's renewed airing of the case in public; Levin approved of the idea of contributions to charity but felt he could never accept a settlement that left him with substantial legal fees; Frank continued to balk at paying any money straight to Levin. In January 1959, Fredman proposed that Levin be given $20,000, outright and unrestricted, in consideration of which he would sell his rights, title, and interest in the play, book, and movie of the *Diary*. Frank would also contribute a sum of his own choice to charity. This too was rejected. In February, Judge Coleman reaffirmed his earlier decision, which left Levin with the option of appealing further or going forward with a new trial. In April, Levin, who had been briefly in the States, returned to Israel, but before leaving he appointed a Committee of Three in New York to act on his behalf, discuss the affair with his adversaries and among themselves, and propose terms of settlement in his absence. He said he would accept their findings and recommendation. The committee consisted of Rabbi Joachim Prinz, president of the American Jewish Congress; Charles Angoff, a writer friend of Levin's; and Abraham Katch, professor of Hebrew and a well-known academic. In the late spring and early summer, the three men discussed the matter on the telephone and in correspondence, but their schedules made it hard for them to meet. Eventually, they decided to turn the problem over to Will Maslow, a lawyer and staff director of the American Jewish Congress, who played an active role in settlement discussions throughout the fall.

Finally, in October 1959, after fourteen months of torturous negotiations, a proposal was with various degrees of reluctance and suspicion accepted by all parties. Frank, anxious to avoid the emotional and financial strain of a new trial, relented and agreed to pay Levin $15,000 outright, in return for which the warrant of attachment of his royalties would be vacated and Levin would assign to him all his alleged rights to the *Diary*. After weeks of argument and revision, during which Levin objected to "thought control" and Frank's attorneys looked for ways to guarantee that Levin would not keep the dispute alive, everybody consented to the following statement for public release:

> The claims made by Meyer Levin with respect to *The Diary of Anne Frank* have been settled with the aid of a committee composed of Rabbi Joachim Prinz, Charles Angoff and Professor Abraham Katch. As part of the settlement, the committee has recommended that Mr. Levin's adaptations of *The Diary*, and his role in connection with it, should no longer be a subject of public or private controversy.

> Both Mr. Levin and Mr. Frank have accepted and approved the settlement recommended by the committee. They consider it an honorable and final solution of the dispute, and join in the committee's recommendation that there be an end to private and public controversy.
>
> Despite his differences with Mr. Frank and Kermit Bloomgarden, the producer of the Broadway production of *The Diary* written by Albert and Frances Hackett, which are now disposed of, Mr. Levin takes this opportunity to state that he believes that both Otto Frank and Kermit Bloomgarden are honorable men, that nothing Mr. Levin has ever said should be construed to the contrary.
>
> Both Mr. Frank and Mr. Bloomgarden take this opportunity to state that nothing they have ever said was intended to be a reflection upon Mr. Levin's talent or capacity as an author or playwright.
>
> All parties regret that the Hacketts received unfortunate publicity as a by-product of the dispute. (26 October 1959, BU)

Given the history of recrimination and distrust, no one felt especially confident that these arrangements would end the controversy, although the legal proceedings were now being brought to a close. Since Levin had strenuously argued against a "silencer" in the joint public statement, an additional document was drawn up in hopes of clarifying the contested matter of "further discussion." Levin signed it on 26 October 1959.

> I want to confirm that I regard the stipulation and the public statement as a final resolution of all the disputes between us. I understand the settlement and the public statement to mean that I will not circularize rabbis or any other groups or persons on the Anne Frank subject or stimulate either public or private controversy about the *Diary* or my part in relation to

it. Of course I retain my right to discuss any literary questions
relating to the *Diary*, but I understand that such literary discussion does not include a discussion of whether or not the
stage adaptation of the *Diary* which I wrote should or should
not have been produced. (BU)

On 1 November, five days after the signing, Otto Frank in
Basel was preparing to cable New York, "Settlement approved,"
when he received a copy of *Evidences* (a journal published by
the American Jewish Committee in Paris), with an article by
Levin expanding his attack on the political motives of all those
involved in the Broadway production of the *Diary*. Although
the piece had been written months before, Frank saw it as
Levin's calculated effort to influence public opinion at the
moment the "no controversy" stipulation went into effect, and
he decided to delay his final endorsement. Almost simultaneously, in New York, reports reached Paul, Weiss that Levin had
spoken again about the case at a city synagogue. Another flurry
of letters and phone calls followed: Paul, Weiss to Fredman;
Fredman and Rabbi Prinz to Levin, accusing him of violating
the commitments he had made in the documents.

As the year 1960 began, developments occurred again on several fronts. Despite the recent flare-ups, Frank decided to sign
the settlement papers; the attorneys brought the legal proceedings to completion; and Edward Costikyan ended a letter to
Samuel Fredman on 13 January with a tart postscript: "Who
owes who a lunch, or should it be a banquet?" But even this
guarded expression of pleasure and relief was premature.
Levin's rage remained unappeasable, and on 21 January, he
wrote Frank that "while the legal phase of our encounter is over

the moral phase is not done. Your behavior will remain forever as a ghastly example of evil returned for good, and of a father's betrayal of his daughter's words." Repudiating his statement that he considered Frank "an honorable man," Levin accused him of a desire to suppress "on stage and screen your daughter's greatest perception" (BU).

At this point, Frank decided to return Levin's letters unopened, and Costikyan told Rabbi Prinz: "I really don't know what can be done with this man. As you can see, he is apparently immune to reason, and totally unconcerned with the value of his word or commitment" (24 February 1960, BU). Fredman, Prinz, and others tried to persuade Levin to abide by the terms of the settlement and to turn his energies to his other writing. But when Frank finally did visit Israel in March, his antagonist published another open letter in the *Jerusalem Post*, asserting that Frank had recently confessed to a journalist on board ship that there had been nothing dramatically wrong with Levin's *Anne Frank* but "he had rejected it because he sought a more 'universal' treatment." At a press conference at the Ramat Hadassah Youth Aliya Centre, Frank denied he had ever said what Levin had reported. Levin countered by claiming the journalist stuck by his story, and again articles and opinion pieces about the sharp exchanges appeared in the Israeli press. For many observers, the quarrel now turned less on legal questions about the dramatization of the *Diary* than on the meaning of Anne Frank as a symbol. In public remarks during his stay in Israel, Frank insisted that his daughter had become an important emblem to the youth of the world, transcending her specific interest to the Jewish people, although he had never attempted to belittle the significance of her Jewishness. Levin

continued to argue that this was a fundamental misreading of
the *Diary* itself and an interpretation that would lead to a dangerous distortion of the most important meaning of the Holocaust. Popular opinion tended to side with Frank. As Philip
Gillon, a columnist for the *Jerusalem Post*, peremptorily put it,
how Otto Frank visualizes the importance of his daughter is his
own business. "By what right can Mr. Levin dictate to a parent
how his daughter shall be presented to the world. . . . Mr.
Levin's attacks are only undignified and irritating. He would
please us far more by writing another *Compulsion* and leaving
poor Anne Frank to develop into whatever sort of symbol she
can" (4 April 1960). Gillon's argument has a commonsense per-
suasiveness about it, but he fails to note that Levin, by warning
of the real dangers of universalizing the Holocaust, is accurately
describing a tendency that was to become increasingly prominent in the following decade and afterward.

When Frank left Israel and continued to refuse Levin's correspondence, the bruising eight-year-old controversy seemed to
be winding down. The lawsuit was over, the public now
showed little interest in the much-exposed quarrel, and the
main participants were in different parts of the world, involved
in other activities. In October 1961, however, the fires were
ignited yet again by an essay, "A Different Kind of Blacklist,"
which appeared in *Congress Bi-Weekly*, the publication of the
American Jewish Congress. In it Levin, recounting a series of
publishing setbacks he had recently experienced (contracts
rescinded, assignments withdrawn, interviews canceled, phone
calls disregarded), argued that the campaign of character and
career assassination begun years before by the Broadway clique

had by this time effectively deprived him of much of his livelihood as a writer. To explain how this had happened, he reca-
pitulated his version of the history of the adaptation of the
Diary and the production of *Compulsion*; and he ended with a
plea to his readers to help end the blacklisting by telling his true
story whenever they heard him described as a troublemaker,
always taking people to court.

Levin's account of the history of the affair was by now familiar, but it included one new paragraph that provoked a set of
indignant responses from the attorneys at Paul, Weiss. In his
description of the settlement agreement, Levin declared that he
had refused to sign a "silencer" that would have prevented him
from ever speaking or writing about the issues involved. Both
Simon Rifkind and Edward Costikyan quickly protested. Writing to Shad Polier, a lawyer active in the American Jewish Congress, Rifkind expressed outrage that an organ of the AJC
should print an abusive article by a pathological liar. Embarrassed, Polier agreed, and he replied by saying that everyone has
the constitutional right to be paranoid, but that freedom of the
press does not apply to the publication of paranoid charges; he
promised to do what he could to rectify the situation (17
November 1960, SHSW).

A revised version of Costikyan's response (reworked after
consultation with Bloomgarden, Hellman, and others) eventually appeared in the February 1962 issue of the magazine.
Declaring that his client, Otto Frank, had for years been "the
victim of one outrageous attack after another from Mr. Levin,"
Costikyan quoted from the settlement agreement to demonstrate that Levin had in fact signed a pledge to end the contro-

versy, and he concluded: "It should be obvious that Mr. Levin by the assertion in his article quoted above, has committed a breach of contract and violation of his solemn word."

In a separate exchange, Costikyan urged the editors to publish an expression of regret and disclaimer of responsibility. Levin, he reported, had been sending reprints of the article, along with "a vituperative covering letter," to a great many people; and the least the magazine's editors could do to "mitigate the damage done to the victims of Mr. Levin's venom" would be to print a clarification. The editors conceded, and in a note following Costikyan's letter, they explained how they had originally published Levin's article in the belief that a reputable writer who thought himself blacklisted was entitled to address the public. But after they learned some key facts from attorneys involved in the case, the editors regretted that they had unwittingly permitted Levin to include statements bearing unfairly upon the *Diary* and the people involved in the dramatization and production. They also deplored the fact that "Mr. Levin is circulating reprints of the article with a personal letter which contains an unjust attack upon Lillian Hellman and renews the controversy about the *Diary*, although he had signed a pledge not to do so."

By this point, however, Levin was surprisingly turning his protest and his creative energies in another direction. He had for some time been planning to explore the implications of the dispute over the *Diary* in an imaginative work. For the next two years, he curtailed the campaign in the mails and the magazines, and he wrote one of his most ambitious and provocative novels, *The Fanatic*, which was published in 1964.

Meyer Levin at seventeen, Chicago 1922–23. [Courtesy of Mikael Levin]

Meyer Levin and his marionettes, 1930. [Photograph by André
Kertèsz; courtesy of and copyright by the estate of André Kertèsz]

A self-portrait marionette by Meyer Levin, c. 1931.
[Courtesy of Mikael Levin]

The Saturday Review
of LITERATURE

XV No. 20   NEW YORK, SATURDAY, MARCH 13, 1937   TEN CENTS A COPY

IN THIS ISSUE

BERNARD DeVOTO
The Pulitzer Prize in History

JAMES T. FARRELL
Reviews "The Old Bunch" by Meyer Levin

HERBERT J. MULLER
Reviews "Very Heaven"
by Richard Aldington

LLOYD C. DOUGLAS
Reviews "We Are Not Alone"
by James Hilton

CRANE BRINTON
Reviews "The Revolution Betrayed"
by Leon Trotsky

MEYER LEVIN   *Samuel Woolf*

"He touches upon the sources and the methods of several generations of novelists, amongst them, Dreiser, Hemingway, Sinclair Lewis, Abraham Cahan, Dos Passos, and F. Scott Fitzgerald. He intelligently organizes material and detail from the fields of domestic relationships, art, science, medicine, university life, capital and labor, real estate and finance"... *(See page 5)*

Meyer Levin on the cover of *The Saturday Review*, 13 March 1937, in which James T. Farrell reviewed *The Old Bunch*.

Anne Frank in the Jewish Lyceum, Amsterdam, 1942, age thirteen.
[Copyright ANNE FRANK–Fonds, Basel/Switzerland]

Meyer Levin (*left*) and Eric Schwab (*right*) as correspondents attached to the U.S. Ninth Air Force, 1944–45. [Courtesy of Mikael Levin]

Meyer Levin's press pass from Overseas News Agency, late 1940s. [The Meyer Levin Collection, Special Collections, Boston University Libraries]

Tereska Torres and Meyer Levin with film for *The Illegals*, 1948. [Courtesy of Tereska Torres]

The New York Times Book Review

JUNE 15, 1952   Copyright 1952 by The New York Times Company   SECTION 7

THE CHILD BEHIND THE SECRET DOOR

ANNE FRANK: The Diary of a Young Girl. Translated from the Dutch by B. M. Mooyaart-Doubleday. Introduction by Eleanor Roosevelt. 285 pp. New York: Doubleday & Co. $3.

An Adolescent Girl's Own Story of How She Hid for Two Years During the Nazi Terror

By MEYER LEVIN

ANNE FRANK'S diary is too tenderly intimate a book to be frozen with the label "classic," and yet no lesser designation serves. For little Anne Frank, spirited, moody, witty, self-desiring, succeeded in communicating in virtually perfect, or classic, form the drama of puberty. But her book is not a classic to be left on the library shelf. It is a warm and stirring confession, to be read over and over for insight and enjoyment.

The diary is a classic on another level, too. It happened that during the two years that mark the most extraordinary changes in a girl's life, Anne Frank lived in astonishing circumstances: she was hidden with seven other people in a secret nest of rooms behind her father's place of business, in Amsterdam. Thus, the diary tells the life of a group of Jews waiting in fear of being taken by the Nazis. It is, in reality, the kind of document that John Hersey invented for "The Wall."

This is no lugubrious ghetto tale, no compilation of horrors. Reality can prove surprisingly different from invented reality, and Anne Frank's diary simply bubbles with amusement, love, discovery. It has its share of disgust, its moments of hatred, but it is as wondrously alive, so near, that one feels overwhelmingly the universalness of human nature. These people might be living next door; their within-the-family emotions, their tensions and satisfactions are those of human character and growth, anywhere.

BECAUSE the diary was not written in retrospect, it contains the freshness of life of every moment.—Anne Frank's voice becomes the voice of six million vanished Jewish souls. It is difficult to say in which respect her book is more "important," but one forgets the double significance of this document in experiencing it as an intimate whole, for one feels the presence of this childbecoming-woman as warmly as though she was snuggled on a near-by sofa.

We meet Anne on her thirteenth birthday, "Quicksilver Anne" to her adored father, but "Miss Chatterbox" and "Miss Quack-Quack," she tells us, to her teacher—for the family is still at liberty. Indeed, her teacher makes her write a self-curing essay on chattering; she turns in a poem that convulses teacher and class, and is allowed to remain her talkative self without further reprimand.

Yet, with the moodiness of adoles-

A journalist and novelist, Mr. Levin recently wrote "In Search: An Autobiography," an examination of the Jewish psyche in the modern world.

Illustration from "Anne Frank: The Diary of a Young Girl."
Anne Frank: A photograph found in her diary.

cence, she feels lonesome "Let me put it more clearly, since no one will believe that a girl of 13 feels herself quite alone in the world, nor is it so. I have darling parents and a sister of 16. I know about thirty people whom one might call friends—I have strings of boy friends, anxious to catch a glimpse of me, who * * * peep at me through mirrors in class. I have relations, aunts, uncles, who are darlings too, a good home, no—I don't seem to lack anything. But it's the same with all my friends, just fun and nothing more. We don't seem to be able to get any closer, that is the root of the whole trouble. Hence, this diary. I want this diary itself to be my friend, and shall call my friend Kitty."

What child of 13 hasn't had these feelings, and resolved to confide in a diary? Anne carried it through, never shrinking from revealing the ugly things about herself.

Her father had already brought the family out of Germany in 1933. In June, 1942, a few weeks after the diary begins, the SS sends a call-up for Anne's sister, Margot, and the family goes into hiding. "I began to pack some of our most vital belongings into a school satchel * * * this diary, then hair curlers, handkerchiefs, schoolbooks, a comb, old letters." The Van Daans, with their 16-year-old son Peter, join the Franks. Later, because "Daddy says we must save another person if we can," an elderly dentist named Dussel is squeezed into the Beret Annex. He gets Anne's bed; she sleeps on a settee lengthened by chairs.

A born writer, Anne zestfully portrays the Annex inhabitants, with all their flaws and virtues. The common

life effect which Mr. Hersey sought to suggest in "The Wall" here flowers with utter spontaneity. But Anne Frank's diary probes far deeper than "The Wall" into the core of human relations, and succeeds better than "The Wall" in bringing us an understanding of life under threat.

And this quality brings it home to any family in the world today. Just as the Franks lived in momentary fear of the Gestapo's knock on their hidden door, so every family today lives in fear of the knock of war. Anne's diary is a great affirmative answer to the life-question of today, for she shows how ordinary people, within this ordeal, consistently hold to the greater human values.

The Frank's Dutch friends in the office on the other side of the secret door sustained them to the end. "Never have we heard one word of the burden which we certainly must be to them. * * * They put on the brightest possible faces, bring flowers and presents for birthdays, risking their own lives to help others." These Dutch friends, Miep, Elli, Kraler, Koophuis, even managed to smuggle in Chanukah gifts, and shyly offered their Christmas remembrances to the hidden Jews.

TWO years passed in disciplined activities. The hidden ones kept busy with smuggled correspondence courses in speed shorthand, in Latin, in nursing; Dussel even attempted dental operations, hilariously described by Anne. She herself studied mythology, ballet, "family trees," while keeping up her schoolwork. She records the family disputes—Mrs. Van Daan violently resisting the sale of her fur coat, only to see it smoked up in black market tobacco! And the comic moments, as when her father lies on the floor trying to overhear an important business conference downstairs; Anne flattens herself beside him, lending a sharp ear. But business is so dull, she falls asleep.

Most wondrous of all is her love affair. Like a flower under a stone fulfilling itself, she came to her first love in her allotted time. "I give myself completely. But one thing. He may touch my face, but no more." All is told, from her potato-fetching devices for going up to Peter's attic lair, to the first misplaced kiss on her ear. And the parents worrying about the youngsters trysting up there in the dusk, sitting by the window over the canal. And her fears that her older sister is lonely and jealous, leading to an amazing exchange of letters between the two girls, in those hidden rooms. Finally, there is even the tender disillusionment with Peter, as Anne reaches toward maturity, and a character understanding replaces the first tug of love. In all this there are perceptions in depth, striv— *(Continued on Page 22)*

Johannes Kleiman, Elfriede Frank-Markovits, Frances Goodrich, Albert Hackett, Otto Frank, and Garson Kanin at 263 Prinsengracht, December 1954. [Copyright ANNE FRANK–Fonds, Basel/Switzerland]

Albert Hackett and Frances Goodrich with the script of the third of eight versions of their play, *The Diary of Anne Frank*, 1955. [Bettmann]

Playbill for the original production of *The Diary of Anne Frank* at the Cort Theatre in New York, October 1955. [Museum of the City of New York; reprinted by permission of PLAYBILL™. PLAYBILL™ is a registered trademark of PLAYBILL Incorporated, NY, NY]

Publicity picture of Joseph Schildkraut and Susan Strasberg, 1955. [Museum of the City of New York]

Otto Frank in 1958. [Museum of the City of New York]

Meyer Levin in 1958. [Photograph by Judith Sheftel; courtesy of
Judith Feiffer]

Tereska and Meyer Levin in the late 1950s. [Photograph by Eric Schwab; courtesy of Tereska Torres]

Meyer Levin and his family in 1957: Tereska, Mikael, Gabriel, Jo (Eli), and Dominique. [Photograph by Judith Sheftel; courtesy of Judith Feiffer]

Meyer and Tereska Levin in Paris, c. 1958–59. [Photograph by Eric Schwab; courtesy of Tereska Torres]

Scene from Israel Soldiers Theatre production of Meyer Levin's
Anne Frank, 1966. [The Meyer Levin Collection, Special
Collections, Boston University Libraries]

Peter Frye and Meyer Levin on stage set of *Anne Frank* in Tel Aviv,
1966. [The Meyer Levin Collection, Special Collections, Boston
University Libraries]

ANNE FRANK
A PLAY BY
MEYER LEVIN
ADAPTED FROM
THE DIARY OF ANNE FRANK

SHOSHANNA ROZEN AND DORI BEN ZEV as ANNE and PETER

*

PRIVATELY PUBLISHED BY THE AUTHOR FOR LITERARY DISCUSSION.

Title page of Meyer Levin's adaptation, printed by the author in 1967. [Courtesy of Tereska Torres]

Scene from Lyric Stage production of Levin's *Anne Frank*, Boston, 1991. James Bodge as Koophuis, Larkin Kennedy as Margot, and Faith Justice as Miep, setting up the rooms before the others arrive. [Courtesy of Sheila Ferrini]

Meyer Levin in his writing studio in Israel, 1969. [Copyright by
Archie Lieberman; all rights reserved]

Dust jacket of *The Obsession*, 1974. [Photograph by Archie Lieberman; courtesy of Tereska Torres]

Meyer Levin on the South Side of Chicago, 11 December 1980. In the background is All Souls Church, built by J. L. Silsbee for the Reverend Jenkin Lloyd Jones, uncle of Frank Lloyd Wright. [Photograph by Archie Lieberman]

› 4

The Fanatic,
Anne Frank in Israel,
and The Obsession

AFTER 1960, NEARLY EVERY creative undertaking in
Levin's life can be seen as an effort to confront, directly or
indirectly, his long, bruising involvement with *The Dairy of a
Young Girl.* In *The Fanatic* (1964), he tried to imagine his way
to an understanding and a release by turning personal history
into fiction; in the staging of his *Anne Frank* in Israel (1966),
he hoped to demonstrate that the script was indeed "playable"
and closer to the inner truth of the girl's book than the
acclaimed Broadway version; and in his memoir, *The Obsession* (1973), he set out to cure and vindicate himself by brooding on and talking through the controversy, revealing what he
believed to be the motives of his adversaries, and demonstrat-
ing precisely how he was victimized and injured. Even in those
works that have nothing to do with Anne Frank—the saga
novels *The Settlers* (1972) and *The Harvest* (1978)—Levin offers
a reading of twentieth-century Jewish history focusing on the
Zionist struggle to ensure a continuity and renewal that were
to be threatened but not destroyed by the Holocaust—an

interpretation of the past on which his adaptation of Anne Frank's book is grounded.

The Fanatic views the subject through the lens of one of the most fascinating stories of Jewish folklore: the plight of the dybbuk, the soul of an unfulfilled dead person who enters the body of someone living and directs his or her conduct. In many versions of the tale, the demon can be exorcised only with great difficulty through the intervention of a Hasidic *tzaddik*, or wonder-worker, with occult powers. Levin's novel is narrated by the dead man, Leo Kahn, a European Jewish poet and intellectual who had been interned by the Nazis in the so-called model camp, Theresienstadt, in Czechoslovakia, and then sent to Auschwitz, from which he miraculously escaped. Hoping to warn the remaining Jews in the first camp about what would happen to them, Leo returned there but was ignored, betrayed, and eventually shipped back to Auschwitz and then to Bergen-Belsen, where he died of typhus.

As narrator of the fiction set in the 1950s, Leo tells the story of the Chicago-born Maury Finklestein, who before the war studied for the rabbinate but avoided the pulpit because of doubts about God and his own fitness to minister, deciding instead to write dramas on biblical themes. When America entered World War II, Finklestein joined the army and was assigned to the chaplain service in Europe. In the spring of 1945, following the liberation of the camps, he worked tirelessly to help survivors. Traveling to Theresienstadt in search of Leo's father, David Kahn, the author of classic texts on Jewish mysticism that had influenced him during his years in seminary, Maury learned that Professor Kahn had been killed; but he met his widow, who was trying to arrange for the publication of a

manuscript called *Good and Evil,* which their son, Leo, had
managed to write and preserve while in the camps. Leo's book,
which combined fiction and impassioned philosophical dia-
logues on the meaning for humanity and God of the Nazi
assault on the Jews, stunned and exhilarated Maury because of
its hard-won affirmation of men, women, and God in the face
of an unflinching confrontation with evil. Maury immediately
offered to try to get the book published in the United States
and then to adapt it for the theater. In Theresienstadt, he had
also met Anika, Leo's sweetheart, whom he helped to conva-
lesce, came to love, and asked to return to New York to marry
him. From this point, the lives of the dead Leo and the living
Maury and Anika become permanently intertwined.

All this is background. The novel actually begins with the
arrival of Maury and Anika at the airport in New York and
then depicts their marriage and his efforts to bring Leo's theod-
icy to the attention of the American public—a plot that in out-
line follows Levin's actual experience but alters chronology,
characters, and events for fictional and didactic purposes. Leo's
manuscript is translated, published in New York, and, thanks
in part to Maury's glowing review, becomes an enormous success. The adaptation, however, is turned down by a producer,
Richard Sharr, on the advice of Robin Adair (né Ruben Adler),
a theatrical gossip columnist, unacknowledged Communist,
and self-hating Jew, who insists Maury's work is nationalist
propaganda, an unstageable Zionist tract. Hollywood writers
are hired to do an authorized version and they produce a well-
made play that moves and inspires huge audiences because of
its "tip-toe aura of reverence" and its easy-to-swallow anti-
fascist, universalist message. The embittered Maury fights for

the right to perform his own script—a battle that the dead Leo
sees as a noble, if quixotic, effort to preserve the true spirit of
Good and Evil, to give the anonymous victims of Nazism their
voices, and to defend individual rights and artistic freedom
against the forces of narrow self-interest and conformity.

Nevertheless, the campaign against "injustice multiplied by
ingratitude" is waged at a frightful personal price. Disapproving
letters to Mrs. Kahn, petitions to rabbis, newspaper ads, TV
appearances, press conferences, protests from the pulpit, a
lengthy lawsuit and court trial, all are damaging to Maury's
health, marriage, friendships, and relationships with people in a
position to publish or produce his work. As the disputes multiply, he develops a conspiracy theory linking his victimization
to the commercial and political schemes of a communist clique
on Broadway and to the liquidation of Jewish writers in the
Soviet Union. Yet, despite the near-ruin of his personal and
professional life (he is denounced as conniving, litigious, red-
baiting, and paranoid), Maury writes a second play, *Job,* another
attempt to explore the contemporary meaning of extreme suffering; this work, too, is appropriated by an unscrupulous producer and his coterie, who stage a heavily edited, vulgarized text
that distorts the playwright's vision. Sick with frustration,
Maury sends to both producers a dime-store knife inscribed
"The Big Knife of Broadway. . . . Use this. It's more humane."
At the climax of the raw, protracted story of rejection, suppression, and ineffectual protest, Maury takes his adversaries to
court and is vindicated by a jury that awards him $100,000 for
wrongful appropriation of ideas. As the novel ends, although
still disillusioned, he receives several small windfalls: an amateur group in New Jersey performs the authentic script of *Job,* a

movie company buys the rights, and the Finklesteins prepare to leave for Israel. In spite of the harm done to Maury's health, marriage, and career, the narrator, Leo, in a series of reflections and prayers, closes by affirming the value and strength of Jewish continuity.

To have this story told by Leo Kahn, a voice from a mass grave in Bergen-Belsen, is certainly a bizarre yet potentially promising narrative design. Given his age, subject matter, observational powers, philosophical cast of mind, and lamentable fate, Leo is a grown-up Anne Frank: a writer who could describe and assess the aspects of the Holocaust that were implied in the girl's diary but not, because Anne Frank wrote it before her arrest and death-camp sufferings, explored there. Not only, then, is Leo the "teller" Levin had been looking for, but he is also potentially the truth teller, the figure who suffered and was there, writing *while* the systematic extermination of Jews was going on. And now, as the narrator of a story that takes place in the 1950s, he should be able to infuse present events with an awareness of the atrocities that killed him and so many others, and to reflect on modern history and the immemorial subject of evil.

At the start, Leo does function in this way. His first descriptions of Maury and Anika arriving in New York are suffused with a haunting sense of the weight of recent catastrophe for victims, survivors, and witnesses. Leo, though, makes it clear that he is not literally the demon from folklore—a hovering, dispossessed, sinful soul—but rather a benign mid-twentieth-century version of the folk figure: an artist seeking to complete his savagely aborted life through a sympathetic connection with someone else who shares his values.

It is not as I sometimes fantasied, half-accepting, half-toying with our legendary; it is not as though an unfulfilled spirit were to enter as a dybbuk into a living being. . . . I have not entered into Anika, nor into this American, into Maury who came and found my Anika. Surely I cannot cause his behavior, I cannot live through him; but he is much like me, there is very much in him that is like what I was, except that he is less ready with anger. . . . But could there be strength of will left in me, it is true that to experience the continuation of my curtailed life, I would exert that life through such a one as he. (22)

Conceiving of Leo Kahn less as an active agent than as a reflecting narrative consciousness, Levin uses him to present the disasters of recent history as a dark shadow over the living and then to explore his fictional characters in terms of their particular relationship to the Jewish concentration-camp dead. Leo himself is a casualty; Anika and Mrs. Kahn are maimed survivors; Maury is a shocked witness with a consuming need to testify; the New York producers, agents, playwrights, lawyers, columnists who determine the theatrical fate of *Good and Evil* either deny or suppress their relationship to the Holocaust and treat Leo's book as a property to be used for their own commercial and ideological purposes. For most of them, as Gary Bossin has said, Maury's script is "an unwanted and uncomfortable reminder of the consequences and responsibilities of Jewish identity" (*The Literary Achievement of Meyer Levin*, 287).

In the mutual identification of Leo Kahn and Maury Finklestein one can locate many of the strengths, weaknesses, and problematic aspects of Levin's novel. So strong is Leo's devotion to telling the story of Maury's quest to publish *Good and*

Evil and transform it into a play that the result is a sharp, sympathetic portrait of Maury as wounded fanatic. We see him in all his admirable idealism and intensity: his love for Anika, his steadfast loyalty to Leo and the murdered Jews of Europe, and his passion for getting their stories told as part of a desire to carry on the time-honored Jewish fight for truth and justice. Yet we also see him as the "rabid rabbi"—obstinate, self-righteous, and self-destructive—refusing to compromise or to admit loss; blurring the fight for justice with an endless campaign for self-justification; endorsing himself in the martyr's role as solitary fighter for artistic and social truth; worsening his wound and then constantly examining it; doing permanent damage to himself, his wife, family, and friends.

But the authenticity and force of Leo's depiction of what it is like to fight these battles and to suffer this fate are diminished by his inability to provide the reader with cogent explanations (or more than intermittent conjectures) about the roots of, and reasons for, Maury's obsessive quest and his inability to relinquish it. Leo traces some of the problems to Maury's childhood insecurities about being Jewish: his fear of beatings from neighborhood kids, his shame at having unpolished immigrant parents, and his deep sense of inadequacy in his early choice of the vocation of rabbi and then of writer. Yet when Leo approaches the event that engendered the obsession—Maury entering the death camps in the days after their liberation—his commentary gradually becomes a form of partisan endorsement rather than balanced analysis and measurement. At first, Leo's descriptions of conditions in Theresienstadt, Auschwitz, and Bergen-Belsen appear to provide a context for understanding some of the extremity of Maury's responses and behavior: after witnessing the effects of Nazi barbarism, a man afflicted by questions of meaning and responsibility might justifiably be called "normal." In fact, though, the narrative ultimately does not work this way. The more drastic Maury's behavior becomes, the more Leo approves of it as a comprehensible and appropriate response, not to the Nazi horror, but to the entirely self-serving conduct of the New York theatrical crowd. For Leo, Maury is at bottom the virtuous man who acts on his inner beliefs, battles for justice against a pack of conformists, and is branded a fanatic for his fervid idealism.

Late in the story, Leo offers an account of events that looks as if it is meant to give the reader the long-sought-for understanding of why Maury is caught in the fierce grip of his conspiracy mania:

> In a letter from his father, there unexpectedly comes to Maury the thread to the source of his long and peculiar ordeal.
>
> Again and again through his troubled connection with my book there has awakened in him the sense of some ulterior source for the persistent hostility directed upon him. Over and over he has traced every thread of motive, to Gaylord [the publisher], or to my translator's greed for a big name, or to Lustig [the lawyer] . . . but he has never been able to understand what happened to Sharr, after that luncheon of acceptance, to turn him to a complete rejection as though Maury were poisonous. Could it all be put down to a sudden personal dislike?
>
> Against all this Maury has been troubled by his persistent sense of the *beshert*, the destined; is it destined that his work should never be seen—perhaps as some punishment? Until he

proves there is another cause, he will be troubled by this self-doubt of his worthiness.

And whether the cause be a divine judgment or a human motivation, his is the sort of mind that must go on seeking the eventual source. (337–38)

In the following paragraphs, however, when Leo explains the meaning and effect of Maury's father's letter, it becomes only too clear that rather than illuminating Maury's condition, he is entering into an evasive plot of his own to validate it. Mr. Finklestein tells his son about recent accounts in the Yiddish press of Soviet persecution of Jewish writers and intellectuals, and within hours Maury finds in these reports the key to the puzzle—the missing motive to explain the virulence in his enemies' rejection and suppression of his work. Stalin's brutal campaign against Jewish culture and identity in the Soviet Union is now being imitated in Communist circles all over the world, and Maury has been targeted as one of its victims! Thus Maury's fanaticism is said again to be the result of external forces: the Broadway insiders are now shown to be products of Cold War conditions—a worldwide Communist conspiracy and the related American anti-Communist conformity of the 1950s.

Compounding the problem of Leo's increasing support of Maury's most extravagant interpretations and conduct is his characterization of the large cast of producers, agents, writers, editors, lawyers, and hangers-on who are united in opposition to the script. Instead of examining the motives and views of Maury's opponents, or probing some of the metaphysical and ethical issues he raised earlier in the novel, Leo becomes as pre-occupied as the playwright himself with the minutia of the controversies and with the need to expose and condemn all the other participants, whom he at times even compares to Hitler's henchmen. As the plot unfolds, Leo sounds more and more like a stand-in for Levin at his most aggrieved and importunate, and less like a fully imagined independent character who might possibly look at the situation from all sides and thus enhance the fiction with detachment and depth. The result is a novel that in the middle almost sinks under the weight of hundreds of melo-dramatic pages detailing the misfortunes of an innocent idealist contending alone against a group of cynical power brokers in a battle of options, rights, and contracts. Levin's request in the book's foreword that the reader approach the story "to seek ideas, meanings, beliefs, rather than to seek personal histories" becomes impossible to comply with. Although some of the satiric exposure is stingingly apt and funny, most readers are likely to agree with David Boroff, who complained in the *New York Times Book Review* that "we participate in [Maury's] vexations almost beyond endurance" and after a while "want only to be quit of this airless world of recriminations and obsessive hate" (26 January 1964, 5).

These problems are further intensified by the flaws of the ending. A reader who has participated in Maury's ordeal and who has accepted Leo's role as a benevolent spirit is going to expect a resolution that evolves convincingly out of the story of chronic possession the dead narrator has been telling. If this is a radical revisioning of a dybbuk's tale (no matter how modern and attenuated the form), Levin would be obliged to invent a conclusion in which some kind of exorcism and release occur.

What he offers instead in four scant pages is a string of inadequately rendered incidents that fail to provide a satisfying emotional and logical finish to the book. First, just after the $100,000 jury award is announced, Maury stands with Anika "bathed in that curious sense of the final goodness of man, of the world, that comes at such rare moments in life . . . when evil has been vanquished"—a Pollyannaish description so inappropriate to the unfolding narrative that the climactic scene dissolves into mawkishness. More convincing is what follows: the "slowly-returning knowledge" that must temper the couple's gratification, "the knowledge of waste and pointlessness." A dispute that began with claims of major moral significance is now being treated by the media and even Maury's friends as a mere money matter, with everyone buzzing about the size of the award and the motions for appeal and dismissal. The disenchanted plaintiff has to look elsewhere for sources of renewal, and after the performance of the original script of *Job*, he pledges to commit himself unstintingly to playwriting, since "this—his work alone—is what can vindicate him." Yet the performance of *Job* at a tiny theater in New Jersey is oddly tangential to the harsh, prolonged main-stage fight for *Good and Evil* and is too small a success to provide much resonance for the optimistic note Levin is so earnestly trying to sound. The Finklesteins' imminent departure for Israel is also meant to signify a new beginning, but since little has been said about the Jewish state earlier in the novel, this too has an inflated ring.

The most jarring note at the end, however, is a more elaborate and unconvincing attempt to reclaim lofty significance for a story that has concentrated for so long on Broadway infighting. In the closing paragraphs of *The Fanatic*, Leo delivers a peroration and blessing designed to celebrate Jewish continuity through the ages.

> And so this account has been written, by myself through Maury, by Maury through me. . . . Is not each consciousness interlaced with thoughts, words, visions from all others, from those we have known, from those we have read, from those who have projected themselves into us through thoughts, visions, ideas they have caused to rise in the world? . . . People live with fragments and with entities of all who have lived before; our people live with the persons who have risen in them from stories and memories of Adam, of Abraham, Leah, Ruth, Moses, David, Jacob called Israel, Isaiah, Maimonides, the Baal Shem; we live with Herzl, with Hannah Szenes, with Einstein, with our nameless companions in Auschwitz.
>
> . . . Let [Maury and Anika] find some peace, let them be dear to each other, and to their children, let them have years of blessing.
>
> . . . And I? Like all, eventually I recede from *I want, I must have, I must be, I must do;* I recede from *I hate, I hurt, I am happy, I am satisfied, I am angry, I am alone;* I recede, and at last I feel that I approach—can it be that I shall soon feel—*I am included, I am?* There remains in me *I love.* (477–78)

Most people reading this passage, thinking about the tribulations of the characters and the author of *The Fanatic*, and of the European Jews with whom they are so closely associated, would be inclined to sympathize with the zeal and desire for reconciliation and release expressed in Leo's finale. The language is so heartfelt, the biblical evocations so sonorous, the aspiration so high. Unfortunately, though, there is little connection between the sentiments and the history of the characters, the fates they have suffered, and the pain they will continue to endure. Not much at the end of the novel can be said to affirm Jewish continuity: the antagonists (most of whom are Jews) remain acutely hostile, and Maury feels betrayed by prominent Jewish organizations that now, after failing to back his earlier protests, invite him to contribute to their charities. Levin's need to affirm his own cherished beliefs results in an ending connected to the plot more by severe authorial hunger than by artistic logic or the facts of the case.

The difficulties Levin had with *The Fanatic* began before and continued after its publication. When he first sent the manuscript to Simon and Schuster late in 1962, his editor Robert Gottlieb responded with compliments, reservations, and serious concern about the prospects of libel. Gottlieb especially liked the sections dealing with Leo in the camps and the "round and real" characterization of Maury throughout the novel, but he was less admiring of the parts in which Levin wrote directly of actual events. "I felt," he told the writer, "that in these matters you stopped being a novelist and became a documenter and propagandizer—the characters stopped being people and became black-and-white counters in your argument. I felt I was being shouted at—*forced*" (9 January 1963, BU). Levin's view of himself was fine, the editor said, it was the others, the villains, he could not believe in. Gottlieb also took pains to insist that he was not partisan and had no judgment about whether "Meyer is right" or "Meyer is nuts" or anything else. But in his view, none of these reactions mattered very much until the firm's attorneys could read the text. He had already spoken with Ephraim London (who was currently representing Levin in a suit brought by Nathan Leopold over *Compulsion*); and the expert on libel law warned that with a novel so clearly based on a well-known controversy involving figures many people could identify, the problems were potentially immense.

After editors and lawyers spent weeks discussing the evidence and legal precedents, Simon and Schuster finally decided (not without apprehensions) to go ahead with publication on the grounds that a plaintiff was rarely able to mount a successful court case against a writer's representation of real-life events in fiction. The situation, however, changed radically in early June, when attorneys at Paul, Weiss read a newspaper report of a forthcoming novel by Meyer Levin about a rejected, suppressed manuscript that resembled his experience with the adaptation of Anne Frank's *Diary*. They telephoned Ephraim London to discuss the agreement of October 1959, in which Levin had pledged not to provoke further controversy about any aspect of the book, the adaptation, or the quarrel with the girl's father.

Both London and Gottlieb were flabbergasted; Levin had never told them that he had signed such a document. When they expressed their chagrin and disappointment, he argued that he had not violated the original agreement, since that covered only such matters as circulating petitions, speaking in synagogues, appearing on television, and sending accusatory letters to Otto Frank and others. He had written *The Fanatic* to interpret life, not to arouse public or private controversy about Frank, Crawford, Bloomgarden, Hellman, or anyone else. The book was not in his view about the infamous "case" (there was no Otto Frank character in it) but was concerned with Jewish cultural issues, problems of faith, and threats to freedom of expression; and he would not accept any restrictions on his right to publish it. But, he said, if the consensus was that the novel did violate the agreement, he was ready to pay back the $15,000, so long as the book could be printed.

Discussions continued in various forms and forums for several months. For Simon and Schuster, the worries about libel were now compounded by the possibility that Paul, Weiss would move to enjoin the book's publication on the grounds of breach of contract. For Levin, the prospect of another suppression was intolerable, and he threatened to protest and even go on a hunger strike if the book were withdrawn. Publication was delayed again. The Committee of Three and others who had been involved in the negotiations four years earlier were contacted. Samuel Fredman upheld Levin's contention that the settlement agreement had never been intended to cover anything Levin planned to write in the way of fiction. After weighing all the arguments and concluding that Otto Frank was not likely to get involved in yet another lawsuit (especially one that would increase the sales of Levin's book), Simon and Schuster decided again to go ahead with publication, and *The Fanatic* appeared in January 1964.

The reception did little to assuage Levin's feelings of anger and frustration. Although the novel was promoted as a dramatization of the Jewish obsession with justice and the relationship of God and the six million, nearly everyone familiar with the writer's history read it as a thinly disguised roman à clef. Reviewers in the popular press could hardly restrain their irritation at what they saw as a recycling of recent scandal and a flagrant example of special pleading. Although David Boroff, in the *New York Times Book Review*, admitted that the novel "conjures up with stunning authority the nightmare world of its protagonist," he remarked that the familiarity of the Levin-Frank feud (and the novelist's lack of proportion and disguise in dealing with it) reduced the book to the merely topical (26 January 1964, 5). Other reviewers were less generous. For David I. Segal, in *Book Week*, *The Fanatic* was simply a bore, the plot manipulated to prove a preconceived thesis, the characters Good Guys versus Bad Guys, the narrative point of view oppressive, and the style full of self-pity and empty rhetoric. Levin, he insisted, "is as guilty as his Communist characters" for narrowing the focus of his novel and using it "as a weapon against only one kind of conspiracy against truth" (2 February 1964, 2). The *Newsweek* critic called the novel "a long tedious whine, possibly of some chest-lightening benefit to the author but dull in the extreme for the blameless reader"; and Stanley Kauffmann, in the *New York Review of Books*, summarily dismissed it as "spurious" and Levin as "an ambitious mechanic who thinks he can bruise and shove his way through reams and reams of paper to Apocalypse" (27 January and 20 February 1964). Half-a-dozen other notices were far more sympathetic and positive, but (with the exception of a piece in *Saturday Review*) these appeared in less widely read and less influential journals, most of which had a religious orientation: the Catholic weekly *America*, the *Christian Science Monitor*, and the Jewish *Congress Bi-Weekly* and *Circle*.

Levin's disappointment with the reviews and sales of *The Fanatic* was keen, but he had predictable, and in part persuasive, explanations for its failure. His wife, friends, and editors had been saying for years that his strident, aggressive actions against Otto Frank and the famous, much-loved play would alienate many people who might otherwise be sympathetic to him and his work. Indeed, his friend Harry Golden told him that suing Anne Frank's father was like suing the father of Joan of Arc, and probably the worst public relations blunder of the century (letter, 30 April 1961, BU). Levin was, in fact, often mocked in New York literary and publishing circles, not only as dogged, humorless, cranky, opportunistic, and ridiculous, but as "Liar Mevin" and as the Professional Jew who had absurdly taken Anne Frank's father to court. Now, with the appearance of *The Fanatic*, the derision that had been heard mostly in conversation began to appear regularly in print. The reviews in the *New York Times, Book Week, Newsweek,* and the *New York Review of Books* were in fact nastier and more personal than any criticism Levin had ever received before. Of course, this shift in tone could be explained by saying that the disapproving reviewers honestly felt *The Fanatic* was a bad novel, or that Levin was inviting attack by publishing a self-justifying book portraying his enemies as cartoonish villains. Yet, for all of this, the ad hominem attacks, the flippancy and scorn—not only at Levin's refusal to relinquish his obsession, but also at his insistence on continuing to dramatize it in public (this time as fiction)—suggest responses in excess of what an author of Levin's accomplishment and reputation deserved. Despite the publicity (which often made him look foolish as well as foolhardy), Levin had been for more than thirty years a humane, dedicated, and serious writer; he had published eleven books and many hundreds of newspaper pieces; and *The Fanatic*, however one measures its flaws, was a deeply felt, carefully wrought work of substantial ambition.

Levin saw the negative reception of *The Fanatic* as further evidence that his career was imperiled by influential people with an active animus against him. The *New York Times Book Review*, he felt, was still angry about his having extolled *Diary of a Young Girl* without declaring an interest in the book; the *New York Review of Books* was edited by Barbara Epstein (formerly Zimmerman), and David Segal worked in Manhattan publishing. Most of the periodicals that praised *The Fanatic* had no ax to grind and were more willing to consider the novel at face value and not to berate the author for his personal behavior. And the majority of them were published outside New York.

The problems that Levin had with the writing, publication, and reception of *The Fanatic* tell us almost as much as the book itself about the character of his obsession at this point in his life. The decision to attempt the novel in the first place attests to the centrality of his preoccupation and his desire to understand and exorcise it. The artistic difficulties he then had with balance and proportion (as the treatment of the Holocaust materials became secondary to the protracted narrative of the Broadway intrigue against him) suggest an essential fact about the fixation itself: that he appeared at times to be more wounded by, or at least more entangled with, the harm that had been done to his career than he was with the atrocities committed against the Jews, or with the misrepresentation of Anne Frank's words in the theater. As Levin's career evolved in the 1960s and 1970s, questions about what he was fighting for and against were asked more frequently, and issues of motivation became increasingly contested.

The idea of "the wound," basic to *The Fanatic*, from this point on also becomes a major theme in Levin's life and work, vital to an understanding of his beliefs and behavior. In the novel, Leo speaks of Maury as "one of those who walk in the world a bit more tenderly than others, because of their inner mark, their ineradicable wound, a wound that can come only through the beloved" (421). Originally, the crime against the Jews and the rejection of his play were Maury's cause, and—as the author puts it—"what began as good will and heroism in the world, with love for a cause, ends in betrayal, in a personal wound, and festers, and becomes a malformation, a thing in itself, an obsession" (222).

Similarly, Levin in his own life perceived a connection between the wound inflicted on him by his opponents through his rejected play and the Nazi crime against the Jewish people. As Maury in the fiction and Levin in the world become enmeshed in their quests for justice, each turns into an injustice collector reluctant to be relieved of his cause. Indeed, neither can seem to let go of his obsession because it has become his cause. Questions about the process by which this happens, the roots of the obsession, and the reasons why Levin cannot relinquish it multiply and become increasingly vexed; they are explored at length in Chapter 5.

Important, too, is the fact that when the reviewers of *The Fanatic* blamed Levin for indulging his obsession and accused him of being unable to transform it into a successful novel, he immediately linked their reactions to the general conspiracy against him and expanded the list of his enemies to include the New York literary as well as the theater establishment. Although he was almost certainly wrong about collusion and scheming among the reviewers, he was responding to an injustice in the extremity of their responses. They condemned him for insisting on writing about a subject they found repellent and for being unable to turn it into the kind of novel they admired. What they could not know, but might have intuited, is Levin's worthy effort in the novel to work through personal and artistic problems he was unable to solve—an effort open to criticism but not censure and contempt.

The writing of *The Fanatic*, then—which had been conceived in part to help Levin understand and perhaps free himself from the Anne Frank labyrinth—now seemed to have had the opposite effect, rekindling his anger and suspicion and intensifying his conviction that he was still being victimized. In the months after the novel's publication, though, he deliberately turned his attention to a number of quite different writing projects to distance himself from the dilemma he could not resolve.

The two longest of these projects were a novel, *The Stronghold* (1965), and a short historical survey for young readers, *The Story of Israel* (1966). Each of these books was an efficient production from the professional writer's desk, but neither opened a new path for future artistic exploration or provided enough distance from the Anne Frank imbroglio to give Levin anything more than temporary relief.

The Story of Israel was one of a series of basic texts on subjects of Jewish history and culture that Levin produced in the 1950s and early 1960s, some in collaboration with scholars, others by himself. Two of the earlier volumes—*The Story of the Jewish Way of Life* and *God and the Story of Judaism*—were designed to be used in synagogues and community centers, but *The Story of Israel*, published by G. P. Putnam, was aimed at a wider audience and was praised by the *New York Times Book Review* and other general-interest journals. Combining an account of a family outing from his home at Kfar Shmaryahu, near Herzliyya, with colorful sketches of figures who shaped the country (Herzl, Weizmann, Ben-Gurion, the agronomist Aaron Aaronson, and others), Levin provides a readable narrative history of the formation of the modern state of Israel from an emphatically Zionist point of view.

A more ambitious and interesting book, *The Stronghold*, Levin's eleventh novel, was based on an actual event the author had witnessed. In the closing days of World War II, the American army freed several French notables (two former premiers, Paul Reynaud and Édouard Daladier, and General Maxime Weygand) who were being held hostage in a fortified castle near Hitler's Berchtesgaden sanctuary in Bavaria. Around this real incident, Levin created a suspense novel that also featured an evolving debate on Europe's treatment of the Jews. The book opens before the liberation, when an Eichmann-like figure, Lieutenant Colonel Kraus of the SS, arrives at the castle with yet another captive former minister, Paul Vered (modeled in part on Léon Blum, twice premier of France in the 1930s), a Jew he had kept from being murdered at Buchenwald. Aware that the Allied victory is near, Kraus (looking for a way to save his skin) asks the prisoners (who also include a priest and a journalist) to testify in a letter that he treated them well. They eventually refuse, but in the process of deliberation they hear for the first time from Vered and others about the death camps and express a range of typical European gentile attitudes toward Jews.

Levin's basic design in *The Stronghold*—to make a celebrity suspense story function as a morality play about questions of guilt and responsibility—is promising; but in practice the two elements do not mesh as well as they might. The action tale of besieged ministers and a vengeful SS man is well paced and engaging, but the characters remain for the most part spokesmen for Levin's summary ideas about anti-Semitism, and the debate itself fades from attention as the rescue plot speeds to its exciting conclusion.

After finishing *The Stronghold* and *The Story of Israel,* Levin began sustained work on a project entirely different from anything he had ever undertaken before: a ribald farce about two hipster protest poets, a Russian and an American, who are hounded by government authorities, flee their homelands, and—after day-and-night sex—meet, improbably, as truck drivers at a fertilizer plant in the Negev just before the Six-Day War. First conceived as a screenplay and then published as a novel in 1968, *Gore and Igor* was a radical departure (a *humorous* book about suppressed writers) that Levin hoped would allow him to get in touch with a previously unexplored side of his talent and take him as far away from genocide and discord as possible. But before he could get into the project in 1966, a chance event again aroused his feelings about the rejection of his play and led to still another widely publicized airing of the quarrel with Otto Frank's attorneys about dramatic rights.

Living in Israel at this time was the fifty-two-year-old Canadian-born theater and film director Peter Frye, who had recently staged works by Ibsen, Lessing, and other classic writers at Habimah, the Chamber Theatre, and Ohel, where he was now artistic manager. Levin, who had met Frye socially, liked his feistiness and independence: "a scrapper, he was always in a row, if not with the rabbinate, then with the critics, the government, or all three together" (*The Obsession,* 258). As they got to know one another, Frye asked about the fight over the *Diary* and Levin gave him a copy of *The Fanatic*, which the director found an arresting personal and cultural record. In subsequent conversations, Levin led Frye to believe that although his play could not be performed in the United States, he still had the option to stage it in Israel, and he suggested they do a reading at his house to determine if the director might be interested in mounting a production. Tereska Torres, who knew that in 1959 her husband had signed away all his rights to the Anne Frank material, decided not to intervene, hoping that the performance of his play might free him from his obsession. In her memoir, she remembers thinking: *"Peut-être le dibbouk qui l'habite quittera enfin Meyer le jour où les paroles d'Anne Frank seront dites sur la scène, exactement telles qu'elle les avait écrites dans le secret de l'Annexe* (160).

Even with a cast of friends and acquaintances, most of whom had little acting experience, the reading at Levin's house absorbed everyone who heard it, and Frye offered to find a public platform for the play. In the weeks that followed, he used a Hebrew translation with his students at Tel Aviv University (where he taught drama) and wrote Levin (who was then in New York) that although the text was too long and needed considerable cutting and revising, it had great potential. The more "I work on it," he said, "the more firmly I am convinced that yours is the more important play. Notice, I don't say 'better' because 'better' is a subjective evaluation, a matter of taste, a matter of cultural development. For example, in terms of American show business theirs may be the 'better' play because it is easier, slicker, more sentimental" (2 May 1966, BU). In this and other letters, Frye continued to argue that "in literary and cultural importance," Levin's work was more significant and less romanticized than the renowned Goodrich and Hackett version, and that he was dedicated to bringing it before the public.

On 9 June, Frye organized a reading at the university that attracted an audience of about three hundred. The presentation, he reported to Levin, was more than adequate: "People responded warmly to every nuance of the play . . . the kids were alright . . . but they will do better." And he continued:

> I am doing this not for your sake. . . . it is difficult to say on paper why I am doing it—I don't want to sound like a philanthropist or like an Evangelist—the reasons for my stubbornness are much deeper than any personal interest or even loyalty to a friend. My loyalty is to the play; my loyalty is to the memory of Anne Frank. (10 June 1966, BU)

During the summer, Frye told Levin that he had gotten a commitment to stage the play from the Soldiers Theatre, a group just established by the Educational and Cultural section of the Israel Defense Forces. He had originally hoped to be able to do the production with top actors in the leading roles and soldiers in minor parts, but this was now not feasible. The actors would consist of young drama-program graduates, a few soldiers chosen by audition, and perhaps one or two older professionals; but people seemed to be inspired by the prospect of putting on the play on a portable stage in Tel Aviv and then touring military bases and civilian settlements around the country. As Tereska Torres recalls the events, Frye's ardor seduced everyone. All thoughts of obstacles vanished; the work could be done; Levin would be cured of his obsession; and even if there were trouble, an Israeli army that could handle Nasser, Hussein, and Arafat would be able to deal with Kermit Bloomgarden's lawyers (*Les maisons hantées de Meyer Levin*, 160–61).

During the rehearsal period, with Levin now present, Frye played a vital role in reshaping the original script. He dramatically opened the production with all the actors huddled under black umbrellas singing "El Ma'alay Rachamim" (God Full of Compassion), a prayer traditionally intoned at a burial or memorial service. This brief requiem tableau introduced a powerful note of sorrow and mourning that persisted through the rest of the play. Frye also added other music, proposed Koophuis as narrator, cut chunks of inert dialogue, and compressed two late scenes to heighten the impact of the ending. In addition, by accentuating Levin's emphasis on Anne's and Peter's relationship to their own Jewishness, he enhanced the clash of values, not of personalities, and sharpened the audience's awareness of the fate of the Jews outside as well as inside the annex. Just as Garson Kanin had helped turn the Goodrich and Hackett script into a heart-rending showpiece, so Frye provided the theatrical savviness that gave Levin's drama a concision, urgency, and beauty that most earlier readers had been unable to perceive in the original draft. Knowing Levin's penchant for conflict, Frye (who wished to engage the audience, not to create scandal) also tried before the opening to keep the playwright from alerting the press or reminding people of the saga of rejection and prohibition.

But the general response to the staging in Tel Aviv and elsewhere made it impossible for Levin to remain silent. During rehearsals, he was thrilled by the promise of a fifteen-year-old dream coming true: the resourcefulness of Frye's direction and the devotion of the cast made him feel that his work captured the strength and meaning of the *Diary* more successfully than the authorized version. Watching the drama come alive for the first time on a stage, he was convinced that people would now be able to see what he had been battling for all these years, and he became as indignant as ever about the treatment of his script in New York. On opening night, he sat transfixed in the last row of the auditorium, and at the final curtain he added his clapping and loud shouts of approval to the audience's applause. Afterward, stunned and exhausted by the experience, he announced to his wife that the Tel Aviv premiere was only a tryout for a professional show on Broadway; and she realized to her dismay that instead of curing his obsession, the Soldiers Theatre performance had intensified it further. When appreciative articles appeared in Israeli newspapers in the weeks after the opening, Levin felt that his vindication was complete and that a new chapter in the annals of his long struggle had just begun.

Heading his *Jerusalem Post* review "Franker Frank," Mendel Kohansky praised the show for its fidelity to the original book, for stressing the psychological element and the relationship between parents and children, and for allowing the authentic personality of the teenage diarist to shine through. "It is," he observed, "on the whole a more honest dramatization than the slickly professional one we have seen before [at Habimah], but a theatrically less exciting one, which is inevitable. The *Diary* is not intrinsically stage stuff; it can be made into conventional theatre only by sacrificing some of its honesty and simplicity— or by presenting it as a reading, which might have been the most satisfying form." Admitting that the performance dragged in spots, and that the professional actors were less effective than the amateurs, Kohansky still singled out for strong commendation the adventurous simplicity of Levin's and Frye's work and the acting of newcomer Shoshana Rosen (13 November 1966, 13).

Dov Bar-Nir, writing in the leftist-labor paper *Al Hamishmar*, also applauded Levin's play for the directness and honesty with which it depicted daily existence in the secret annex. "There is no moralizing," he said, "no terrors, persecutions, tortures, trials. . . . In two hours at the Soldiers Theatre we live the short life of Anne Frank, moving, exciting, authentic." Like several other commentators (Sara Frankel in *Hayom*, for instance), Bar-Nir expressed gratitude to Levin for bringing the Anne Frank story to a young Israeli audience, most of whom had been born after 1945 and knew little about the history of the Nazi era.

These complimentary articles and praise from playgoers made Levin feel that he had to proclaim his triumph and renew efforts to regain performance and perhaps even publishing rights to his own creative work. Although he had promised Peter Frye not to revive the old animosity, he now insisted that to keep silent was an act of moral cowardice—like appeasing Hitler in Munich—and he called a press conference of Israeli and foreign journalists to describe the contentious history; to repeat his charge that he was a victim of censorship by a Stalinist, anti-Zionist cabal; and to assert that the merit of his work had been at long last publicly confirmed.

Within days, newspapers in several countries had printed stories about the opening, the press conference, and the renewed controversy. The *New York Times* article, "Anne Frank

Play Staged in Israel," reported that Israeli critics had found
Levin's rendering less theatrical but more honest than the
Broadway play produced in 1955 by Kermit Bloomgarden. Noting that Dr. Emil Feuerstein, president of the Israeli Association of Drama Critics, found the Levin adaptation "infinitely
superior to the Hackett version, which had put aiming for a hit
above faithfulness to the source," the *Times* correspondent went
on to announce Levin's intention to continue his fight to have
Anne Frank shown in the United States and to establish it as a
"permanent institution in the theatrical literature" around the
world (27 November 1966).

On 6 December, attorneys from Paul, Weiss in New York
cabled the Israel Defense Forces, demanding an immediate halt
to the Soldiers Theatre production because it infringed Otto
Frank's copyright and other property rights. According to the
settlement of October 1959, they said, Levin had transferred all
rights to his adaptation—including Israeli rights—to Frank. In
response to this and other telegrams, Levin and his lawyer
argued that the Israeli rights still belonged to him and that the
Jewish people had an immutable prerogative to its own cultural
material. Peter Frye and administrators also used various tactics to keep the show running, which they managed to do for
more than fifty performances. By early January, however, after
Paul, Weiss announced that they would institute legal action
in Israel to protect Otto Frank's copyright, the army decided
to withdraw the play. Ironically, the last performance took
place on 18 January 1967 at Kibbutz Meshek Yagur, near Haifa,
where Levin had lived and worked on his first extended visits to
Palestine forty years earlier. David Zinder, who played Dussel,
recalls that Levin was very unstable: "Somebody in the dress-

ing-room asked a question about why Otto Frank was behaving in this way and Meyer had an hysterical attack, screaming and uncontrolled, yelling—red in the face. The whole unhappy story pouring out" (letter, January 1994, TF).

During the weeks of renewed conflict, however, Levin received further support for his actions. The labor daily, *Davar*, ran an article congratulating the writer, expressing a preference for his work over Goodrich and Hackett's, and arguing that "*The Diary of Anne Frank* is not the personal property of the heirs and the legal action against Levin and his dramatization was unjustified, because the Soldiers Theatre chose the Jewish version which was more faithful to its source" (23 December 1966, 8). Levin also received many personal letters of support, among them a note from Yehiel Dinur, who—under the name of Ka-Tzetnik (from the German acronym KZ for *Konzentrationslager*)—had written some of the most searing, widely read stories of the death camps. Ka-Tzetnik, who had become an internationally known figure after testifying at the Eichmann trial, saw Levin's drama and wrote him: "I was distressed to learn that Anne Frank is again condemned to oblivion. When I saw your play at Soldiers Theatre in Tel Aviv I felt the magnetic pull between the audience and Anne Frank on stage. It is a shame that questions of a non-literary nature can sometimes come between an artist and his audience in expressing the human condition. You have my deepest sympathies" (18 January 1967, BU). Elie Wiesel wrote a similar letter of support a few weeks later.

After the exchange of telegrams with attorneys in New York, and the encouragement he was getting from people in Israel and elsewhere, Levin took the closing of the army production as a new stimulus to increase his efforts to get public recognition for his play. Two months earlier (just after the premiere in Tel Aviv), he had received an inquiry from the lecture bureau of the National Jewish Welfare Board in New York about a U.S. tour of the Soldiers Theatre production. Although such an arrangement was impossible, he now felt the time was ripe to press his claims even more resolutely than he had done before.

Late in 1966 and through the early months of 1967, Levin wrote scores of letters to influential figures in American and Israeli legal, artistic, publishing, and philanthropic circles, urging them to back his cause. He asked Will Maslow of the American Jewish Congress (who had helped negotiate the 1959 settlement) to "consider the real issue" before he condemned him as "a contract breaker." The agreement, Levin insisted, did not stipulate that his creative work should be destroyed. He had as much right to keep the play alive "as any Jew had to keep himself alive when the Nazis tried to kill him. The Nazis too attempted 'legalism' in their suppression of life, and to me—as to Anne Frank—a work of art has the same right to life as a human being" (7 December 1966, BU). In an exchange with his friend Rabbi Jacob Weinstein of Chicago (who had written the anti-Bloomgarden article "The Betrayal of Anne Frank" in 1957), Levin admitted that the Soldiers Theatre performances violated earlier agreements, but he now felt that he had "to recognize a higher law in this respect," and he asked Weinstein to seek official authorization to perform the play and to urge others to do the same. Using similar arguments, Levin also wrote to editors and publishers (including Ken McCormick of Doubleday), proposing they issue a dual edition of his text and the Goodrich and Hackett play, or an edition in English or Hebrew of his work alone; and he sent copies of the play to the producer Jean Dalrymple at City Center Drama Company, to the director Harold Clurman, and to other theater notables, asking them to consider putting it on.

Levin also tried to find ways to influence Otto Frank more directly. He contacted Walter Pick, husband of Hannah Pick-Goslar (the Lies Goosens of the *Diary* and one of the last people to see Anne Frank alive through the barbed wire of Bergen-Belsen), and asked him and his wife to intercede on his behalf. His play, he told Pick, was more faithful and more important for Jews and Israel than the Broadway version. Pick replied that while Levin's claim might be true, his wife was so tied by affection and history to Otto Frank (she had known him before the war, and he had helped her emigrate to Israel afterward) that she could not intervene. To her mind, no abstract speculation about Levin's obligation to fight for the prerogative of the Jewish people to its cultural material could change Frank's basic right to approve or disapprove of adaptations as he saw fit. Pick also spoke of Otto Frank as "a rare specimen of a good and sunny human being," expressing a wish that the seventy-seven-year-old man not be hounded for his honestly held opinions. Levin, irritated by Pick's reaction, wrote back that "the phrase 'to hound an old man for his honestly held opinions' is just another insult which I may add to those which this old man has had to absorb for *his* honestly held opinions" (7 and 9 December 1966, BU).

Several of the friends with whom Levin corresponded at this time replied with understanding, empathy, and concern but undertook to persuade him—despite his rage and disappointment—to abandon a fight he could not legally win and to focus his attention on his other writing. Among the most candid and forceful were Rabbi Weinstein and Rabbi Joachim Prinz. In late January 1967, Weinstein told Levin that the quarrel was "eating you like a cancer" and that "hate and self-pity" have deprived "your recent work of the creative fire" that characterized *The Old Bunch, In Search,* and *Compulsion.* He begged "an old dear friend" to turn his mind to other subjects (29 January 1967, BU). A few days later Rabbi Prinz, responding to an earlier entreaty, told Levin:

> Legally you are completely wrong. The agreement is quite clear. You have abdicated your right to have your play performed in any form whatsoever. You accepted money from your opponents as a token of this agreement, and you have obligated yourself in such clear terms that there is no court in the world that would approve any action not in accordance with this agreement. This is the legal part of it. It is important, but it is not the only consideration.
>
> My consideration is for you as a human being. You have permitted yourself to be maneuvered into an almost paranoid state of mind. It might be very well that my letter is not going to cure you from it. But I must make the attempt. It might very well be that you need some psychiatric help because you have made yourself sick. This kind of sickness in a man of your importance and talent is not merely a concern for Meyer Levin but for all of us. The more you concentrate on violating the agreement, the sicker you get. (31 January 1967, BU)

Levin's response to these and other such appeals was usually to admit his obsession but to argue vigorously that to be obsessed was not necessarily to be wrong, and to urge the correspondent to accept his point of view. His play was unjustly proscribed for doctrinaire reasons; his reputation was severely damaged; and he would continue to make every effort to get the ban lifted and to have the work freely performed by any-one who wished to stage it. "It is with a great shock that I read your letter," he replied to Jacob Weinstein:

> Though it is written with great warmth and sympathy, and though I am sure you remain my friend as I remain yours, I would have thought you would take a broader view of what happened. Your view amounts to saying that a contract is eternally binding, above justice and life itself, not subject to review or change when basic circumstances change. . . . The basic circumstance changed. The basic circumstance was the assumption that my play was no good, unactable. It has now been proven that it is not only actable and a very good play but probably a work of true permanent value. (3 February 1967, BU)

As the months passed, Levin recognized that his efforts to organize support for his cause were unavailing, and he decided—against the advice of his agent and others—to print five thousand copies of *Anne Frank*, privately at his own expense, which he would then distribute "for literary discus-sion" to libraries, individuals, theater groups, and community centers. To introduce the text, he wrote a fourteen-page "Pref-ace to a Forbidden Play," offering his view of the dispute. This Preface, like so much of his writing on the Anne Frank affair, is a vigorous polemic mixing persuasive arguments about artistic freedom, the influence of commercial factors on Broadway, and the merit of his own play with unproven intrigue theories, aggressive attacks on his enemies, and a partially distorted account of what occurred between 1952 and 1959. In some paragraphs, he provides a cogent critique of the flaws of the Goodrich and Hackett *Diary* and an explanation of what he aimed for in his own work, especially on the subject of universality versus Jewish particularism; but in other places, his need for self-justification leads him to misrepresent Otto Frank's actions and his own. (Levin claims erroneously, for instance, that Frank "authorized and approved his play," and that as author he offered to withdraw his original script to make way for a world-famous dramatist who never materialized. He also reports misleadingly that throughout the trial, he offered to drop his charges if his play were given noncommercial performance rights.)

For all its shrill rhetoric, exaggeration, and distortion, Levin's preface does present a powerful image of a writer obsessed with a perceived injustice, and it makes a forceful case that his drama be permitted noncommercial production:

> I must repeat that I have never asked that this play be substituted for the other. I have simply insisted that those who wish, should be able to present it. . . . To the producer and authors of the other play I would say, You have had the greatest possible gratification in world-wide performances, in earnings, in prizes—isn't that enough? Can't you now allow the public the right to see a different version if they want to? (p. xiii)

Levin's adversaries, however, had for many years been dismissive of his appeals. Not only did they have the law on their side (Levin *had* freely and with the advice of counsel signed the agreements and accepted money for the rights to his play), but they also maintained that his claims were baseless, his charges of political machinations preposterous, and his obstructive actions over fifteen years personally damaging to them and others. Therefore they felt entirely justified in not yielding on the matter of performance. Besides, if they did yield and permitted his work to be staged, they were convinced he would begin other protests and litigation. As Levin sent out thousands of copies of *Anne Frank* to libraries, groups, and individuals—and as requests for permission to perform the play significantly increased—the attorneys at Paul, Weiss considered various options with Frank, Bloomgarden, and the Hacketts. Close to eighty, and busy with other legal entanglements related to his daughter's world-famous book, Otto Frank had no desire to get involved again in a lawsuit with Levin, which he felt would lead to more recriminations and attacks. Since the private distribution of the printed play did not appear to endanger anyone's fundamental rights, the decision was made to ignore Levin and to have Paul, Weiss answer all applications for performance rights to his play with a five-page form letter of refusal describing the background of the dispute and the various contracts and agreements signed by the parties involved. The letter ends:

> Notwithstanding these agreements, and in violation of them, Mr. Levin has continued to claim the right to produce and to have the version of The Diary which he wrote produced. He has continued to publish and distribute copies of it. He has continued to circularize Rabbis and other groups and persons on the Anne Frank subject. He has continued to stimulate public and private controversy about The Diary and

his part in relation to it. And he has continued to not only discuss whether or not the stage adaptation of The Diary which he wrote should or should not have been produced, but to stimulate repeated requests from various people for the right to produce it. In 1966, Mr. Levin violated his commitments wholesale by stimulating a production by the Soldiers Theatre in Israel. . . .

In these circumstances, it simply is not possible to grant your request: there are too many individuals with interests in the dramatic rights who would find such a performance objectionable. Moreover, in light of the relationship between Mr. Frank and Mr. Levin, Mr. Frank is simply not inclined to authorize productions which will just give rise to a renewal of the ancient and unpleasant controversy. (BU)

Despite the futility of his efforts to gain permission to have his play performed, Levin continued to distribute copies and to plead his cause. He also engaged in confessional, self-justifying correspondence with friends. One of the most fascinating of these exchanges took place in November 1968 with Martha Gellhorn, the reporter, novelist, and former wife of Ernest Hemingway, whom he had met when they both covered the Spanish Civil War and World War II. Levin had sent Gellhorn a copy of his privately printed play, and on 13 November she acknowledged it with what she later called "awful frankness":

You'll never forgive me for telling you truthfully that you have wasted your nerves, gaiety, energy, and surely your wife, on nonsense: it simply isn't a very good play, Meyer; not that the one shown on the stage was very good either, though they are astoundingly similar. That the author of *Compulsion* could have written this play is in itself odd: like two different people, and the author of *Compulsion* is a tremendous writer. Whereas the author of *Anne Frank* is a good honest man, who has made a pedestrian play and stuffed such boring speeches into the mouth of a 13-year-old that one can't quite believe what one reads.

Gellhorn concludes by telling Levin how disturbed she is to see how "you have cooped [yourself] up . . . in your own mind, obsessed with this second-rate work, doomed yourself to a self-made prison; been your own devil" (BU).

Levin, who admired Gellhorn and responded to her criticism with respect, set out four days later "to explain . . . old Meyer Levin's obsession":

> I have tried with two analysts and am on the third so probably incurable. But when you daintily remind me it is not a very good play or mediocre and much like the other you touch on several dubious points. First, the question of whether it was or was not a good play was the heart of the disturbance for a few years because the only way one could find out was on the stage. In the Israel performance I at last found out. With a lousy cast, except for the two principal kids, the thing played beautifully and after seeing it about fifty times I was convinced. It is a good play. Kind of in the Chekhov manner as I had hoped . . . that is how it comes out on the stage. As to the other play being something like it, of course it is, they swiped it from me. They copied the whole staging, the structure, etc. only left out the Jewish heart.

At this point in his letter to Gellhorn, Levin offers his habitual argument about political plotting, accusing Hellman, Bloomgarden, and the Hacketts but also going on to include a sharp attack on "my own people, my own Jews, the same lousy community to which I directed my entire writing career," for turning away and not helping him.

> Why? Because Otto Frank was a remote cousin of the Strauses of Macy's, and because his lawyer, Rifkind and Co., was president of the American Jewish Committee. In other words, the Jewish establishment refuses to support a Jewish writer and a Jewish cultural cause because the other side has family connections. It is all slightly redolent of the worst of the Jewish Community Committees set up by the Nazis to make lists and assign priorities and preside over the liquidation. (BU)

In Moscow, he goes on, they would have put the "nutty Levin" in a writers' lunatic asylum, but in America he is "branded as paranoic and lectures are canceled." Acknowledging that he is in the clutch of a mania from which he cannot extricate himself, Levin closes by admitting some of the dismal consequences of his obsession and offering one interpretation of its meaning:

> It has about killed my marriage to the charming Tereska because we cannot talk about this subject as it makes her shudder and so I can hardly talk about anything at all since this subject stands in front of me most of the time.
>
> In a peculiar way, this is my masochistic mechanism for identifying with the Holocaust. I know it. I see myself as a Jew who created something that was then handed over to a couple of non-Jewish front people, and the more I protest the more I am vilified.

In her response on 23 November, Gellhorn stands her ground:

Your letter made me sad; you are like an alcoholic who
cherishes, excuses, justifies, and denies his addiction. I am,
you will be maddened to hear, sorry for you; but a damn sight
sorrier for Tereska and the children. Since an obsession may
be painful to the one obsessed but can be nothing except a
deadly murderous sickening bore to those who have to live
near it. And you used to be quite a funny guy; such a waste,
to degenerate into this.

Then Gellhorn goes on to tell Levin that in her view he is not
fighting artistic censorship: "It's the censorship of *you*—you've
isolated yourself in a cage of self-concern. . . . You even resent
the fury people feel about sending Russian writers to prison—
who sent you to prison, chum—because what is driving you is
not a universal ill or injustice, it's *you* not getting a square deal."
And she closes with a poignant postscript: "I remember you in
a jeep in the snow in Luxembourg and—perhaps shamefully
surely selfishly—it is one of my gayest memories. Find your
way back to being a brave, disinterested man."

Gellhorn's mix of blunt realism and compassion is also evi-
dent in letters she was writing to Tereska Torres at the same
time. Explaining how distraught she was after spending four
months looking after her ninety-year-old mother in St. Louis,
Gellhorn shares her most recent letter to Levin with his wife,
her friend, and concludes: "I can't take him on; I am not a doctor. . . . I've done my best, such as it is." But even as she talks of
withdrawing, Gellhorn continues to be concerned and tries to
be helpful. She offers the name of a doctor in Israel, discusses
medication, shares her thoughts about Levin's personality and
problems, praises Torres's loyalty, and sympathizes with what
she has had to put up with: "He's got the busy-ness and the

blazing comfort of being ego-mad with his own trouble; you
only have the grisly role of watching this needless and ugly
ruin." And, in talking about medication, she recalls going
through a similar experience with Hemingway:

> I agree with you about medication; and there is indeed the
> chance that various medications, acting like shock treatment,
> do and can shake loose obsessions. I know nothing about
> Ernest in his last years, have only heard; it seems clear he was
> quite insane. But I noticed this long before; terrible suspicions
> of people (mad and ugly) and a sense of persecution—he who
> was the favorite of the Gods—and total unreliability in
> emotion; his greatest friend this week, too great a friend, was
> suddenly denounced as a swine and enemy the next week.
> I thought it was just a filthy nature—and there is that too—
> but also clearly clinical madness.
>
> I think Meyer's nature is basically sweet, or so it seems to
> me. You have been loyal and enduring, beyond belief. But I'd
> think a certain loneliness must set in for absolutely nothing
> bores people so much as the obsessions of others. I wonder
> how Meyer managed to clear his mind enough to write that
> gay book about Gore and Igor. A romp. Cheered me to think
> he'd cheered up. (18 November, no year, TT)

Gellhorn's candid, tough-minded reactions to Levin's play
and predicament carry the refreshing authority of common
sense; her image of him as a kind of ideological alcoholic and
her remarks about egotism and self-concern are keen and
painfully pertinent. But at the same time, her dismissal of both
plays as worthless and of the entire affair as "nonsense" suggests
a high-mindedness of her own; she seems unable to credit the
weight of the issues Levin has been struggling with, or the mis-

ery of his having lost what he helped to create and worked on so ardently (and it is not even clear she has read Anne Frank's *Diary*). Even allowing for his typical hyperbole, Levin's answers have a valuable candor of their own; his comment about masochistic identification with the suffering of the European Jews offers an insight that is of permanent relevance to an understanding of his condition.

Gellhorn's last comment on *Gore and Igor* serves as a reminder that Levin, at the same time he relentlessly pursued the justification of his own position and tried to get his play performed, was also writing fiction that suggested both a desire and an ability to escape for a time from the restrictions of what Gellhorn calls "a cage of self-concern." *Gore and Igor*—the extravagant spoof about peaceniks, folksinger–protest poets, and sexual hijinks in the 1960s—now seems self-indulgent, heavy-handed, and a lot less funny than it must have been at the time, but for Levin it provided a gratifying, if only tempo-rary, sense of release. Reviewing the novel in 1968, Wallace Markfield expressed understandable delight at having come unexpectedly on "zippy, zany farce" and "irreverent kibitzing of Israel" from "this tough old Zionist troubleshooter," at find-ing "broad, bawdy hints of black humor in a writer who has been put down as a gritty naturalist, a kind of Jewish James T. Farrell" (*Life*, 16 February, 6). Most other reviewers, though, found the shaggy poet story merely silly, the frankness smut, not wit. Some objected that the novel was an exploitation rather than a satiric commentary of the unbuttoned behavior of sixties radicals. *Gore and Igor* had only modest sales, and Levin did not try to work again in a comic vein—which is, in retrospect, a pity, since it might have led him to see (and to

use) what many onlookers saw: the elements of slapstick farce
(as well as seriousness and suffering) in his sixteen-year-old feud
with Otto Frank. In *The Obsession*, six years later, a sharp perception of comic travesty *does* occasionally break through, and
it is one of the things that makes that original book so memorable.

After the writing of *Gore and Igor*, however, Levin turned
his creative energies to still another markedly different undertaking: a massive, old-fashioned historical novel about a pio-
neer Jewish family that fled pogroms in Russia to settle in
Turkish-ruled Palestine at the beginning of the Second Aliyah
(the wave of immigration that brought some forty thousand
Jews to the territory between 1904 and 1914). Levin had been
thinking about this project for most of his life, and it had deep
meaning for him. Inspired by the activist family of Yitzhak
Chizik, one of his roommates in Chicago in the late 1920s, *The
Settlers* was written (as the dedication to Chizik declares) "in
promise, and in remembrance." Both the ambition and the
design of the book were large. Working on the manuscript
steadily between 1967 and 1971, Levin set out to portray the
dreams and struggles of the fictional Chaimovitch family (parents and nine children) through one of the most tumultuous
periods of modern history: the early Zionist efforts to reestab-
lish Jewish roots in Palestine, the rise of Arab nationalism, the
outbreak of World War I, the Russian Revolution, and the
events that led to the Balfour Declaration, the British defeat of
the Turks, and a new alignment of power in the Middle East.
The Settlers would be *The Old Bunch* writ large: the chronicle of
young Jews in Chicago would now be followed by a saga of
Jews in the modern world. Not only would the domestic and

international be blended, but the book would also have an expanding allegorical implication. The Chaimovitches (whose name is derived from the Hebrew for "life") settle at Mishkan Yaacov ("the dwelling place of Jacob"), on the banks of the Jordan in the Galilee. The father is named Yankel (a Yiddish diminutive for Jacob), and the strivings of his sons and daughters are often reminiscent of those of the children of the biblical patriarch. By telling the Chaimovitch story against the background of world events from 1907 to 1920, Levin hoped to celebrate the power and actualization of the Zionist dream as well as the aspirations of the Jews throughout history. After twenty-five years of preoccupation with Jewish victimization, he would now offer (in what could well be his last major effort) a heartening story about Jews having prevailed.

Not that the anger over the Anne Frank affair had been stilled. While reading proofs of *The Settlers*, the sixty-six-year-old Levin felt the "ancient devilment" spring out at him again (*Obsession*, 11). He started making plans for new protests, appeals to writers' groups, and even legal action, stimulated in part by regular requests from people wanting to stage the play. Since *The Settlers* looked as if it might be a big hit, however, he was worried that a flare-up of the old dispute could threaten the book's reception. In hopes of controlling his desire to incite trouble, he once again sought psychiatric help. Meanwhile, prepublication anticipation for *The Settlers* was indeed high. Simon and Schuster saw that the book might become Levin's first national bestseller since *Compulsion* fifteen years earlier. Instead of a historical thriller based on a spectacular murder case, he had now given them a densely inhabited panoramic novel that embodied many of his most passionate concerns

about the continuity of the Jews—a work that might tap the
market for earnest, colorful, narrative-driven chronicles popu-
larized by such writers as James Michener, Herman Wouk,
Leon Uris, and Chaim Potok. The publisher's first advertising
heralded the novel as an engrossing, inspirational saga, a broad
family story about triumph over adversity, enriched by heroic
figures and happenings from life (the deeds of the one-armed
soldier Joseph Trumpeldor and the fiery Zionist revisionist
Vladimir Jabotinsky, who formed the Zion Mule Corps at Gal-
lipoli; the escapades of the Nili underground intelligence
group, and the liberation of Jerusalem). A striking, two-page
spread in the *New York Times Book Review* set quotes from
Norman Mailer, Isaac Bashevis Singer, Frederick Morton, Ger-
ald Green, and Gerold Frank alongside a boxed endorsement
from Prime Minister Golda Meir of Israel. Mailer called Levin
"one of the two or three best living American writers working
in the naturalistic tradition"; *The Settlers* was "his magnum
opus." Meir claimed that the novelist's intimacy with the subject and his sympathetic understanding of his many characters
made *The Settlers* "a remarkably impressive recreation of one of
the great chapters in modern and Jewish history" (23 April
1972).

Within a few months of its publication, the novel sold close
to fifty thousand copies, appeared on several bestseller lists,
brought lots of fan mail, and earned $350,000 for paperback
rights. Nevertheless, Levin saw a sinister pattern in the way the
book was written about around the country. Acclaimed as an
absorbing story of breadth and power by reviewers in Chicago,
Philadelphia, Los Angeles, and elsewhere, it was perfunctorily
discussed and grudgingly praised by Granville Hicks in the

back pages of the *New York Times Book Review* and ignored by *Newsweek, Life, Time,* the *New Yorker, Saturday Review, Harper's,* the *Atlantic,* and other national journals. New York radio and television talk-show hosts, who customarily interviewed Levin when a work of his was about to appear, also disregarded him. Although his publishers, family, and friends tried to convince him that the reception of *The Settlers* was in fact excellent and that there was no dark plot against it, he took the lackluster piece by Hicks and the silence of the mostly New York–based national journals as the latest example of the anti-Israel metropolitan intelligentsia working to harm his career by misrepresenting or ignoring him. Although some of the critics who did review the book complained of tedious writing, one-dimensional characters, and popular history with a Hollywood flavor prevailing over art, it was the absence of reviews in New York that distressed and provoked Levin most of all.

On 12 October 1972, five months after *The Settlers* was published and had established itself as a success, Levin took out a half-page ad in the daily *New York Times,* headed CAN A LITERARY MAFIA AFFECT YOUR CHOICE OF BOOKS? Noting that critics across the country had called *The Settlers* his best novel, he went on to protest again that because of his having dared to fight against the prohibition of his Anne Frank play, the New York literary establishment continued to conspire against him by refusing to acknowledge and discuss his work in public and denigrating it in private. The existence of such a scheme was confirmed by those close to him even as they denied it: "My publisher takes the position that there is no such mafia, but that for me to fight it will prove disastrous!" Admitting that *The Settlers* had been a top bestseller in Chicago and Los Angeles, and number seven nationally, and had been chosen by the Book-of-the-Month Club as a featured fiction alternate, Levin explained that nonetheless his hatred of censorship and his desire for the widest possible audience led him to pay for this pronouncement and urge people to read his book.

A month later, after getting letters of support, he placed a second advertisement in the *Times*, this one titled WHAT IS "TOO JEWISH"? Here he elaborated on his indictment that the silent treatment accorded *The Settlers* "culminated a campaign of literary disparagement and character assassination" that had begun twenty years before, when his dramatization of Anne Frank's *Diary* was stifled for being "too Jewish." Concluding that "even my ad about the silent treatment got the silent treatment," he ended with a warning about "mind-manipulation through purposeful omissions and silences" and told readers where they could get copies of his original notice and his new novel (15 November 1972).

For many people at the time, Levin's behavior only reinforced the view that he was often a ludicrous figure, out of touch with the reality of his own literary status and with the way literary reputations were customarily made. For them, he was an independent, frequently published, widely read novelist (his books had sold several million copies in hard and soft covers in many languages); and his insistence on broadcasting shrill claims of Stalinist, anti-Zionist repression and on comparing his situation to the plight of Jewish writers in Russia only revealed the depth of his vanity and delusion. For Levin himself, however, the self-inflicted opening of the old wound led to thoughts of writing about it again, but in another form: a work that would disclose his side of the story in detail, without recourse to masks and fictions.

When Levin began *The Obsession* in 1971, he was sixty-five, and he had come to believe that the twenty-year fixation with *The Diary of a Young Girl* was the defining fact of his later life, "the inevitable expression of all I ever was, all I ever did, as a writer and as a Jew" (7). This memoir (perhaps his last major book) would be a confessional summing-up, an effort to vent his still-pent-up feelings, to examine their roots, consequences, and implications, to unmask his enemies, and to offer a cautionary moral tale about ideological manipulation in midcentury American society. The book would stand as his *Anatomy of Obsession*, a flagrantly candid, hopefully instructive exposure of himself and his adversaries that might recall his play from banishment and free him from the Anne Frank ordeal.

As a representation of what it is actually like for a very talented, prolific writer to be enmeshed for years in a compulsive preoccupation, the memoir is a bold and unforgettably affecting piece of work. When it was published, Jerome Greenfield fairly praised its "unique power" and said that not since Fitzgerald's *The Crack-Up* "had an established American author exposed his milieu and himself in public so nakedly" (*American Zionist*, March–April 1974, 38). The very design of the book is obsessional, and it inevitably prompts the same extreme range of responses from readers that Levin himself often elicited from the people he knew and met. He opens with an extraordinary, almost outlandish, but undeniably riveting description of his experience as a kind of epic descent:

> In the middle of life I fell into a trouble that was to grip, occupy, haunt, and all but devour me, these twenty years. I've used the word "fall." It implies something accidental, a stumbling, but we also use the word in speaking of "falling in

love," in which there is a sense of elevation, and where a fatedness is implied, a feeling of being inevitably bound in through all the mysterious components of character to this expression of the life process, whether in the end beautifully gratifying, or predominantly painful. In my "fall," too, there lurks the powerful sense of the inevitable. Through the years of this grim affair it has always seemed that the process had to come, that it was the inevitable expression of all I ever was, all I ever did, as a writer and as a Jew; that it was in itself virtually artistic in its construction, its hidden elements, its gradual summoning up and revelation of character both in myself and others, and in its exposition of social forces. (7)

The language here—with its evocation of the opening of *The Divine Comedy* and its reflection on the word "fall"—is clearly drawn from Dante, the Bible, and *Paradise Lost* (was the Fall calamitous or fortunate?). The intention is immediately to enhance the twenty-year-old trauma by placing it in the context of renowned epic stories that are among the emblematic narratives of our history and culture. The tone and attitude— poised, distanced, striving for objectivity and fullness—is clearly meant to imply that the author has reached a point at which he can finally put the tumult of the recent past into perspective and consider it from above the fray. To say that the affair was itself "virtually artistic in its construction" is to suggest a control that comes from understanding, perhaps even mastery. This formulation is also a deft, insinuating way of bringing Levin's travail into parallel relationship with that of Anne Frank, for her story (with its unities of time and place, its foreordained doom, its theme of the fine soul wasted, and its status as a symbolic narrative of a people) has intriguing connections with Greek tragedy.

What the writer hopes to do, he tells us (continuing his use of mythological imagery), is "to unravel the three-threaded intertwinings of fate, manipulation, and one's own will," so as to understand "what happened to me."

> "Exactly how did it, how could it have come about?" we demand. Was all this from within myself? one asks, or from outside? Was there some hidden secret force working on me so that no matter what I did through the normal ways of society I could not prevail?—Ah! paranoia!—But if I trace back and find that there really was such a force?—Witches! Demons! The conspiratorial view of history! (8)

Notable here is the rapid giving way of studied distance in the opening paragraph to a more intimate, emotional point of view; blunt phrases, question marks, dashes, and exclamation points introduce the startling specter of paranoia and conspiratorial views of history that will be at the center of the zigzagging narrative from now on. The unexpected shift in tone and perspective continues as Levin casually tells us that he has consulted four psychoanalysts and therapists on many occasions in the past decades, and it soon becomes clear that it is psychoanalysis, not mythology or classical literature, that will provide a vital frame for the confessional memoir.

As the urgent narrative proceeds, we learn a good deal more about Levin's experiences with the four analysts. The first, identified as Dr. A, was a woman in Israel who treated him at intervals there and in New York for twenty-five years. Most important, he had consulted her in 1951 at the time of the suicide of Mable, his first wife; since his involvement with the Anne Frank *Diary* began around then, they later talked a great deal about the possibility that his obsession was a guilty, self-punishing response to Mable's death. Levin stubbornly insisted that he had no more personal reaction to Anne than he did to any other victim; he was merely a writer fighting against artistic suppression, as all writers must. In the middle 1950s, Dr. A. told him that she feared he was in danger of succumbing to a ruinous paranoia, and when he kept resisting her diagnosis, she suggested he consult someone else, perhaps a man. Levin, who blamed her for "failing with Mable" ("everyone failed with Mable"), agreed and consulted a Dr. Sulzberger.

As Levin tells it, Sulzberger, who was a maverick member of the German-Jewish newspaper family that owned the *New York Times*, treated him in 1957, at the time of his troubles with the dramatization of *Compulsion* and the beginning of the trial against Frank, Crawford, and Bloomgarden. Levin and Sulzberger focused on Levin's street terrors from childhood and spoke mostly about different ways of responding to persecution. Although Levin admired the doctor's knowledge of literary and theatrical matters, he felt their discussions were superficial and soon ended the treatment, remembering Sulzberger fondly for urging him to "fight with joy . . . enjoy the fight." "He thought," Levin wryly observes, that "he could turn me into an Irishman."

Around 1970, when he was having trouble writing *The Settlers*, Levin went to the third analyst, an elderly Polish Jew named Bychovsky. As he describes it:

> So . . . once more the rehearsal of early years, marriage and divorce, the suicide. The absorption in things Jewish, perhaps overcompensation for that first marriage to a gentile? And the second marriage to the daughter of a converted Jew, herself

baptized at birth. Rebellion, guilt, and hence my obstinacy
over the Jewish content of the Diary? And so the whole Anne
Frank story all over again in all its wanderings. (301)

According to Levin, Bychovsky eventually told him that all
artists are "somewhat" paranoid but that his essential problems
were quite a different thing from paranoia. "The enemies you
tell of are undoubtedly real. The question is, are they worth all
the trouble you give yourself over them?" (16). Bychovsky pre-
scribed Ritalin, which Levin felt helped him get on with and
finish his saga novel.

Shortly afterward, Levin went to the fourth analyst (a
woman identified as Dr. Erika) with one immediate objective:
he wished to be able to control his actions when *The Settlers*
was published, so as not to jeopardize its reception. With her he
explored his motives for wanting to renew the Anne Frank
campaign at the time of the publication of what could be his
major novel: Was it "the old masochism, the self-destructive
mechanism?" During the course of treatment they talked again
about his early life and relationship with his family: "My father,
the little tailor, my mother with her hysteria, my sisters, and
how Bess got herself a nice young Jewish doctor, and how her
Meyer and I became close friends" (21).

In a session with Dr. Erika an event occurred that Levin in
the memoir uses to create considerable emotional effect and
dramatic suspense. On the second page of the book, he
describes how a short time before he began writing, he was
telling his fourth analyst about an incident involving his sister
Bess on the very day that her husband died suddenly of a heart
attack in Chicago, which was also the last day of the Levin-

Frank trial in New York. He had told this story many times
before, but when he tried to utter the key words to Dr. Erika,
he choked, broke down in sobs, and could not get them out.
Placed at the very start of the narrative, the report is deliberately truncated, and the unspoken words become a clue to an
important mystery that is not in fact cleared up until 192 pages
later. (In *this* history it will be considered shortly.)

The brief but suggestive vignettes of many sessions with four
different analysts, woven into Levin's narrative without regard
to chronology or consistency, are essential to the book's impact
and meaning. On the most basic level, they often establish
sympathy for the teller. After all, he tried so often and so hard
to get help with his affliction—a trouble that is the outcome
of his idealistic concern for getting the story of the European
Jews faithfully told and for protecting the integrity of Anne
Frank's words. In addition to creating sympathy for himself,
Levin, in quick scenes from the psychiatric inner sanctum, dra-
matizes (with great novelistic flair) some of his most intimate
and intense feelings and gives the reader tantalizing glimpses of
four analysts and the analysand trying to understand the roots
and meaning of his fever. We see them, ever so fleetingly, discussing Levin's parents, his emotionally privileged childhood,
his early ambivalence toward Judaism, his marriages, first to a
gentile and then to the young Jewish daughter of an influential sculptor friend who had converted to Catholicism, his insecurities as a man and writer, his entering the concentration
camps, his subsequent identification with the fate of the Jews,
and much else.

The psychoanalytical vignettes let the memoirist reveal himself as seen by others and at the same time show him grappling

with theories and suppositions about his extravagant conduct. In the episodes that view the writer through the eyes of others, *The Obsession* takes on the qualities of a richly comic novel, a miniature *Portnoy's Complaint*—boisterous, prodigal, uncomfortably and insinuatingly funny. His antagonists are imagined on the Westchester estate of Nathan Straus, tearing to shreds the "Russian-Jewish nobody," the "scheming, greedy incompetent writer," who had gotten his "hooks on poor Otto in Europe." The Broadway crowd scoffs at "that boob Levin," who naively signed away his rights when he was told it would be in the best interests of Anne if a world-famous playwright did the dramatization of the *Diary*. Some people mock him as a red-baiting McCarthyite spotting Communists under every bed: "Call the asylum. A crazy Jewish writer is making false accusations" (87). Others dismiss his disappointment as crudely commercial: "Come on, Levin, aren't you really sore because you had your hands on a 'property' that was worth millions, and let it be taken away from you" (37). Still others, more benign, say the *Diary* is doing so much good, "Why tarnish the image? Perhaps Levin wasn't handled right from the start, but why let that interfere with a play that is loved all over the world . . . a play that has done wonders against anti-Semitism? He lost out that's all. Well, he's being paid" (203). Many friends avoid him; others look on at parties with wonderment and compassion as the irrepressibly aggrieved Levin pours out the story for the thousandth time, desperately pulling papers from his pockets with "proof" of his wildest assertions. And even his doctors occasionally chide him for his excess: "So I had been to the justice figures. Run to papa. Run to mama. Run to the rabbi" (138).

In the other scenes from the psychiatric sessions, we see Levin responding to speculations about shame, father fixations, Jewish righteousness, Jewish self-hatred, and conjectures about his need for punishment (as a failed husband, for the suicide of Mable and the troubles in his marriage to Tereska, or as a survivor who guiltily identifies with the murdered Jews of Europe). We see him questioning why he clings to his sickness, why he seems to look for excuses to prolong the nasty confrontation with his enemies. For all the wild comedy of some of the psychiatric vignettes, the sight of Levin struggling with the most profound issues raised by his character and conduct is both disturbing and surprisingly invigorating; he can be a clownish figure, but he is also at times a courageous old battler: Levin agonistes, affirming above all his commitment to justice and to the continuity of the Jews, in spite of the high personal cost.

As the narrative of *The Obsession* unfolds, Levin comes to reject psychoanalysis even as he submits himself to it ("Self-entrapment?" "No, too pat, not everything is masochism"); and near the end of the book, he asks:

> What is really known of the mysterious process of analysis? Some detective-story-like cases we know, cases in which the clue came in a word, a dream, an incident recovered from prememory, and a trauma was dissolved away. And yes, I did know a few persons who had been helped by analysis. I had in the past in some way myself been helped by Dr. A, mostly in the early sessions in Jerusalem. Now I was stuck. . . . (288)

Levin's rejection of psychoanalysis can be seen of course as yet another confirmation of the commanding power of his obsession, but it is also accompanied by a more serious and consequential refusal—a refusal of analysis in the broader meaning of the word. Throughout the memoir, he remains unwavering in his belief that his *Anne Frank* was rejected and suppressed for political reasons by Stalinists and anti-Zionists, and he is unable to allow the possibility that his opponents had motives other than the ones he accuses them of having (whether commercial, aesthetic, or something else). To substantiate a political plot, he offers hearsay and suspicions but no documentation that can count as hard, conclusive evidence. Late in the memoir, he reports a 1972 conversation with Francis Price, in which the former Doubleday editor claimed to have heard Otto Frank admit that he was told Levin's play could not be done because it was "too Jewish." But the alleged conversation between Price and Frank (reported twenty years afterwards) is shrouded in mystery and difficult to evaluate. Even if it did take place, it cannot be taken as confirmation of a widespread intrigue.

Levin's extended description of the conduct of Frank, Crawford, Bloomgarden, and the lawyers at Paul, Weiss, moreover, is often marked by inaccuracies, distortions, and self-justifying rearrangements of what actually happened between 1950 and 1970. Because he reads the past through the lens of a later-arrived-at conspiracy theory, Levin provides an account that is mistaken in many of its details and unconvincing in its overall emphasis and final judgment. Take, for instance, his opening description of the source of his troubles:

> The case in court had arisen from my difficulties over *The Diary of a Young Girl* by Anne Frank. Continuing from my

war correspondent experiences my intense absorption with
the Holocaust, I had helped Otto Frank to secure publication
for the Diary in English, and had dramatized it. Mr. Frank
had come to New York, to see to the authenticity of the
staging, but at that point the prominent playwright Lillian
Hellman and her producer, Kermit Bloomgarden, had persuaded him, he told me, that as a novelist I was no dramatist,
that my work was unstageworthy, that it had to be discarded
and another version written.

From the start I had strongly suspected that some doctrinaire formulation rather than pure dramatic judgment had
caused Miss Hellman's attack on my play, and after the
substitute work written under her tutelage was produced, I
became convinced that I had been barred because I and my
work were in her political view "too Jewish." (8–9)

In fact, Levin did not "help secure" the publication of the
Diary (although he was instrumental in its great success). Otto
Frank did not come to New York "to see to the authenticity of
the staging"; he had been invited by Doubleday in June 1952
to help resolve the dispute between the firm and Levin on the
choice of the adapter. When Frank finally did arrive in September, Doubleday was long out of the picture, but he was still
waiting for Cheryl Crawford to decide whether or not Levin
would be the playwright. It was far too early to discuss questions of staging, which in fact Frank was to have nothing to do
with in any case. Hellman and Bloomgarden did not persuade
Frank to reject Levin's script; Crawford did. At that point,
Hellman had advised Crawford but was intensely preoccupied
with her own affairs: the fallout from her recent testimony to
the House Un-American Activities Committee, troubles with

the Internal Revenue Service, and a commitment to direct a revival of *The Children's Hour*. Bloomgarden was not yet involved. Levin did not at that time express any suspicion that "some doctrinaire formulation" caused Hellman to attack his play; in fact, it is unlikely that he knew she had discussed his script with Crawford until several years later. His specific accusations about ideology, de-Judaizing, and sinister manipulations were not made for at least three years after the refusal of his script.

Other errors occur elsewhere in the memoir. Levin writes that the crucial Goodrich and Hackett article, "Diary of the *Diary*" (which led him to solidify his suspicions about Hellman), was published at the time of the Broadway opening of the play, when it actually appeared twelve months later. Reporting on other happenings at the time of the opening, Levin contends that he had not then considered and did not take legal action. But he had begun talking with attorneys nearly two years earlier and actually started litigation in December 1954, ten months before *The Diary of Anne Frank* opened at the Cort Theatre. Some of these errors may seem minor, but taken together (and with other inaccuracies) they make up a significant pattern of misrepresentation and seriously damage his case.

In the last analysis, then, Levin's memoir, written *de profundis*, can be said to succeed brilliantly as an anatomy of the dynamics of obsession, but to fail as an exposé and a cure. Levin does not prove his charge of conspiracy, nor does he rid himself of his compulsive preoccupation. In fact, he ends by reaffirming his disturbance as an expression of aspects of his best self: a lifelong passion for justice and a love of the pure in heart. The incident about his sister Bess that had been mysteri-

ously held for revelation at the close is now carefully positioned
to support and celebrate this view. The words the sobbing
Levin could not say to Dr. Erika had been spoken by his sister
Bess Steinberg. On the last day of the Levin-Frank trial in New
York, a message arrived that Meyer Steinberg had died of a
heart attack in Chicago, but given the climactic moment in
court, Levin had to delay leaving and missed the funeral. Soon
after he arrived, however, standing in the Steinbergs' kitchen,
he received a phone call from his lawyer reporting the jury's
verdict in his favor. At that moment, his sister said: "I know it
was my Meyer that did it. He went straight to heaven and
asked for justice for you."

Levin reflects on this incident in the last pages of *The Obsession*:

> It was for the pure in heart that I had wept. For those like
> my brother-in-law Meyer Steinberg, the good little doctor, for
> their departure, for the horror of their absence in the world.
> I had wept because of Bess's belief, and her Meyer's belief in
> me, and in justice from God, in that world where one en-
> counters only betrayals and hostility from so many, even from
> those who should be most understanding. And so I was
> choked with my grief for such love, the rare love of the pure
> in heart that still manifests itself at times in our besmirched
> and murderous world of man.
>
> Was it because Anne Frank, too, had symbolized for me
> the pure in heart? (311–12)

Levin then ends *The Obsession* with an account of his own
visit to the Anne Frank House in Amsterdam and his perception that even there the meaning of her life and diary was falsified by the compulsion to universalize and deny the particular

fate of the Jews—a disillusionment he uses to warn readers again of the perils of political manipulation and to reaffirm his commitment to fight against it:

> Thus there developed my justice obsession. The obsessive
> aspect is perhaps now more manageable, but I would not
> want to lose its concomitant, the search for justice. Yes,
> I cling to it. . . . (316)

Despite the rhetorical excess and moralizing, the aspects of Levin's best self (his passion for justice and the continuity of Jewish life) do come through in these closing pages; but so do the qualities for which he was so often criticized and belittled: his relentless, often unsubstantiated attacks on those with whom he disagreed; his embittered self-righteousness and self-justification; and, of course, his obsessiveness (now viewed by him as a virtue). The vivid complexity of the demon-ridden self-portrait that Levin paints in *The Obsession* was the subject of many of the reviews in the weeks after the publication of the book; but so were the singularity, extravagance, and dubiousness of his charges of conspiracy. In a meticulous, widely discussed piece for the *New York Times Book Review*, Victor S. Navasky (lawyer, author, and later editor of the *Nation*) begins by trying to sort out the historical facts and define the obsession in what he calls this "disturbing, strangely involving book." He first lays out the way Levin saw himself as a triple victim of the upper-class German-Jewish Establishment, of Stalinism (which in 1952 was engaged in an annihilation campaign against Jewish writers), and of reverse-McCarthyism; and then he frames the basic questions raised by Levin's compelling narrative: "Am I victim or am I crazy? And whichever I am, is it right to suppress a play which . . . was called 'infinitely superior to the Hackett version'. . . . and anyway, doesn't art have its own moral imperatives which supervene contracts, legal agreements, technicalities negotiated under stress, especially when that art encapsulates the mystery of the Holocaust?"

Whatever the answers to these questions may be, Navasky continues, "one will not find them in a book whose power comes precisely from the fact that Levin sees the world from the cave of his preoccupations, call them what you will, and what he is describing are shadows on his wall." Nonetheless, Navasky goes on to ask a series of questions aimed at probing Levin's account of his victimization, and he concludes by expressing doubts about the existence of a conspiracy: "Not even the weighted evidence Levin has provided . . . convinces me that if the producers thought they could either make money or get strong notices that they would not have gone ahead with it." Nor, according to Navasky, does Levin (in spite of his superb discussion of the atmosphere of the McCarthy period) satisfactorily document his contention that Hellman opposed his play for ideological rather than dramaturgical reasons (3 February 1974, 5–6).

Navasky's review provoked many letters, two of which the *Times Book Review* printed: one from Levin, the other from Kermit Bloomgarden. Levin challenges Navasky on several points, notably the matter of documentation, repeating the account of his conversation with Francis Price in which Otto Frank is quoted as admitting he was told by the producer that the play could not be staged because it was too Jewish. Strongly protesting Navasky's efforts "to whitewash the Hellman contingent while expressing sympathy for my ordeal," Levin ends by insisting that he wrote *The Obsession*, not because of the Anne Frank affair alone, but because it is "an amazing example of hidden censorship and may serve as a warning. All I ask is that it be read." In his letter Bloomgarden expresses gratitude to Navasky for seeing "through many of Mr. Levin's deceptions" but insists they are greater than the reviewer could possibly know. He offers his own account of the history of the rejection of Levin's play and goes on to call the writer's belief that there is a political plot against him "total, ugly nonsense. No politics were ever involved. Nor did any of us ever think of the play or ourselves as 'too Jewish' or not Jewish enough." At the close, Bloomgarden calls Levin's "obsession" a cloak for "vindictive falsehoods and old-fashioned red-baiting under a pious claim of noble motives," and he expresses shock that Simon and Schuster would publish a book whose contents they knew were based on a contractual violation and whose attacks "on innocent people they could have checked" (3 March 1974).

The severe hostility expressed here continued as long as all the parties to the controversy lived. In the last seven years of his life, Levin wrote two long novels, *The Harvest* (a 1978 sequel to *The Settlers*) and *The Architect* (based on the life of Frank Lloyd Wright and published just after Levin died in 1981); but he also kept up his protest activities to the very end. He urged friends to form a group called the Committee for Historical Honesty to raise money to help publicize his cause. He continued to petition various professional and Jewish organizations (PEN, ACLU, ADL, AJC, etc.). He spoke often with lawyers (including Leonard Schroeter, Edward Katz, Arnold Forster, and Shale D. Stiller) to find out whether he had any legal avenues to explore, mainly on the grounds that he was deceived

when he signed the settlement agreement in 1959. He tried also
to gather testimony from members of his Committee of Three
to confirm his belief that they had never met. Attorneys, however, told him that his having signed the settlement agreement
in full consultation with his lawyer made going to court risky
and most likely futile. Schroeter, a friend who admired Levin's
courage and accomplishments, also reminded him of the emotional and fiscal costs of litigation. Shale Stiller advised him not
to attack the 1959 assignment of rights but rather to try to persuade Paul, Weiss to allow his play to be done because participants in the quarrel were dead or old, and he was not looking
for financial reward. Otto Frank died in 1980, but in the same
year Levin raised the possibility of pursuing a class-action suit
for the Jewish people's right to a faithful dramatic version of
Anne Frank's book; and he continued to encourage community groups to request permission to put on his play as a test
case. Most approaches to Frank's attorneys, however, were met
by letters rehearsing the history and asserting that Levin's
claims had no validity, that he violated written agreements, and
that the present copyright situation was too complicated to
think about granting production rights. To some inquirers,
Paul, Weiss also wrote that Levin engaged in outrageously con-
frontational behavior and venomously accused Otto Frank and
others of being anti-Semites, Communists, and literary mur-
derers. On occasion, some of the attorneys also tried to convince Levin's supporters to be patient and wait a little longer.
When the participants in the controversy were dead, they said,
there was likely to be little opposition to the performance of
the disputed play—an attempt at consolation that only further
infuriated the writer.

In 1979 (the fiftieth anniversary of the birth of Anne Frank and the year of revivals of the Goodrich and Hackett *Diary*), Levin mounted his last major protest effort, circulating many hundreds of copies of "The Suppression of Anne Frank," a document he called an ethical will. He asked recipients to create a chain letter by sending it on to friends and associates. In 1980, after reading *The Ghost Writer*, Philip Roth's brilliant fantasy on the Anne Frank story, Levin told friends that he resisted such "intellectualized toying with the material," although he admitted that the basic invention of an Anne Frank alive in the Berkshires should be taken as the fictional Nathan Zuckerman's, not Roth's. In April of 1981, a few months before he died, he read about a current scandal involving an unearned Pulitzer Prize and wrote to Richard T. Baker, the administrator of the program, asking him to reconsider the 1956 award to Goodrich and Hackett. Baker answered that there was no likelihood whatsoever of any reconsideration of the award, since *The Diary of Anne Frank* was a legitimate entry of a very moving play. "Your quarrel," he told Levin, "is with the authors and producers, not with us" (28 April 1981, BU). In the last weeks of his life, Levin also wrote about the Pulitzer award to Martin Peretz at the *New Republic*, Benjamin Bradlee at the *Washington Post*, and other people in journalism and publishing.

In these efforts, Levin was met by occasional approval but mostly by silence, apathy, resistance, or at best sympathetic efforts to get him to give up what almost everyone else felt was by then a lost cause. From time to time, someone tried to support his crusade in print. In 1976, Benno Weiser Varon, a diplomat and journalist, created a stir with a long polemical essay, "The Haunting of Meyer Levin" (*Midstream*, August–September, 7–23). Varon, who received most of his information and his basic interpretation of the case from Levin, denounced Lillian Hellman, the New York Marxist intellectual clique around *Partisan Review*, and the Epstein empire at the *New York Review of Books* for the neglect and denigration of Levin's major writings on Jewish life. The article generated a lot of mail both pro and con Levin, but it offered no new evidence or corroboration of its familiar claims. In August 1980, to celebrate Levin's upcoming seventy-fifth birthday, the *Jewish Week–American Examiner* ran an article by Philip Hochstein on the controversy, under the heading "De-Judaizing Holocaust Is Major Issue," and they reprinted "The Suppression of Anne Frank." Again, the details and the main thrust came from the accounts Levin had been offering for more than twenty years.

Levin's last protests and the efforts and articles supporting him had little appreciable effect on what he most wanted to accomplish: to get the prohibition lifted on his play and to convince people that there had been an outrage perpetrated on him and on the Jewish people. When he died in July 1981, most obituaries described his many accomplishments as a novelist and journalist over half-a-century and paid tribute to his passionate dedication to writing positively about Jewish life. Nearly every one mentioned the long, bitter conflict over the dramatization of Anne Frank's *Diary*, a battle he was considered to have lost.

> 5
Don Quixote
and the Star of David

IN 1991, TEN YEARS AFTER the death of her husband, Tereska Torres published in Paris *Les maisons hantées de Meyer Levin*, a memoir-novel in which she depicts what it felt like and meant for her to share the life of an obsession-gripped writer for nearly all of their thirty-three-year marriage. Structured more like a prose poem than either a conventional memoir or novel, the book is a striking phantasmagorical confession: very short sections of intense lyrical recollection mingle with factual narrative, passages of reverie, conjectures about cause, descriptive sketches, and feverish dreams. From these highly charged, intimate segments come many suggestive images and ideas that provide further insight into a consideration of the private and public significance of Levin's involvement with Anne Frank's book and life, and especially his role in helping to shape American attitudes toward the Holocaust.

The picture of Levin that emerges from Torres's work is partial but exceptionally distinct. We see him first at thirty-eight, a handsome journalist in wartime London, dancing with a

woman half his age who is a volunteer with the Women's Army
Corps of de Gaulle's Free French Forces in exile. He had
known Tereska Szwarc as a small child in Paris, when he was
friends with her sculptor father, Marek, a Polish Jew secretly
converted to Catholicism. Now, to her astonishment, with the
sounds of bombs in the background, Levin suddenly proposes
marriage; and she, alarmed by his romantic recklessness and
involved with another man, resists him. He woos her with
ardent stories about a fateful resemblance to his first teenage
flame and with the gift of a Chinese silk nightgown he had
been carrying around the globe. She is intrigued but wants a
love that would free, not devour her; and they part. She marries
Georges Torres, within months is widowed by the war, has a
child, meets Levin again, joins him on a trip to ancestral
Poland, and plays an active role in the clandestine, inspirational
filming of *The Illegals.* In the spring of 1948 they marry.

In Torres's finely etched presentation, the Levin of these
years is a captivating figure. When they met in 1943, she had
known of his reputation as a novelist, foreign correspondent,
and founder of a marionette theater in Chicago that staged
Strindberg and O'Neill. He had been with Hemingway in
Madrid, had had an affair with a well-known black actress, and
was about to get divorced from someone else. After the war
ended, she saw him as an artist, activist, and lover: a romantic
idealist for whom the word "impossible" had the same meaning
as "dangerous." We get scenes of the steadfast Levin reporting
on the Nazi destruction of European Jewry and laboring to aid
the survivors, giving everything, receiving nothing. Torres
reveals him strolling, buying presents, smiling shyly and
sweetly, bright with the look she remembers from a photograph

of him as a boy of nine: "a look full of the hope of a marvelous future that he believed he was promised." Then comes the fateful day in Antibes when she gives him the French translation of the Dutch girl's diary, after which everything is elegiacally divided into two epochs—Before Anne Frank, After Anne Frank.

After 1950, there are periods of happiness associated with the excitement of meeting the dead child's father, reviewing and then adapting the *Diary*; and later, with times of solitary creation, escaping into books, being rewarded and honored for his writing. He travels, loves his wife, plays with their children, enjoys friendships, and tries to build a new life half the year in Israel. But for most of Torres's book, we view the man familiar from the Anne Frank tribulations described earlier in this study: an aspiring, driven combatant among producers, agents, lawyers, theater people, fighting real and imagined enemies. Torres, who does not believe her husband was cheated of his rights and victimized by a conspiracy, is sympathetic to his ideals and sufferings but not to his emotional outbursts and unrestrained behavior, and she records fierce quarrels at home: about tactics, legalities, literary and cultural values, and the effects of the prolonged controversy—the rage and rancor, the misunderstandings—on their marriage, the children, and his creative work. Often, she tries to convince him to give up for his own good a hopeless, self-destructive fight that will ruin his health and career; and she keeps insisting that it is not Anne Frank's words he is fighting for, but his own, since her words can still be read in the *Diary*, even if they have been falsified on the stage. Although she admits he has been badly treated, she accuses him at different moments of inordinate ambition and cruelty; and she protests to friends who, thinking they are offering support, feed him hearsay to arouse his suspicions. Throughout the memoir, Torres gives us glimpses of their restless private lives during the Anne Frank years, the most vivid of which is her sketch of a recurring nightmare in which a fat, ugly, naked girl lies in bed between herself and her husband— an image she comes to recognize as the distended form of Anne Frank that Levin's fixation has placed between them. She recalls speaking often of the dead girl as her rival and challenging him to choose, just as Levin had come to think of Otto Frank as his rival in an Oedipal struggle over the dead daughter. Once, in the heat of a fight about enemies and competitors, he cried out, "If you really love me, you will take a gun and kill Otto Frank."

Also memorable are scenes in which Torres records efforts to get her husband to talk about what Anne Frank signified to him. Once, driving between Tel Aviv and Haifa, she brings up the old subject. The car swerves, tires screech, Levin roars: "She signifies nothing to me, nothing. What are you insinuating? . . . Shut up, I don't identify with Anne Frank. I fight the way I would fight to defend any censured, suppressed writer . . . there is no other reason." Throughout the book, Torres reports her husband's insistence at different periods that Anne Frank the child didn't mean anything to him, that he was always fighting a battle for or against *something else*: for morality, Jewish identity, free expression, justice; against de-Judaizing the *Diary*, blacklisting, suppressing art, injustice.

Although Torres sometimes compares the Anne Frank disputes to a marionette show in which the strings are hopelessly snarled and the meaning never clear, she does speculate about the possible origins of her husband's fixation. Reflecting, not arguing, she emphasizes two subjects: the particularities of his Jewish childhood in Chicago and his adolescent romance with a girl named Doris. Struck, as everyone is, by Levin's confession in *In Search* that his dominant early memory is the fear and shame of being a Jew, Torres sees one significant source of his troubles in his having been treated as the precocious, privileged child by anxious immigrant parents. The elder Levins, notably the overbearing mother, put up with his capriciousness and usually gave in to him when he became angry. The spoiled boy grew up to be at once self-confident, ambitious, and insecure, eager to succeed but, because of his ambivalence toward his parents and background, unable to deal satisfactorily with persistent feelings of inferiority and with the normal setbacks of everyday life. Bad luck, opposition, and criticism were unexpected and seen by the zealous but self-doubting Levin mainly as resistance to his talent and his Jewishness motivated by widespread hostility, ultimately perceived to be conspiratorial.

For Torres, the teenage romance is equally important in understanding the roots of Levin's attachment to the dead girl's book. At fifteen, he met and was infatuated with a girl, the sister of a male friend, with whom he then had an intense but unconsummated relationship for more than six years. Influenced by her status-conscious bourgeois family, Doris rejected the "undependable" young artist and married a mutual friend, who became a doctor and later figured in *The Old Bunch* and *Citizens*. Over the next forty years, Levin and Doris occasionally met or corresponded and kept up an unspoken fantasy that they might have been each other's predestined "true," but necessarily lost, love. (As time passed, he, at least, seemed to prefer the idea of Doris to the reality.) In Torres's view, this fascination with shadowy conceptions of the one fated first love and the traumatic influence of lost romance made Levin particularly susceptible to the power of his encounter with Anne Frank, the quintessential innocent lost girl. Torres does not explore the biographical fact that after his separation from the Jewish Doris, Levin had a series of unsuccessful affairs with mostly gentile women and eventually married a non-Jew and then Torres herself, the baptized daughter of Jewish converts to Catholicism, whom he first met and admired when she was a four-year-old child. Both his wives were very young; each had been married before and had been widowed within months of her wedding. But this history clearly reinforces the centrality of his image of Doris—the idealized woman he never possessed—in understanding Levin's preoccupation with Anne Frank.

From these speculations about childhood and adolescence, Torres draws a compelling portrait of Levin as an impetuous romantic idealist haunted by lost and dead women and by the loss of other people's innocence, and his own. His encounter with the death camps and his subsequent desire to bear witness to the sufferings of the guiltless six million is seen as inevitably connected to his fundamental idealism and innocence, traits that link him for her in ironical ways to one of the most celebrated of possessed romantic idealists, Don Quixote. In a remarkable sequence midway through the memoir, Torres describes going alone on Broadway to see the old film of S. Anski's famous play *The Dybbuk*, which provoked in her a near hallucinatory series of reflections about the possibility that the soul of Anne Frank had inhabited her husband's body the day he looked into the mass graves at Bergen-Belsen. Brooding about possession and exorcism, she asks why Levin had been sent to defend the affirmations of Jewish identity written by Anne Frank in the Amsterdam annex and why one diary page about suffering should have assumed such momentous importance, causing him to spend thirty years defending her words. Addressing her husband with a mix of love and despair, she asks: "*Don Quichotte, les ailes de ton moulin sont en forme d'é-toile de David. Pourquoi?*" (82). Pondering the vital question why the wings of his windmill were shaped like the Star of David, Torres circles back to Levin's own confession that his dominant memory from childhood was the fear and shame of being Jewish.[1]

In many ways, the image of Don Quixote and the Star of David does have potency and suggestiveness as a gloss on Levin's thirty-year engagement with Anne Frank's life and book, and it is also useful in beginning to assess his contributions to an expanding American awareness of the Holocaust in the 1950s and afterwards. Levin's romantic impetuosity was from early on one of the dominant features of his personality. His announcement at nine that he would be a writer, like Dreiser or Dostoyevsky; his garish adolescent stories that turned on dismemberment and a longing for punishment; his postgraduation trip to Europe at nineteen, in which he looked not only for adventure but also for a larger surrogate commu-

---

1. For another provocative argument about Levin's troubled relationship to his own Jewishness, see Sander Gilman's "The Dead Child Speaks: Reading *The Diary of Anne Frank*," in *Jewish Self-Hatred*, 345–60. Gilman speaks of Levin's involvement with Anne Frank's book as "one of the most complex creations of a projection of self-hatred by a twentieth-century Jewish writer" (346).

nity of writers and artists to substitute for what he felt to be the constrictions of family, school, and journalism in Chicago—these expressions of his romantic bent have already been mentioned.

This inclination to interpret reality in terms of his own passionate needs and aspirations was also clearly expressed during the late 1920s, when he wrote a mystical novel, *He, Israel* (which has never been published). Here, a young American Jew is jolted into self-awareness as he comes to recognize the distance between himself and his upper-class gentile girlfriend. Setting off on a spiritual journey, he travels through Europe and eventually arrives in Palestine, where he identifies the Jewish people itself with the Messiah and comes to see the return of the Jews to Eretz Israel as the completion of all that had been embodied in the figure of the personal redeemer. Levin's actual discovery of Palestine had been almost accidental (he was asked by the *Menorah Journal* to write about the opening of the Hebrew University in 1925), but it was an exhilarating revelation that fed his appetite for heroism. In the lives of the early Zionist settlers he found an energy and purpose—a vibrant new idealism—that spoke to his craving for a grand affirmation. It also, however, unnerved him, for he had already decided that he wanted to be a major American writer, and when his first two novels were accepted for publication, he left the kibbutz, where he had lived for three months in 1927, to pursue his career back home. (He returned to the kibbutz two years later, but again his stay was brief.) The evolving decision to try to be a bicultural writer—to speak to America about the Jews in Palestine and vice versa—was also a lofty gesture, and the writing of *Yehuda* (1931) and the compiling of Hasidic stories in *The Golden Mountain* (1932) were admirably bold (if perhaps quixotic) ventures to undertake at the start of a worldwide depression.

Certainly the most consequential of such decisions was his resolve in 1945, after entering Ohrdruf, Buchenwald, and Bergen-Belsen, to bear witness to the fate of the European Jews—an aspiration that was itself noble but posed complex questions for him about his own Jewishness. Encountering the camps was traumatic for many reasons. The visceral terror of discovery itself was heightened by Levin's own history. In some ways, the experience seemed to confirm his lifelong feelings of inferiority and his fright: Might this in fact be what the world wanted to do to the Jews? Could it even be a punishment that was deserved? Yet at the same time, the encounter authenticated Levin's desire to solidify his connection to the Jewish people and to work for their survival and future renewal. The shock clarified for good his previously uncertain attitude toward the ancient injunction in Psalm 137 against the desertion of one's people: "If I forget thee, O Jerusalem, may my right hand forget its cunning." The trauma also galvanized him as a writer and filmmaker, and the work he did for the next three years (the battlefield dispatches, the filming of *My Father's House* and *The Illegals*) reveals some of the finest aspects of his character: courage, devotion, magnanimity, imaginative daring, and a passion for justice. Although conditions under which the filming was done (the lack of money and equipment, the plight of the survivors, the threat of injury and arrest) now make the results seem rough, the works were among the valuable post-

war efforts to alert people to the consequences of Nazi barbarism.[2]

Levin's initial enthusiastic commitment to Anne Frank's
Diary in 1950 was also a product of his romantic idealism, but
of much else as well. Coming at a time when his need to bear
witness was profound and the future of his literary career wor-
risome, the book looked like both a great revelation and a fine
opportunity. In the girl's vibrant renderings of event and emotion, Levin perceived what Philip Roth was later to call "the
incarnation of millions of unlived years robbed from the murdered Jews"—an embodiment for which he had been search-
ing for so long. He felt, too, that her work might be the creative occasion that would make his reputation and bring
financial security, especially if it could be staged and filmed as
well as published. Levin's conception of a girl's diary as the possible instrument of his moral and economic fulfillment is itself
an imposing romantic idea and is central to an understanding
of both his determination to spread the story of the fate of the
Jews and his long Anne Frank ordeal.

The fervor and high stakes involved in his commitment to
the *Diary* led him simultaneously to recognize and to exagger-
ate its value and importance. As keenly as any of its first readers, he saw the uniqueness of the book as a particular human
document *and* as a representative story of the mass destruction
of a people simply for being who they were. With his early promotional efforts and his brilliant pieces in the *New York Times*

---

2. In 1985, the historian Robert Abzug paid tribute to Levin's contributions by titling his authoritative book on Americans and the liberation of the
Nazi concentration camps *Inside the Vicious Heart,* a phrase from *In Search.*

Book Review, Congress Weekly, and elsewhere, he contributed more than anyone else to its extraordinary success in America. He also took the full measure of the child: her wit and irrepressibility, the dynamic unfolding of her character under duress, her dawning perceptions about being a Jew and a writer, and the anguish of her fate at Auschwitz and Bergen-Belsen.

Yet, at the same time, the intensity of his dedication caused him to argue that the stature of the book as symbolic narrative was in excess of what it actually represented, thus contributing to the questionable mythologizing of Anne Frank that was so prevalent during the 1950s. A fourteen-year-old Dutch girl could not possibly be "the voice of the six million"; no single person could. She was a privileged, well-liked teenager whose diary revealed wonderful powers of observation and pleasing self-display; but only at stark (if unforgettable) moments did it hint at the nature and implications of what the Nazis were doing day after day to the Jews. A girl's journal about her family in hiding that ends with an editor's note about their fate cannot convey the full actuality or meaning of a catastrophe in which millions of individuals and much of their culture were obliterated in camps built and operated by one of the great nations of Europe. Although Levin said that the survivors were like people who had acquired the hearing "of a whole range of tones outside normal human hearing," he insisted on choosing a story *within* the range of normal hearing to communicate an unprecedented historical horror.[3] The impulse in the decade

3. The same point is made by Sidra Ezrahi in her fine book *By Words Alone: The Holocaust in Literature,* 201–2.

after the war to gain some consolation by turning an ordinary, innocent victim into a symbolic Holocaust martyr and a cultural icon (a Jewish Anne of the Beatitudes) was probably irresistible, and Levin felt it to a degree, though far less than Frances Goodrich, Albert Hackett, Garson Kanin, and a great many others. But it was a dubious kind of consolation. Anne Frank's spirit lives on because of the accidental survival of her luminous book; the overwhelming majority of murdered Jews are anonymous as individuals and exist now only as part of an appalling number.

Levin's first reactions to Cheryl Crawford's rejection of his play in October 1952 also should be understood in light of just how much he had invested in the adaptation and what he felt was at stake. For a good part of two years he had promoted and written about the *Diary*, soliciting hundreds of editors, agents, filmmakers, and others to interest them in its prospects. When the book was finally published and his review helped make it an instant bestseller, he (like everyone else) was quickly caught up in the excitement about its surprising success and seemingly unlimited future. All his writing life, he had struggled against reluctant and resistant responses to his work; now, he saw an opportunity for a moral and financial success that could give him the preeminence as a writer on Jewish subjects that he had been trying to establish for decades.

Writing by and about Jews, moreover, was moving slowly from the periphery to the center of the postwar cultural scene. A new generation of very talented Jewish writers was emerging. Saul Bellow had published *Dangling Man* in 1944, and five years later his disturbing novel about anti-Semitism, *The Vic-*

tim; and he was just about to become famous with *The Adventures of Augie March* (1953), the first of his popular Yiddish-inflected American novels. Delmore Schwartz, Isaac Rosenfeld, Paul Goodman, and Bernard Malamud were all beginning to attract attention for their fresh stories of contemporary Jewish life; and in a more popular vein, so was Herman Wouk.[4] To further complicate Levin's situation, the younger writers (as different as they were) were more critical of their subject matter, more assimilationist in temperament, and more radical in their use of new narrative forms. Several of them also had the advantage of being associated with *Partisan Review*, one of the most highly regarded, influential magazines of the period; whereas Levin, having been mostly in Europe between 1942 and 1950, was a marginal figure on the literary scene with no base at a journal, publishing house, or university. *Citizens*, his last novel on an American subject, had appeared in 1940, and his earlier work (with the exception of *The Old Bunch*) was neglected or dismissed as old-fashioned. His association with Zionism and his aggressive anticommunism set him off from some of the dominant left-wing ideologies of the time, and his reputation for contentiousness further alienated him from writers and publishing people who "mattered." Despite these obstacles and concerns, he believed that a successful theatrical adaptation of a

4. Levin himself commented on one aspect of the trend in a piece he wrote for *Commentary* in October 1953, titled "The East Side Gangsters of the Paperbacks: The 'Jewish' Novels That Millions Buy." He objected to the lurid portraits of Jews in increasingly popular mass-market fiction by such writers as Harold Robbins and Irving Shulman.

notable book about the European Jews (a subject most American writers were hesitant to touch or willing to treat only indirectly) might now still have the impact he wished.

The sudden refusals and rebuffs in the fall of 1952 fed Levin's increasing disillusionment and anger. Crawford's unexpected rejection of the script as "unplayable," the failure of the fourteen additional producers to express interest in staging it, the confrontations with top-line lawyers, the signing away of rights to the material, the prospect of Carson McCullers's being named adapter, the swift deterioration of his friendship with Otto Frank, the assignment of the option to Bloomgarden, and the hiring of Goodrich and Hackett—all these developments precipitated Levin's loss of what he felt to be the grandest literary opportunity of his life: the chance to be a spokesman for the Jewish dead, to get a play on Broadway, and to achieve a success that might establish his reputation as an important writer.

Levin's one defense against all these difficulties was his faith in the potential of his own work. He had written a serious adaptation that aimed to convey the complexity of the *Diary* and its context. If it was a preliminary script—unpolished, too long, static in places, occasionally preachy—its problems could be solved in collaboration with more experienced theater people. The negative responses of Crawford and the other producers could be attributed to shortsightedness, timidity, box-office anxiety, bad advice, and worries over his disagreements with Otto Frank and others. Levin's belief in the potential of his own play, although sometimes undermined by doubt, was at the heart of nearly everything he did in the disputes over the next twenty-nine years, and much of that faith was justifiable.

Assessing Levin's play now is difficult because there really is no one play. The draft of 1952, various subsequent revisions, the 1966 version staged by Peter Frye, the volume privately printed a year later, and the texts used in Boston and elsewhere in the 1980s and 1990s make it necessary to speak of his drama as a blueprint or working text for a production. Seen this way, it was and remains a play that can be successfully performed by a director and cast willing to flesh out a faithful, affecting dramatic version of the *Diary*. It is unlikely that it would have been (or ever will be) a popular work, or a staple of the repertoire, but it has an authenticity and enough theatrical virtues to merit staging.

As Mordecai S. Kaplan demonstrated in his 1983 and 1991 productions at the Lyric Stage in Boston, Levin's *Anne Frank* can move an audience and earn praise. Many playgoers and reviewers testified that in Kaplan's staging, the work came closer than the celebrated Broadway version to embodying the essence of the *Diary* (as Levin's play had done when Peter Frye directed it in Tel Aviv in 1966). Working in a shoe-box-sized playing space, the Lyric Stage company was able to communicate with great effectiveness the fright and claustrophobia of the inhabitants entombed in the hiding place, and much of the meaning of what happened to them there and afterward. That the two families and Dussel are Jewish is fundamental to that meaning. The Germans persecuted them for only one reason, and this single fact shapes their response to their predicament. Margot, a sketchy figure in the Goodrich and Hackett *Diary*, is filled out here, especially when she talks about wanting to become a nurse in Palestine after the war. Anne, too, mentions her Zionist bent and reflects at length about Jewish identity, but she finally affirms a more universalist point of view: she wants to be something "in the world," do "something for mankind," without masking her Jewishness. The elder Franks are shown discussing the implications of their assimilation, wondering if the present dilemma has anything to do with their not giving their daughters a traditional Jewish education, and thus offending God. Edith Frank is portrayed as devout and even a bit mystical, whereas her husband is a decent, honorable, caring man, but nothing like the paragon of strength, domestic responsibility, and stoic virtue that he is in the better-known play. Peter Van Daan is also characterized principally in terms of his perplexity about his Jewishness.

Equally important to the presentation of the theme of Jewish identity is Levin's insistence that the audience never be allowed to ignore the monstrousness of the Nazi assault. The narrator, Koophuis, charts the progress of "the final solution" year by year, and the family members often talk about roundups, arrests, deportations, death marches, and gassings. If Anne is portrayed as the life-affirming girl maturing into womanhood and the budding writer playing with language, the audience is always aware of who is threatening her efforts at self-realization, and who will soon murder her. The equation between the Nazis and death is made very early on and is present throughout the action; so is the note of lamentation, struck at the opening by the intoning of the mourner's prayer, El Ma'alay Rachamim, heard at different points, and mixed with a rising battle crescendo at the end.

Levin's play is most admirable in its loyalty to the child and to history: its forthright attempt to convey the vitality, terror, and anguish of the Anne Frank story. In this regard, Levin was uncommonly courageous in resisting the evasive, if consoling, platitudes of so many American responses to the *Diary* in the fifties and sixties, particularly the general talk about "man's inhumanity to man," the child's "gift of hope," and "the eternal verities of the immortal human spirit" (although he himself was not always immune from such phrases). That he should eventually have believed his problems to be the result of a political and cultural conspiracy can also be seen as a response, although extreme, to the times in which he lived, as well as a product of his own personality. An aspiring progressive Jewish writer coming to artistic maturity during the 1930s had reasons enough to be suspicious of the way editors and audiences responded to his work. By the late 1940s, Levin's troublesome experiences in the literary marketplace had made him even more susceptible to translating neglect and silence into animosity, and negative criticism into ideological opposition. (His friend Arnold Gingrich of *Esquire* liked to say that "other writers got rejection slips, but Meyer got suppressed.")

The fact that *The Diary of a Young Girl* was published in 1952 when America was in the midst of a Cold War fever about communism, security, and loyalty only heightened Levin's tendency to look for subterranean political connections. (The Rosenbergs were tried the year before and executed the year after; Senator McCarthy was on the attack throughout the early fifties; and special investigating committees seemed to be operating everywhere.) In *The Obsession*, Levin himself has provided an especially astute description of the temper of the times:

> In the Depression . . . you clearly knew the physical supporting element that was pulled out from under you—a job.

In the McCarthy era it wasn't the loss of a job alone that
projected you into the abyss, for you lost also the psychological supporting sense of knowing what was true. We were
confronted with the manipulation of truth on a massive,
pervasive scale. An insinuation became a truth. To have
associated socially with a communist friend, or, in the new
language—with someone suspected of "subversion," became
disloyalty to America. Even more deeply disturbing than loss
of employment was the loss of life-orientation.

There was created the pervasive atmosphere of a conspiratorial world, in which you could never be sure you were being
told the truth in matters that affected your friendships, your
employment, or your beliefs. (46)

In this "Red Scare" environment, Levin (and many others)
could find a great deal to be distrustful about. Even if Lillian
Hellman was not involved in an elaborate intrigue to sabotage
his play, she did advise Cheryl Crawford, recommend
Goodrich and Hackett to Bloomgarden, and make suggestions
about the adaptation as it was being written. That she also was
an assimilated German-Jew, an anti-Zionist, and a former Stalinist, who had recently received enormous publicity for not
naming names before the House Un-American Activities Committee made her a ripe candidate for "villain" in Levin's tem-
pestuous response to his misfortunes; so did her reputation for
bearing grudges and being contemptuous of people with whom
she disagreed. Although Levin was not, as he thought, the victim of a conspiracy, his career and reputation were certainly
impaired by the opposition and mockery of those who did not
respect his beliefs about Jewishness and his opposition to Russian Communism. He was also thwarted by something less tan-

gible but more pervasive than an overt conspiracy: the coming together of powerful elements in the Zeitgeist—the commercial imperatives of Broadway, the resistance of audiences to disagreeable (not to mention harrowing) subjects, the American craving for universalism and broad consensus, the assimilationist mood among many Jews, the postwar pressure to reconstruct, not offend Germany, and the reverse McCarthyism in some left-wing intellectual circles that gave anticommunism a bad name.

That the materialism, political fear, conformity, and simplistic pieties of American society in the 1950s, as well as Levin's own often hapless, self-defeating behavior, obscured his play and his efforts to deepen public understanding of the significance of what was done to the Jews of Europe is one of the most plangent facts of his thirty-year involvement with Anne Frank's book. Yet in a strange, ironical way, that involvement can also be read as one of Levin's most engrossing, wide-ranging, and resonant stories, a story he in part created, tried to write himself out of, but could never actually write. As he said in his memoir, the affair "was the inevitable expression of all I ever was, all I ever did, as a writer and as a Jew" (7); and the implications of that story continue to have important private and public reverberations.

An American Jewish writer of high talent, ambition, and heightened social consciousness is present at the liberation of the Nazi camps and sets out to convey the significance of the atrocities by writing dispatches, making films about the struggles of survivors, and publishing a blunt autobiographical memoir in which he probes the dilemma of being an "unbelonging" Jew at midcentury. He then proposes adapting for the theater a remarkable diary kept by one of the innocent young victims, hoping that his play will allow him to reach a large audience with its serious message. In his enthusiasm, he writes a draft that faithfully yet awkwardly conveys the book's essence, but the script is summarily rejected as unsuitable for the commercial stage, without his being given a chance to explore and develop its possibilities with the help of experienced theater people. The drama that is chosen achieves enormous success and esteem, quickening the process by which its protagonist becomes one of the best-known, most-loved figures in history and a cultural symbol of lost possibility but of hope as well. Embittered by the loss of the auspicious project he created and by the rejection of his work, the writer undertakes a strenuous campaign to get his version accepted and performed, a campaign motivated by a desire for truth, justice, and freedom of expression, but also by dashed hopes, frustrated ambition, vanity, envy, rage, and unresolved tensions related to his family, heritage, and profession. The campaign eventually brings him into conflict with a cast that includes the respected father of the dead author and eminent people in the worlds of publishing, theater, literature, journalism, politics, religion, and law (many of whom are themselves Jewish). As resistance to his claims intensifies and the stakes get higher, he repudiates agreements, writes abusive letters, distorts past events, develops a conspiracy theory, takes out accusatory newspaper ads, initiates litigation, stirs public scandal, and causes great distress to himself, his adversaries, his family, and his friends. His obsessive battle, which he sees as a fight for truth, justice, and personal redemption as an artist and a Jew, becomes blurred by what many others perceive as an endless, ego-driven, paranoid campaign for self-justification. With so much of his energy and imagination devoted to confronting real and invented enemies, he becomes increasingly isolated. His other writing suffers; much of his later fiction is characterized by tendentiousness and the absence of the imagination, drama, and complexity that mark his best earlier books, except for one novel and a memoir in which the subject is the obsession itself. His family life suffers too; his wife speaks of watching him sink "deeper and deeper into the quicksand" of his Anne Frank obsession as "the most heart-breaking sorrow of my life" (undated letter, late 1970s, BU).

Years later, recalling the effects of the Anne Frank affair on their family life, Levin's adopted daughter remembered his many acts of kindness and generosity, but she also spoke of herself and her brothers as being, in some ways, like battered children who never talked about the traumatic events through which they had lived. In 1991, after reading their mother's book, they were astonished to discover the meaning and consequences of the turbulence that had gone on around them for so long.

Despite the effects, the writer cannot relinquish his cause and free himself of his fixation because over the years they have come to embody, for better and worse, so much of his personality and being. His original cause—to bear witness to the Holocaust—was motivated primarily by shock, outrage, grief, bewilderment, ambivalence about his own heritage, and an idealistic need to now find personal redemption in renewing his connection to the past and the future of the Jewish people. By choosing Anne Frank's *Diary* as the instrument for his own fulfillment, he innocently selects a book that is both well- and ill-suited for the task; and he sets out to enact his redemptive drama in an environment (the American entertainment world) that inevitably turns it into a bruising tragic farce. The wound of the European Jews does become his wound, but in endlessly ironical and diminished ways; and his history testifies to the enormous difficulty, if not the impossibility, of finding an authentic way to bear witness to the Holocaust in a society governed by money, popular taste, media hype, democratic optimism, and a susceptibility to easy consolation. In the process, the writer's wound often seems self-inflicted, a punishment he administered to himself out of guilt and shame about being Jewish, and from disillusionment at being "betrayed" by Otto Frank, the father of "the lost girl" and his surrogate father and rival as well. But, in fact, the wound was caused by unresolvable tensions between his romantic desire for self-fulfillment as a Jew and a writer, his personal limitations as a man and a writer, and the material, political, and cultural conditions of the world in which he lived.

After his death, it becomes clear that he was in vital ways more reliable as a reader of the girl's book than those who helped create the sentimental mystique in America. His drama, while not as theatrical, is a more accurate response to the child and her history than is the acclaimed version. (Indeed, some of his most important insights have been reflected in recent revised versions of the Goodrich and Hackett play, designed to make it more realistic and less uplifting.) But fifteen years after his death, nearly all of his books are out of print; his play is rarely done, even in minor theaters; and he is remembered—if at all—mostly as the writer who fought a strident, interminable, losing battle against Anne Frank's father. In the 1990s, even his valuable early contributions to the success of the *Diary* in America have been unfairly criticized for paying more attention to the specific qualities of the book and its writer than to the particular crime the Nazis committed against the Jews.[5]

Reflecting on this reading of the history, one feels the force of a fine comment by Levin's editor and friend Robert Gottlieb: "I was very fond of him, and admired both his energy and his abilities. But in his quarrelsome and provocative mode he always reminded me of a figure from Molière, about whom one doesn't know whether to laugh or cry."[6] Now, however, from a distance, if we look closely at, and then past, the quarrels and provocations, Levin's accomplishments appear more substantial. Even if recollections of his outrageous behavior can still provoke sadness, laughter, or pain, his cause seems in important ways less lost. He wrote a number of books that deserve to be kept in print: *The Old Bunch, Citizens, In Search, Compulsion,* and *The Obsession.* His prohibited play deserves to be published and performed. He challenged people, often in uncomfortable ways, to think about and act on the meaning and responsibilities of contemporary Jewish identity; and he made essential contributions over a thirty-year period to an understanding of Anne Frank's *Diary* and its connections to the Holocaust.

5. See Alvin H. Rosenfeld, "Popularization and Memory: The Case of Anne Frank," in *Lessons and Legacies,* 249–51; and Edward Alexander, *The Holocaust and the War of Ideas,* 1–53.

6. Letter to author, 17 February 1994.

> BIBLIOGRAPHY

As indicated in the text and notes to the book, the author cites a number of unpublished sources (further information on which can be found in the List of Abbreviations at the front of the book), as well as published sources, which are listed below.

Abzug, Robert. *Inside the Vicious Heart: Americans and the Liberation of the Nazi Concentration Camps.* New York: Oxford University Press, 1985.

Alexander, Edward. *The Holocaust and the War of Ideas.* New Brunswick, N.J.: Transaction, 1994.

Berkow, Ira. *Maxwell Street.* New York: Doubleday, 1977.

Bossin, Gary. *The Literary Achievement of Meyer Levin.* Ph.D. dissertation, Kent State University, 1980.

Doneson, Judith. "The American History of Anne Frank's Diary." *Holocaust and Genocide Studies* 2:1 (1987): 149–60.

Ezrahi, Sidra. *By Words Alone: The Holocaust in Literature.* Chicago: University of Chicago Press, 1980.

Fife, Stephen. "Meyer Levin's Obsession." *New Republic,* August 2, 1982, 26–30.

Frank, Anne. *The Diary of a Young Girl.* New York: Doubleday, 1952.

———. *The Diary of a Young Girl: The Definitive Edition.* Edited by Otto H. Frank and Mirjam Pressler. New York: Doubleday, 1995.

———. *The Diary of Anne Frank: The Critical Edition.* Edited by David Barnouw and Gerrold Van Der Stroom. New York: Doubleday, 1989.

Friedlander, Saul. *Memory, History, and the Extermination of the Jews of Europe.* Bloomington: Indiana University Press, 1993.

Fuchs, Daniel. *Three Novels.* New York: Basic Books, 1961.

Gilman, Sander. "The Dead Child Speaks: Reading *The Diary of Anne Frank.*" In *Jewish Self-Hatred.* Baltimore: Johns Hopkins University Press, 1986.

Goodrich, Frances, and Albert Hackett. *The Diary of Anne Frank.* New York: Random House, 1956.

Langer, Lawrence. "The Americanization of the Holocaust." In *From Hester Street to Hollywood,* edited by Sarah B. Cohen. Bloomington: Indiana University Press, 1983.

Levin, Meyer. *Anne Frank.* Privately printed by the author, 1967.

———. *Compulsion.* New York: Simon and Schuster, 1956.

———. *The Fanatic.* New York: Simon and Schuster, 1964.

———. *Gore and Igor.* New York: Simon and Schuster, 1967.

———. *In Love.* Unpublished memoir. Boston University, Mugar Memorial Library.

———. *In Search.* Paris: Authors Press, 1950.

———. *The Obsession.* New York: Simon and Schuster, 1973.

———. *The Old Bunch.* New York: Viking, 1937.

———. *The Settlers.* New York: Simon and Schuster, 1972.

———. *The Stronghold.* New York: Simon and Schuster, 1965.

Levin, Meyer, and Charles Angoff, eds. *The Rise of American Jewish Literature.* New York: Simon and Schuster, 1970.

Lindwer, Willy. *The Last Seven Months of Anne Frank.* New York: Pantheon, 1991.

Rosenfeld, Alvin H. "Anne Frank—and Us: Finding the Right Words." *Reconstruction* 2:2 (1993): 86–91.

———. "Popularization and Memory: The Case of Anne Frank." In *Lessons and Legacies: The Meaning of the Holocaust in a Changing World,* edited by Peter Hayes. Evanston: Northwestern University Press, 1991.

Rubin, Steven J. *Meyer Levin.* Boston: Twayne, 1981.

Torres, Tereska. *The Converts.* New York: Alfred Knopf, 1970.

———. *Les Maisons hantées de Meyer Levin.* Paris: Éditions Denoël, 1991.

Verhoeven, Rian, and Ruud van der Rol. *Anne Frank: Beyond the Diary.* New York: Viking, 1993.

Designer: Barbara Jellow

Compositor: ComCom, Inc.

Text: 11/15 Adobe Garamond

Display: Adobe Garamond

Printer: Haddon Craftsmen, Inc.

Binder: Haddon Craftsmen, Inc.